ENERGY AND ECONOMIC REFORM IN THE FORMER SOVIET UNION

Also by Leslie Dienes

SOVIET ASIA: Economic Development and National Policy Choices

THE SOVIET ENERGY SYSTEM: Resource Use and Policies (*with Theodore Showboat*)

Also by Istvan Dobozi

THE HUNGARIAN ECONOMY IN THE 1980s: Reforming the System and Adjusting to External Shocks (*with Josef C. Brada*)

MONEY, INCENTIVES AND EFFICIENCY IN THE HUNGARIAN ECONOMIC REFORM (*with Josef C. Brada*)

PRIMARY COMMODITIES IN THE WORLD ECONOMY

Also by Marian Radetzki

A GUIDE TO PRIMARY COMMODITIES IN THE WORLD ECONOMY

AID AND DEVELOPMENT

FINANCING MINING PROJECTS IN DEVELOPING COUNTRIES (*with Stephen A. Zorn*)

INTERNATIONAL COMMODITY MARKET ARRANGEMENTS

MINERAL PROCESSING IN DEVELOPING COUNTRIES (*with Stephen A. Zorn*)

STATE MINERAL ENTERPRISES: An Investigation into their Impact on International Mineral Markets

URANIUM: A Strategic Source of Energy

Energy and Economic Reform in the Former Soviet Union

Implications for Production, Consumption and Exports, and for the International Energy Markets

Leslie Dienes
Professor of Geography
University of Kansas

Istvan Dobozi
Energy Economist
World Bank, Washington, DC

Marian Radetzki
Professor of Economics
University of Luleå, and
Director of SNS Energy, Stockholm

St. Martin's Press

First published in Great Britain 1994 by
THE MACMILLAN PRESS LTD
Houndmills, Basingstoke, Hampshire RG21 2XS
and London
Companies and representatives
throughout the world

A catalogue record for this book is available from the British Library.

ISBN 0–333–60634–5

Printed in Great Britain by
Ipswich Book Co Ltd
Ipswich, Suffolk

First published in the United States of America 1994 by
Scholarly and Reference Division,
ST. MARTIN'S PRESS, INC.,
175 Fifth Avenue,
New York, N.Y. 10010

ISBN 0–312–12014–1

Library of Congress Cataloging-in-Publication Data
Dienes, Leslie.
Energy and economic reform in the Former Soviet Union :
implications for production, consumption and exports, and for the
international energy markets / Leslie Dienes, Istvan Dobozi, Marian
Radetzki.
p.   cm.
"The study presented on the following pages was conceived at a
conference organized by SNS Energy in Stockholm late in 1990."
Includes bibliographical references and index.
ISBN 0–312–12014–1 .
1. Energy policy—Former Soviet republics—Congresses.   2. Energy
industries—Former Soviet republics—Congresses.   I. Dobozi,
Istvan.   II. Radetzki, Marian.   III. SNS Energy.   IV. Title.
HD9502.F67D54   1994
333. 79' 0947—dc20   93–31487
                                                           CIP

Contents

Contents

List of Tables, Figures and Maps

Tables

Acknowledgements

The study presented on the following pages was conceived at a conference organised by SNS Energy in Stockholm in late 1990. Work began in July 1991 and went on until the end of 1992. Though the manuscript is the result of a joint effort by the three authors, the main responsibility for Chapter 2 rests with Dienes, Chapters 1 and 3 with Dobozi and Chapter 4 with Radetzki. Radetzki also undertook a thorough editing of the entire text.

Generous financial support from the following sources made the work possible: BITS (Swedish Agency for International Technical and Economic Cooperation); NUTEK (Swedish National Board for Industrial and Technical Development); and two divisions in the World Bank, viz., the Industry and Energy Division in the Technical Department Europe, Middle East & North Africa Region, and the International Trade Division in the International Economics Department. The authors wish to express their sincere gratitude for this support.

Consecutive versions of the manuscript have been reviewed in seminars at BITS, SNS Energy, University of Luleå and the World Bank. Valuable comments received at these seminars are gratefully acknowledged. Special thanks are due to Ziad Alahdad, Shigeru Kubota and Harold Wackman, all with the World Bank, whose continuous advice was of great help in improving the quality of the work.

Anita Angelryd and Susanne Holmer at SNS Energy, from where the work was administered, processed the words, tables and graphs with great energy and unfailing enthusiasm into a legible shape.

MARIAN RADETZKI

Abbreviations

BCM	Billion cubic meters
BITS	Swedish Agency for International Technical and Economic Cooperation
bl	Barrel
BTU (mmBTU)	British thermal units (million BTU)
CIA	Central Intelligence Agency (of the USA)
COMECON	Council for Mutual Economic Assistance (an association of communist countries)
EOR	Enhanced oil recovery
FSU	Former Soviet Union
GDP	Gross domestic product
IMF	International Monetary Fund
Kcal	Kilocalories
KTOE	Thousand tons of oil equivalent
mbd	Million barrels per day
mboed	Million barrels of oil equivalent per day
MDS	Multidimensional scaling
MTOE	Million tons of oil equivalent
NUTEK	Swedish National Board for Industrial and Technical Development
OECD	Organization for Economic Cooperation and Development
PPP	Purchasing power parity
Rbl	Ruble
TOE	Tons of oil equivalent
TPES	Total primary energy supply
VAT	Value-added tax

Fuel Conversion Rates

Most energy quantities are expressed in tons of oil equivalent, TOE. One TOE equals roughly 10 million Kcal and 40 million BTU.

Actual tonnages of coal are converted into TOE, in accordance with their heat content. In the FSU case, between 1.5 and 3.5 tons of coal correspond to 1 TOE.

Volumes of gas, too, are converted into TOE according to their heat content. Between 11000 and 14000 cubic meters of natural gas correspond to 1 TOE (1.1–1.4 BCM = 1 MTOE).

In value terms, one dollar per mmBTU roughly corresponds to 28 dollars per thousand cubic meters, to 40 dollars per ton of oil and to 5.46 dollars per barrel of oil.

Summary of Major Conclusions

The aim of this study is to explore the likely paths for the former Soviet Union's (FSU) hydrocarbon production, consumption and exports under alternative political and economic scenarios until 2005, and to analyse the implications of shifting FSU exports for world energy markets in general, and for Eastern Europe in particular.

ALTERNATIVE REFORM SCENARIOS

For a coherent analysis of the above issues it is necessary to make assumptions about the reform process in FSU countries, and the macroeconomic implications. Four scenarios are presented: (1) *shock therapy*, which posits rapid moves towards simultaneous macroeconomic stabilisation and structural reforms; (2) *gradual market reforms*, which assumes the establishment of a market economy to proceed more slowly; (3) *reform impasse*, in which political problems and intra-FSU rivalries defer the initiation of comprehensive economic reforms until after the middle of the 1990s; and (4) *reform impasse and internal war*, which assumes an internal war of one year's duration superimposed on the pessimistic outlook of Scenario 3. The fourth scenario and its implications have not been worked out in detail.

Continued GDP contraction is anticipated in the early 1990s in all four scenarios. The turnaround to positive growth and the speed of subsequent expansion will be fastest in Scenario 1 and slowest in Scenarios 3 and 4.

The evolution of actual events until the end of 1992, as the study is being concluded, suggests a somewhat greater likelihood for macroeconomic developments akin to those of Scenario 2.

ENERGY PRICES

Rational energy pricing is of overriding importance for economically efficient production and for minimising wasteful consumption practices. Hence considerable attention is devoted to pricing issues.

1

With the recent establishment of parallel energy markets, a multitude of functional oil, gas and coal prices have emerged. In 1992 the bulk of energy trade still took place at state-controlled prices. After several major price revisions effected in that year, the state-set prices moved closer to those prevailing in the parallel markets. A sizable gap still exists between these prices and international price levels, especially if the unrealistically low commercial exchange rate for the ruble (115 rubles per dollar in June 1992, rising to about 1000 rubles per dollar in the Autumn of 1993) is applied. Even at the more realistic rate of 30 rubles per dollar in the the first half of 1992 (based either on purchasing-power parities or on conditions in the entire tradable sector), the state-set prices are very low in an international comparison. For example, in June 1992 the official wholesale prices of crude oil and natural gas were only 12–13 per cent of the international price (commercial exchange rate), and 45–53 per cent of the international price (PPP exchange rate).

Energy prices in real terms are posited to move up in all scenarios, until parity with the world market is reached. Using the 'realistic' exchange rate (Rbl 30 per dollar in first half of 1992, adjusted for future inflation differentials), world-market levels are assumed to be reached only by 1995 in Scenario 1 and substantially later in the other scenarios.

Given the importance of energy and the hyperinflationary macro-economic environment in the FSU, energy-price decontrol through a single stroke is not a realistic option. Even under the best of circumstances it is unlikely that parity between domestic and international prices could be achieved before the mid-1990s.

Attempts to force a convergence of domestic energy prices with international ones, using the inflated commercial exchange rate of the ruble, may have a questionable macroeconomic utility. Nevertheless, pricing reform, implemented in parallel with macroeconomic stabilisation, is crucial for creating effective incentives, both to relieve exessive energy consumption and to halt the decline in oil production and hasten petroleum output growth.

HYDROCARBON PRODUCTION

Between 1989 and 1991, mainly as a consequence of the macroeconomic disorder, the FSU's output of oil fell by 95 million tons, or 17 per cent. Virtually all of this decline occurred in Russia, with West

Siberia most severely affected by ruptured logistics and labour flight. In the same period, coal output fell by 51 MTOE, or 16 per cent. Russia accounted for one half of this total. Further declines in the output of both fuels were recorded during 1992. Production of gas, in contrast, experienced some increase in this period.

Fundamental to the analysis of future production is a combination of constraints imposed by (a) geology and geography, (b) the cost of output at the margin, and (c) institutional, political and social requirements.

In all scenarios, total projected fuel production until 2005 remains below the 1989 peak. The rapid output increases in the 1980s were based on overuse of extremely favourable West-Siberian oil and gas deposits. The oil and coal production levels of earlier years cannot continue in the 1990s. Only the natural-gas industry is physically capable of sizable expansion of output in the present decade.

Restoration of closed oil wells and the release of concealed oil with the application of superior technological equipment might raise annual output by some 30 million tons (0.6 mbd), corresponding to roughly one fifth of the production decline between 1989 and 1992. On account of ongoing depletion, such an improvement could not be sustained for more than 3–4 years.

The giant oil fields in West Siberia are more than 60 per cent depleted, and are past their production peaks. Newly discovered reserves are of smaller size and are less easy to exploit. Because of steeply increasing costs of the marginal output, production levels above 500 million tons (10 mbd) during this century are economically prohibitive when a 'realistic' exchange rate is applied.

Maintenance of oil and condensate output at an annual level of around 440 million tons between 1993 and 2000 will require a total investment expenditure of $70 billion, or some $8 billion per year (constant 1990 money). Raising output by another 50 million tons per year will augment investment expenditure much more than proportionately.

Gas output is far less constrained by physical/geological barriers. Production is projected to decline during the first half of the 1990s, mainly because of inadequate domestic demand and the constraints imposed by export pipelines and foreign willingness to buy more FSU gas, but to rise briskly during the ensuing ten years. By the end of the century Scenario 1 forecasts an output level of 710 MTOE (850 BCM), 8 per cent above the 1990 peak, with the total cost of marginal output roughly equal to price. By 2005, Scenarios 1 and 2 presuppose a sizable contribution from the as yet undeveloped Yamal fields to make up for ongoing depletion of exploited deposits. However the costs and economics of Yamal are highly uncertain.

Investment requirements in gas extraction, treatment, pipelines and storage, to attain the production level projected in Scenario 1 for the FSU as a whole, are assessed at $1.5 billion per year in the period 1992–5. In the subsequent five years the annual sum (excluding Yamal) rises to $2.5 billion annually. The development of Yamal (including pipelines), mainly in the next century, would carry an aggregate investment cost of close to $40 billion. All figures are in constant 1990 money.

The FSU's coal reserves greatly exaggerate the true production potential. The inferior location and economic quality of the reserves will suppress output in all scenarios to around 200 MTOE by the mid-1990s, down by about one third from the 1989–90 level. Even after this decline substantial subsidies will be needed to keep marginal output economically viable. Such subsidies are seen to be politically and socially prompted by the very high unemployment in coal-producing areas that would otherwise ensue.

Large infusions of Western technology are indispensable for attaining the relatively elevated production levels projected in Scenarios 1 and 2. But foreign capital and technology inflows will not take place on any large scale until an appropriate institutional infrastructure has been established and an economically reasonable and stable legislation governing foreign involvement has been put in place. Political opposition to foreign direct investment in Russian energy is a further deterrent to technology and capital inflows.

In the near future restoration of closed oil wells and extraction of bypassed oil will offer the easiest prospects and the least political opposition to foreign investor participation. Maintenance of gas pipelines and the need to build a new export pipe in the 1990s to secure the FSU's market share in Europe offer other suitable opportunities for foreign involvement, with startup in the first half of the 1990s. Foreign investment prospects in oil and gas-field development in the near future are greater in Azerbayjan and Kazakhstan than in Russia because of less restrictive political attitudes to such involvements in the former countries.

While massive foreign technology and capital infusions are critical for energy production developments in the long term, they can not fully compensate for the severe geological deterioration of reserves in the 1990s. Furthermore the introduction of foreign equipment to oil and gas production will be a time-consuming task. Experiences from the United States suggest that assimilation of novel techniques by production crews takes at least several years. Reliability of well-known domestic input supply will be more important for maintaining the FSU's production in the medium term. Foreign participation in the domestic manufacture of standard oil and gas industry inputs in the FSU could be a useful supplement to direct foreign investments in energy production.

Output will be hard to maintain without close political and economic cooperation between the new states. Virtually all FSU republics are critically dependent on the Russian energy supply. At the same time the energy producers in Russia rely heavily on inputs from other republics. The sharp changes in the relative prices of inputs and outputs of the energy producers, envisaged under the price reforms, will create a fertile ground for conflict between suppliers and buyers. All the projected production levels depend on reasonable resolution of such intra-FSU conflicts and tensions.

ENERGY CONSUMPTION

The FSU countries are extremely wasteful of energy. An estimate of 'systemic energy waste' shows that they used 60 per cent more energy than they would have done if they had behaved like typical market economies. For 1990 this amounted to a staggering 500 MTOE (10 mboed). In the early 1990s energy wastage increased to even higher levels.

A disaggregated analysis of energy waste points to industry as the sector with the largest savings prospects. Within industry, metallurgy exhibits the most blatant energy inefficiency. The residential/municipal sector, too, offers scope for very large energy savings.

Based on assumptions consistent with Scenarios 1–3, quantitative projections have been prepared for energy consumption from 1992–2005. The first half of the 1990s is marked by a large contraction in consumption caused by the sharp economic slump and, in Scenarios 1 and 2, by the intense energy price shock. The falloff in consumption varies across fuels, the least pronounced being in natural gas and the sharpest in coal. In Scenarios 1 and 2 total fuel consumption begins to trend upward from the middle of the 1990s. In Scenario 3 the turnaround comes somewhat later.

The findings suggest that market reforms can generate rapid and significant reductions in energy intensity, given the large reservoir of untapped energy efficiency and the scope for restructuring the economy. Energy-intensity trends display a marked downturn in the projections. In Scenario 1 the decrease in the energy/GDP ratio works out to an average 2.6 per cent a year for the period 1990–2005, the same as observed in Japan between 1973 and 1990. In Scenario 2 the decline is 1.9 per cent, which suggests that a noticeable reduction in long-standing high energy intensity is possible even under phased reforms.

EXPORT PROSPECTS

Production and consumption figures for recent years, as well as projections until 2005, for the FSU as a whole, and for Russia, are detailed in Tables A and B. Figures A and B present the data for oil and gas in graphical form. Projected export volumes are derived as the residual between production and consumption. Gas-production estimates in the 1990s were reduced below potential capacity in some cases to reflect the limitations of export potential. The aggregate figures reveal that reduced consumption will be the major driving force determining export performance, expecially in the longer term.

FSU oil exports (excluding intra-FSU trade) are forecast to decline until the mid-1990s, down to about zero in Scenarios 2 and 3, where slow or paralysed reforms cause production to contract, while the consumption savings potential remains underutilised. A recovery is seen to begin in the latter half of the decade, on the assumption that eventually the reform process will gather speed and incentives to produce more and consume less will be reinforced.

Gas exports from the FSU in the first two scenarios are projected at high levels through the time horizon of the study. In Scenario 1 the willingness of foreign buyers to absorb FSU gas, not the ability to produce it, becomes the effective constraint on exports. A 'gas bubble', defined as unused production potential, develops in this scenario during the 1990s as a consequence of declining domestic consumption and insufficient expansion of exports. Foreign sales of gas in this scenario are nevertheless seen to increase briskly, from 87 MTOE (104 BCM) in 1990 to 115 MTOE (138 BCM) in 1995 and 160 MTOE (192 BCM) in 2000.

Table A FSU Energy: projections of production, consumption and exports under alternative scenarios (MTOE)

	Total fossil fuels			Oil			Gas			Coal		
	Prod.	Cons.	Exp.	Prod.	Cons.	Exp.	Prod.	Cons.	Exp.	Prod.	Cons.	Exp.
1989	1567	1298	269	610	442	168	644	555	89	313	301	12
1990	1527	1271	256	570	414	156	660	572	88	297	285	12
1991	1435	1242	193	515	413	102	658	572	86	262	257	5
Scenario 1: shock therapy												
1995	1170	975	195	390	330	60	580	465	115	200	180	20
2000	1375	990	385	460	290	170	710	550	160	205	150	55
2005	1550	1100	450	550	310	240	800	650	150	200	140	60
Scenario 2: gradual reforms												
1995	1235	1125	110	390	390	0	620	520	100	225	215	10
2000	1330	1055	275	450	340	110	660	540	120	220	175	45
2005	1485	1125	360	520	330	190	760	640	120	205	155	50
Scenario 3: reform impasse												
1995	1200	1105	95	380	390	-10	615	540	75	205	175	30
2000	1290	1145	145	430	380	50	670	610	60	190	155	35
2005	1385	1180	205	500	350	150	705	700	5	180	130	50
Scenario 4: reform impasse and war												
1993	–	–	20	–	–	0	–	–	20	–	–	5
1995	–	–	50	–	–	0	–	–	40	–	–	10
2000	–	–	105	–	–	20	–	–	60	–	–	25
2005	–	–	175	–	–	120	–	–	5	–	–	50

Table B Energy in Russia: projections of production, consumption and exports under alternative scenarios (MTOE)

	Total Fossil Fuels			Oil			Gas			Coal		
	Prod	Cons	Exp	Prod	Cons	Exp	Prod	Cons	Exp	Prod	Cons	Exp
1989	1214	802	412	555	277	278	495	355	140	164	170	−6
1990	1187	796	391	516	268	248	515	366	149	156	162	−6
1991	1116	786	330	461	268	193	517	370	147	138	148	−10
Scenario 1: shock therapy												
1995	894	617	277	335	213	122	463	300	163	96	104	−8
2000	1050	631	419	380	187	193	560	355	205	110	89	21
2005	1207	703	504	460	200	260	632	421	211	115	82	33
Scenario 2: gradual reforms												
1995	948	712	236	340	252	88	498	337	161	110	123	−13
2000	1006	671	335	370	219	151	521	351	170	115	101	14
2005	1150	718	432	440	217	223	595	413	182	115	88	27
Scenario 3: reform impasse												
1995	929	699	230	332	252	80	492	347	145	105	100	5
2000	1005	725	280	370	243	127	530	392	138	105	90	15
2005	1075	756	319	420	229	191	555	451	104	100	76	24

Figure A   FSU oil and gas: projections of production, consumption and exports under alternative scenarios (MTOE)

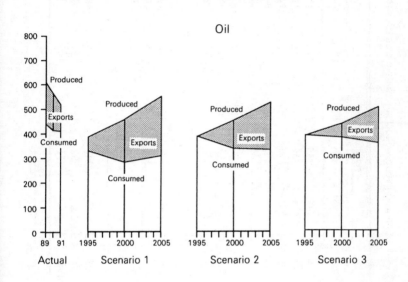

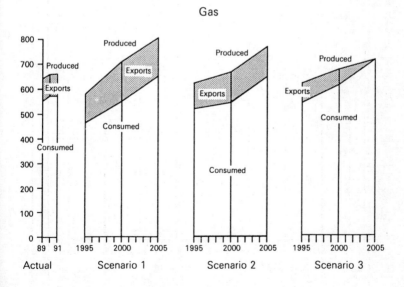

Summary of Major Conclusions

Figure B   Russian oil and gas: projections of production, consumption and exports under alternative scenarios (MTOE)

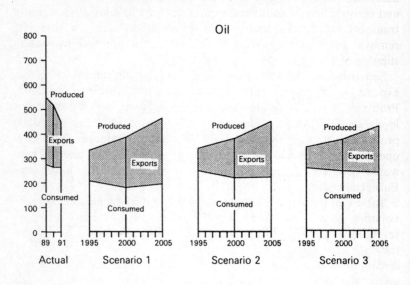

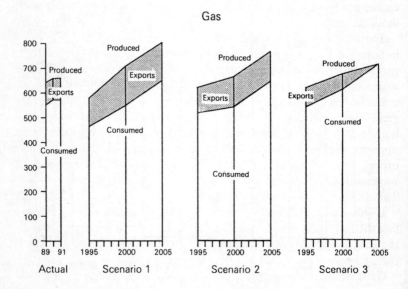

Foreign support to liquidate the 'gas bubble' arising from successful economic and political reforms would strengthen the FSU's foreign-currency earnings, and thus reduce the need for non-commercial assistance from the West. Such support could involve the financing and construction of additional export pipelines to relax any emerging transport bottlenecks, and – even more importantly – a complete removal of remaining West European restrictions on increasing supplies of FSU gas.

Scenario 3, on the other hand, depicts a gradual decline in FSU gas exports, with foreign sales shrinking to insignificance by 2005. Problems in expanding production and continuing high consumption levels are both at play. European importers of FSU gas would be profoundly affected by the projected export performance, and European gas prices would rise far above equivalence with oil prices. There would be a need to rethink the role of gas in the East- and West-European energy mix.

Table C summarises the revenue implications of the projected export volumes, using the World Bank's energy-price forecasts. Export revenues vary considerably over time and across the scenarios. For the FSU, exports reach a trough in the mid-1990s. The consequences of discontinued oil exports will be very severe for the FSU's economy, given that oil has traditionally been the main earner of foreign exchange. Export revenues expand substantially in subsequent years in all scenarios.

The FSU's export-revenue levels (again excluding intra-FSU trade) in Scenario 1 are more than twice as high as in Scenario 3 through the period under investigation. From the turn of the century the difference works out at more than $30 billion per year. This finding points to the dramatic importance of reforms for export performance. But given the great significance of energy production and trade in the macroeconomies of some FSU countries, the causal relationship operates in the opposite direction too. A healthy energy sector generating sizable export revenues is a crucial precondition for the maintenance of successful economic and political reforms in Russia, Kazakhstan and Turkmenia, the main energy exporters.

Ukraine and other energy-importing FSU countries, in contrast, will face difficult adjustments in all scenarios, akin to those experienced by the East-European nations since 1990, as the prices they pay for their energy imports are raised to international levels.

Geographical disaggregations of production, consumption and exports reveal the continued dominance of Russia in FSU totals.

Table C   Projected export revenue from fossil-fuel sales under alternative scenarios (billion 1990 $)

	FSU				Russia			
	Oil	*Gas*	*Coal*	*Total*	*Oil*	*Gas*	*Coal*	*Total*
Scenario 1								
1995	7.5	10.8	1.2	19.5	15.3	15.3	−0.5	30.1
2000	26.9	19.0	3.6	49.5	30.5	24.4	1.4	56.3
2005	36.0	17.0	4.0	57.0	39.0	23.8	2.2	65.0
Scenario 2								
1995	0	9.4	0.6	10.0	11.0	15.1	−0.8	25.3
2000	17.4	14.3	3.0	44.7	23.9	20.2	0.9	45.0
2005	28.5	13.6	3.3	45.4	33.5	20.6	1.8	55.9
Scenario 3								
1995	−1.3	7.1	1.8	7.6	10.0	13.6	0.3	23.9
2000	7.9	7.1	2.3	17.3	20.1	16.4	1.0	37.5
2005	22.5	0.6	3.3	26.4	28.7	11.8	1.6	42.1

Russian exportable surpluses are much larger than those of the FSU as a whole, reflecting its sizable supplies to the importing FSU republics.

Ukraine is by far the largest energy importer in the FSU. Roughly one quarter of the total energy surpluses generated by Russia in recent years have been absorbed by Ukraine. The magnitude of Ukraine's energy-import needs is projected to remain broadly unchanged through the forecast horizon.

Table C also shows the projected Russian energy-export proceeds, based on the assumption that all exports, including those within the FSU, will be sold at international prices. For Russia, too, the figures reveal the stark importance of successful reforms for the energy sector's performance.

Kazakhstan and Turkmenia account for virtually all the remaining energy surpluses generated in the FSU. Though Russia's dominance is projected to remain unchallenged, Kazakhstan's share of these surpluses is forecast to increase from 5 per cent of the FSU total to 10 per cent over the projection period. Early next century, Kazakhstan and Turkmenia are seen to emerge as the most energy export dependent republics in the FSU, that is the ones with the highest ratio of energy exports to GDP.

IMPLICATIONS FOR INTERNATIONAL MARKETS

The fluctuating volumes of coal and oil exports emerging under the alternative scenarios are deemed to have only a temporary and limited impact on the international prices of these products. The price elasticity of international coal supply is high and the FSU's share of the market is small. In oil, the supply decisions of Middle-East oil producers will overwhelm the impact of any changes in the FSU's sales.

Very different conclusions emerge in the case of gas. Deliveries of this fuel from the FSU play a crucial role in the isolated European market, and fluctuations in that supply could have sharp and lasting implications for price.

The East-European countries present a special case, given their very heavy traditional dependence on energy imports from the FSU and infrastructural installations geared to FSU supplies. The degree of Eastern Europe's dependence and extent of vulnerability to potential FSU supply failures is least in coal. In the case of oil, the versatility of the international market and existing harbour and oil terminal facilities offer a fair degree of flexibility to most of the countries for substituting FSU oil for deliveries from elsewhere.

Natural gas again stands out among the fuels, since existing pipeline systems do not permit the East-European countries to import from elsewhere in the event of FSU supply failures. Elaborate plans are under discussion to reduce the detrimental consequences of such failure through the opening up of alternative sources of supply, by pipe or as liquefied natural gas. Many of these plans involve very large investments and would take several years to implement. The incertitude of FSU supply could well have been resolved by the time the new sources become operational. Furthermore the cost of alternative gas supplies is higher than the cost of FSU gas in most cases. For instance, replacement of 30 BCM of FSU gas by gas obtained elsewhere by the turn of the century is assessed to raise the total cost of production and transport of the delivered gas by some $700 million per year. This additional cost would have to be weighed against the presumed greater security of supply from diversified gas imports.

A two-pronged approach seems appropriate in the East European efforts to suppress dependence on FSU energy. Some of the plans to diversify have strong justification in economic and security terms, and should therefore be carried out. These plans ought to be supplemented by forceful efforts to reduce the very large and widespread energy waste. In many cases, energy savings should provide a highly economical approach to limiting an excessive dependence on the somewhat uncertain energy supply from the FSU.

Introduction

By the late 1980s the Soviet Union had developed into the world's largest exporter of energy, and its important role as energy supplier to the rest of the world was seen as continuing into the foreseeable future. This position was dramatically altered in the early 1990s. The profound political and economic change of Soviet society gained speed in 1990 and led to a division of the union into a number of independent republics. Output of energy in the former Soviet Union (FSU) first stalled and then declined sharply, partly in consequence of political disintegration and the incoherence of the initial economic reforms, but also because of more fundamental problems in the energy sector. The oil industry fared worst in the process. Traditionally very high consumption levels of energy were not much reduced, despite a dramatic contraction of GDP after 1989. The result was a drastic shrinkage of the FSU's energy exports.

The sharp change in the fortunes of the energy sector in the FSU has been largely unanticipated, and the outlook for its future performance is extremely unclear. What may happen to energy production, consumption and exports in the former Soviet republics is of utmost importance to their general economic progress. Ample and reliable domestic energy availability is crucial to the smooth restructuring of these republics' economies, a precondition for sustainable economic growth. The domestic importance of energy is further exacerbated by the fact that fossil fuels have long provided the dominant source of foreign exchange, another key prerequisite for economic transformation and growth. What may happen to future energy production and consumption in the FSU is also of crucial significance to the world markets for energy, given the recent importance of Soviet supply to these markets.

The unclear outcome of ongoing change in FSU energy, and the importance of that outcome for the FSU itself and for world energy markets, provide the justification for undertaking the present study.

A crucial objective of the following investigations is to explore what may happen to energy production and consumption in the FSU until beyond the turn of the century under alternative scenarios for political and macroeconomic development. The dramatic importance of reforms for the energy sector's performance emerges starkly from the ensuing discourse. But the analysis also points to the recursive nature of the relationship. Given the significance of energy in the macroeconomy of the FSU, maintenance of successful reforms is crucially dependent on large and expanding energy-export revenues. A further objective of the work is to clarify the implications for international energy markets of the varying export flows from the FSU that will result from the alternative energy-production and consumption developments.

The subject is complex and hard to tackle. There is no experience to draw upon about the process to transform communist societies into market-oriented ones. The economic and political thrust of ongoing reforms in the FSU is under constant change, and it is not always easy to determine its long-term direction. Statistical services in the FSU have disintegrated, so it is hard to update historical series. Costs and prices under the old central planning were, by and large, void of economic meaning, and it is difficult to perceive the structure of costs and prices likely to emerge as a market economy is introduced. This problem is further aggravated by the exceedingly high rates of inflation that have reigned throughout the FSU since the beginning of the 1990s, and the erratic and unrealistically low rate of exchange of the ruble quoted in emergent marginal markets in the recent past.

A thorough analysis of the prospects for energy in the FSU that seriously tackles these complications is especially warranted, given the definitive statements based on highly superficial analysis of this topical subject that have proliferated since the beginning of the 1990s.

The following study, completed at the end of 1992, limits its time horizon to 2005. It focuses on the three major fossil fuels: oil, natural gas and coal. The consecutive steps of the deliberations are outlined below.

Chapter 1 provides the political and macroeconomic framework to the ensuing analysis of energy production and consumption. It outlines three alternative scenarios for political and economic reform, and sketches a fourth one. The most optimistic, in terms of both macroeconomic performance and energy exports, is Scenario 1, shock therapy; the most pessimistic is Scenario 4, reform impasse combined with a period of internal war. All the scenarios envisage contracting GDP levels until the mid-1990s, followed by fast recovery in Scenarios 1 and 2, and a much slower pickup under reform impasse. A crucial assumption in the scenarios concerns the speed with which heavily depressed internal energy prices in the FSU are raised towards international market levels. The scenarios are not alternative forecasts of what may happen to the reform process. Rather they should be seen as analytical tools to facilitate analysis of what may happen to energy in the FSU.

Chapter 2 looks in detail at the prospects for energy production. It identifies and assesses the constraints to output of each fuel imposed by the legacy of past production patterns, by geology, geography and technology, and by the cost of marginal output. Plausible levels of production over time are established for each scenario, both for the FSU as a whole and for major producing republics and republican groups.

Though the focus of Chapter 3 is on prospects for consumption, the agenda is much wider. The chapter begins by scrutinising the consumption patterns and levels in the old Soviet Union and assessing the extent of systemic energy waste under the old centrally planned regime. It then takes a detailed look at the evolution of energy prices during the early phases of reform, from 1990 until mid-1992. Future consumption levels under the alternative scenarios are then determined with the help of an econometric model and plausible assumptions about economic growth, structural change and the price and income elasticities of energy demand. The consumption projections, too, are disaggregated by major republic and republican group.

Chapter 4 concludes the study by looking at the international implications of the alternative developments of energy production and consumption in the FSU. Projections of exports for each fuel under each scenario are first established by comparing the production and consumption paths identified in Chapters 2 and 3. Quantitative and qualitative approaches are then employed to gauge the impact on international prices from alternative developments of energy exports from the FSU. The chapter ends by taking a closer look at Eastern Europe. This region is heavily and inflexibly dependent on supplies of FSU energy. Hence there is a case for exploring the measures that could reduce the vulnerabilities of failed FSU energy supplies.

An important technical matter requires attention in this introductory note. The ensuing analyses have had to cope with the difficult issue of choosing the appropriate ruble/dollar exchange rate, for instance in determining whether the FSU's costs of production are internationally competitive, and in assessing the price increase needed to align domestic energy prices with international ones. This issue assumes particular complexity in periods of very high inflation, such as that which characterised the FSU economy during 1992.

The 'commercial' exchange rate (115 rubles per dollar in June 1992, rising to 330 rubles per dollar in mid-October, and to about 1000 rubles per dollar in the Autumn of 1993) is unrealistic because it reflects an extreme undervaluation of the ruble in purchasing power parity (PPP) terms, and a severe one even with respect to the tradable sector as a whole. A recent Russian investigation found that at the prices prevailing on 1 May 1992 the PPP exchange rate was seven rubles per dollar in relation to GDP, 10 rubles per dollar in relation to exports, 25 rubles per dollar in relation to imports; and 30 and 22 rubles per dollar in relation to oil and natural gas, respectively (*Ekonomika i zhizn'*, no. 25, June 1992). For July 1992 a PlanEcon report estimates the PPP rate at six rubles per dollar. The report notes that in Eastern Europe the ratio of commercial/PPP exchange rates has never exceeded a multiple of five in the period since 1989. On this basis it concludes that the commercial exchange rate of the ruble should be defensible in the region of 30–50 rubles per dollar (PlanEcon, 1992).

For a realistic approximation of the exchange rate in the context of the entire tradable sector, the implicit ruble/dollar cross-rate of Hungary, has been chosen. This rate, set by the National Bank of Hungary, stood at 3.2 rubles per dollar in the fourth quarter of 1990. The bank followed an active and reasonably realistic exchange-rate policy vis-à-vis both the ruble and the US dollar, but it stopped quoting the ruble in 1991. After adjusting for the domestic–external inflation differentials in 1991 and 1992 (first two quarters), the average cross-rate for the first half of 1992 works out at 30 rubles per dollar. The realistic nature of this rate is supported by the implied valuation of the ruble in fuels trade on Russian commodity exchanges (see Chapter 3).

In following chapters this more realistic exchange rate (3.2 rubles per dollar in 1990; 30 rubles per dollar in the first half of 1992) is frequently employed in converting ruble costs and prices into dollars, but it must be stressed that the issue of ruble exchange rates is surrounded by a large degree of ambiguity, and that it is by no means clear that the chosen rate (adjusted for inflation differences) would assure payments equilibrium for the tradable sector over time. It should also be noted that the 30 rubles per dollar exchange rate is 'realistic' only during the first half of 1992. Given the sharp divergence of Russian and external inflation trends, the inflation-adjusted rubles per dollar rate must be higher in the post-June 1992 period.

1 Alternative Scenarios for the FSU Reform Process

1.1 INTRODUCTION

Because the FSU can be assumed to function as a reasonably distinct common market for trade and possibly as a common-currency zone, we believe that it retains its relevance as a unit of analysis beyond a purely geographic unit.

What will happen to energy production and consumption in the FSU, and to export capability in the medium- to long-term, depends crucially on political and economic developments, and on the ensuing path and speed of the reform process. The purpose of this chapter is to delineate a few plausible scenarios for these developments, and so to provide alternative starting points for the ensuing analyses of production and consumption prospects.

The path of future events is highly uncertain. The range of possible futures is exceedingly wide. We have formulated only four so as to make the analysis of production, consumption and exports prospects a manageable task. The scenarios considered on the following pages comprise: (1) radical market reforms (shock therapy); (2) gradual market reforms; (3) extended period of reform impasse; and (4) reform impasse and internal war. Only the first three are worked out in some detail. The macroeconomic implications are discussed briefly under each scenario. Figure 1.1 summarises the growth paths of GDP over the period under study. Given the disparate growth trajectories, by the year 2000, total output in Scenarios 2 and 3 works out at 14 per cent and 45 per cent below that of Scenario 1. By 2005, the respective GDP shortfalls are 18 per cent and 50 per cent below the outcome in Scenario 1. Real energy prices in all scenarios are seen to increase at varying speeds until they reach the international market level. This is posited to happen by 1995 in Scenario 1, by 2000 in Scenario 2, but only by 2005 in Scenarios 3 and 4. Chapter 3 provides further details of the extent and speed of these price increases.

These scenarios, along with their indicated macroeconomic outcomes, should not be regarded as forecasts. Rather they should be seen

Figure 1.1   Growth profiles of FSU GDP under Scenarios 1–3

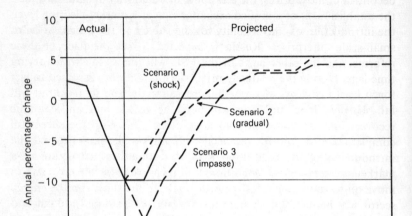

as analytical tools to facilitate the main objective of our study. The indications of where production, consumption and export capability would go in each case are summarised in Table 1.1 at the end of the chapter. The quantitative results that we reach in later chapters of the study do not stand or fall with the actual occurrence of one of the selected scenarios. For although only four plausible development paths have been outlined, among the infinite number of possibilities it would appear that the chosen set provides the full range of plausible energy-export outcomes, from the most buoyant, associated with Scenario 1, to the bleakest one resulting from Scenario 4.

1.2   SCENARIO 1: RADICAL MARKET REFORMS (SHOCK THERAPY)

Scenario 1 assumes the implementation of a comprehensive and radical reform programme, beginning at the end of 1992 or in early 1993. This programme simultaneously combines a strong macroeconomic stabilisation policy with drastic structural reforms such as the immediate decontrol of most prices, the scrapping of a majority of state subsidies, the establishment of a unified exchange rate at a market-clearing level, the introduction of convertibility for the ruble and the privatisation of small-scale enterprises. Russia is expected to set the pace of these reforms, and the other parts of the FSU will follow suit with varying time lags. During the relatively brief transition period, assumed to last for at least two years, prices will increase rapidly and total output will fall sharply. Soon, inflation will begin to recede and an economic recovery will get under way no later than 1995. With the successful completion of a forceful financial stabilisation programme, and the introduction of the basic legal and institutional infrastructure of a market-oriented regime, conditions will be in place for the economy to move on to a sustained, fast-growth track. In the short run the energy sector will be hard hit as state investment and subsidies are cut and domestic demand for energy contracts. Declines in aggregate energy production will continue throughout the mid-1990s. But recession and price-induced savings in oil consumption may reduce the oil-export decline. Although uncertainty surrounds the extent of energy-supply response to systemic reforms in the longer run, this scenario assumes that it will be favourable and therefore, together with the vast scope for price-driven energy savings, energy-export prospects, particularly for natural gas, look promising.

1.2.1 Management System

While centralised controls over state-owned enterprises will be quickly eliminated in most of the economy, fears about the possibility of excessive disruptions in the supply and distribution of energy will prolong some administrative control, notably state orders or similar arrangements, over energy producers during the transition period. By about the end of 1994, these administrative mechanisms will be eliminated for energy too. Right from the outset the process of demonopolisation will proceed speedily. The giant energy associations with monopoly power will be broken up into smaller units, which will be allowed to set their output levels and other parameters independently. In the first year of reforms subsidies to unprofitable energy producers will be reduced at a single stroke, and further reductions will be phased in for the following years. Any remaining subsidies will be defined by specific objectives and viewed as transitional and subject to annual reconsideration. Even in the face of higher domestic prices for energy, the elimination of subsidies will require a substantial reduction in production costs of many producers (especially in the coal industry) as a precondition for survival. This scenario implies a relatively high number of closures of energy-producing units over time, but especially in the early stages of the reform process. Cross-subsidisation, earlier a major form of bailing out inefficient units within the large energy associations, will be less extensive as a result of splitting up the oversized producer organisations. This will contribute to the high incidence of closures.

1.2.2 Supply System

Except for the brief period of transition, decentralised energy producers will be free to negotiate contracts with domestic (later on also with foreign) customers and to sell an increasing share of their output on the commodity exchanges. Thus the distribution of energy will soon resemble a regular wholesale trading system, free of direct administrative controls. In the transition stage selective administrative mechanisms will remain to ensure some continuity in supply and distribution links and to meet the essential requirements of the government, including foreign-exchange needs to service external-debt obligations. Even the remaining state orders, however, may be negotiable with the authorities. Later on state-supply orders may become optional or be eliminated altogether.

1.2.3 Ownership Relations

While privatisation will proceed rapidly in the rest of the economy, energy enterprises, in view of their strategic importance and large book value, will be kept under predominantly public ownership. Later on, however, smaller and even medium-sized units may end up in private or quasi-private hands through outright sales to individuals (particularly employees) or cooperatives, long-term leases, and so on. Quasi-private-property rights will emerge mainly in the form of joint-stock companies, into which a large number of the existing energy enterprises will be transformed. State-owned shares in these companies will be held initially by public holding companies operating on strictly commercial criteria. With the institutions of market economy firmly in place, including adequate legal protection for foreign investors, the inflow of foreign direct investment can play an important role in the privatisation of the energy sector, especially from the middle of the 1990s.

1.2.4 Investment

Energy enterprises will be required to generate funding for investment through self-financing, commercial credits, consumer contributions or joint ventures with foreign companies. To avoid the danger of serious underinvestment, particularly in the early years of reform, the government is assumed to play an important role in securing investment funds until energy producers achieve financial strength through higher domestic prices and an increase in efficiency. From the mid-1990s the generally favourable economic climate, including clear ownership rights, adequate legal protection and the establishment of special economic zones, is assumed to stimulate large-scale foreign investment in rebuilding, modernising and expanding the energy sector. The oil and gas industries will emerge as prime targets for foreign investors as their underlying strong comparative advantage becomes more transparent under market-clearing prices and exchange rates.

1.2.5 Prices

A key feature of this scenario is that, at the outset, virtually all prices will be freed from control. For a brief period energy will be an exception, as the authorities will maintain some price controls (mostly in the form of setting ranges within which 'official' prices will be allowed to move) in order to temper the intensity of the overall price shock. Thus, in the state-regulated segment of the energy market, price revisions will be stretched over three years to bring domestic energy prices in to line (at a realistic exchange rate) with world prices by the middle of the decade. In the free-market sector – commodity exchanges, non-state-order deliveries, barters and so on – energy prices are assumed to reach market-clearing levels much sooner. Prices of some energy products, especially those purchased predominantly by households, will be decontrolled more gradually, but even in these cases prices will reach market levels in an established time-frame, say within four to five years. To prevent monopolistic abuse, price regulation will be maintained in those areas (electricity, gas and heat) where neither domestic nor foreign competition exists to a meaningful extent. In these instances, prices are expected to reflect long-term marginal costs.

1.2.6   External Relations

Early in the transition exchange rates will be unified at a realistic level. This implies significant revaluation of the ruble relative to its deflated levels registered in 1993. With comprehensive price reform and the establishment of a unified exchange rate at a market-clearing level, rapid progress can be made toward convertibility of the ruble. This process can be completed by 1995. Convertibility at a realistic exchange rate is assumed to be a key factor in opening up the FSU's energy sector to the world energy markets, including import competition and foreign investment.

An integral part of this scenario is a relatively early decentralisation of foreign trade in energy by providing registered agents, including energy producers, with direct trading rights. To cushion the initial shocks that can possibly result from rapid moves toward an open-trade regime in energy, some mechanism of export licensing will be maintained, together with foreign-exchange retention quotas (until convertibility is established) and a set of border taxes which will decline gradually with the convergence of domestic energy prices toward export prices.

1.2.7   Macroeconomic Performance

The dramatic emergency stabilisation measures taken at the outset of this scenario will cause a sharp downturn in total output for at least two years. A vigorous recovery will get under way from 1995. By then the conditions for efficient allocation of resources will, by and large, have been put in place and the economy will be able to move on to a sustained fast-growth track at a 5 per cent average rate of GDP growth over the 1995–2005 period. The severe short-term economic depression is expected to dampen domestic energy demand considerably, thus freeing more energy for exports. The net export effect, however, will depend also on the severity of the output decline affecting the energy industries themselves. In the long run the sustained rapid economic growth, taken in isolation, would reduce the available export surplus of energy. However this impact may be overridden by the combined effects of large efficiency gains in energy utilisation and the expansion of energy output in response to much higher energy prices, efficiency improvements in production, and the inflow of foreign investment capital, technology and management skills.

1.3   SCENARIO 2: GRADUAL MARKET REFORMS

Following political consolidation, the establishment of a market-based economy proceeds step by step. Initially some key aspects of central planning (such as state orders and controlled prices) will continue for fear of protracted excessive inflation and a collapse in production. While market reforms move ahead on a slow track, efforts will be made to attain reasonable macroeconomic stability within three years by reducing the budget deficit, curbing the money supply and slashing subsidies and state-financed investment. As a result the economy's recently experienced decline will continue. A modest recovery will get under way from 1996 onward, as the salutary growth effects of macroeconomic stability and partial market reforms begin to materialise. The administrative controls over the energy sector are expected to remain in place longer than in the rest of the economy, and even after the transition period the process of marketisation will proceed at a more gradual pace than elsewhere. Overall this scenario indicates a guardedly optimistic outcome for FSU energy exports as market reforms stimulate supply and dampen domestic demand, the latter's relative importance being the larger.

1.3.1   Management System

In this scenario a gradual decentralisation of decision-making takes place. Large state-owned firms, which continue to be dominant actors, are expected to behave as profit maximisers under a regime of full financial accountability and self-financing. Budget constraints facing both energy producers and consumers will harden considerably compared with the historical pattern. Particularly in the early stage of reforms, several administrative mechanisms of the old central-planning machinery will remain in place, including state orders. The relative importance of the latter will gradually decline, and sometime during the second half of the 1990s producers are expected to be freed from them. Moreover, within a few years, state orders will become negotiable, unlike the existing system of state orders, which is mandatory.

Organisationally the enterprise reform involves a phased demono-polisation of the oversized production associations through their transformation into financially viable smaller production units, a process which has already started in the coal and oil industries.

In view of the continued dominance of state ownership, price controls and informal interference with enterprise autonomy, subsidies will continue to be provided to financially troubled enterprises, but on a more selective basis and with stricter conditions than in the past. Consequently closures of unprofitable production units will gradually increase.

1.3.2 Supply System

In the early stage of the reforms considerable continuity will remain in supply and distribution ties. For fear of possible disruptions in supply and unchecked price hikes on the part of largely monopolistic energy enterprises, the authorities will control a significant proportion of the distribution of energy products. During this period, running until about the mid-1990s, the energy-supply system will resemble a semi-market scheme in which competition among suppliers shows some increase, but on the whole remains largely circumscribed. Over time, however, the administrative controls will diminish in importance as new supply and distribution links are formed among enterprises. Even while the system of state orders remains in effect, energy producers will be allowed to freely dispose of output above state order, and it is expected that with the evolution of a more balanced supply–demand situation in the energy market the share of output freely contracted with customers will rise. From the second half of the 1990s the supply system as a whole will evolve toward a situation in which energy products are increasingly traded as regular wholesale items.

1.3.3 Ownership Relations

While a progressively greater part of the economy will be privatised, the energy sector will mainly remain in state hands. Prospects for private involvement in the ownership of energy enterprises is especially bleak in the short and medium term (until about 1995). Although a large part of the energy industry will be transformed to joint-stock companies, the shares will be owned almost entirely by the state (for instance, coal-producing enterprises will sell shares to power generators, which also remain in public ownership). Later, when the mechanisms of a market-oriented economy become more deeply rooted, private involvement will become significant through the inflow of foreign investment.

1.3.4 Investment

In this scenario it is not realistic to expect that energy producers will be able to secure all the necessary investment finance through self-financing and commercial credit. This may become possible in the longer term when prices are raised to economic levels, energy producers achieve financial viability and the commercial banking system is firmly in place. In the interim, however, the government has a major role to play in meeting the essential investment needs of the energy sector. Government withdrawal from energy investment financing would involve the risk of serious underinvestment for a substantial period, with damaging consequences for both the satisfaction of domestic demand and exports. During the transition period (until 1995), even with continued government funding the volume of energy investment is expected, at best, to remain at the level observed in 1990–2. From the mid-1990s, however, Russia and the other oil- and gas-rich republics will be able to count on greater foreign investment. Although it is assumed that realised FDI in energy will be substantial, some remaining unfavourable aspects of this scenario – notably continued dominance of state ownership, foreign investors' perception of unfair competition from state enterprises, the risk of government intervention in the management of state enterprises with which foreign investors are working in joint ventures – will prevent a potentially much larger capital inflow.

1.3.5 Prices

A multi-tier energy-pricing system will evolve: prices relating to state orders will continue to be administered while those in the parallel markets will be more or less determined by supply and demand. Periodically, administered prices will be subject to upward revision, but they will continue to lag far behind true scarcity prices. In the early period considerable distortions will also remain in relative prices for different fuels and between industrial and household prices. From the mid-1990s onward, in the more consolidated macroeconomic environment and in the face of more responsive consumer behaviour, decontrol of energy prices may accelerate, so that by the year 2000 domestic prices are expected to be brought in to line with the then prevailing world prices. Even after extensive marketisation efforts competition is expected to remain very limited in some sectors of the energy market. In these areas regulated pricing regimes will be necessary on the basis of long-term marginal costs of supply.

1.3.6 External Relations

The early stage of the reform will continue to operate with widely disparate multiple exchange rates. By the middle of the 1990s it may become possible to establish a unified exchange rate that is close to the rate registered in the free currency markets. Limited (internal) convertibility can be achieved in a few years into the reform programme, but introduction of full (external) convertibility at realistic exchange rates is not likely before 1996–7. For several years government authorities will maintain most of the currently existing administrative restrictions on foreign trade in energy. Over time, energy export and import licensing will be progressively liberalised. With the unification of exchange rates, the introduction of external convertibility and the gradual convergence of domestic and international energy prices, the country will be able to shift to an energy market that is open to exports and imports. In the interim special arrangements will be maintained: energy exports will remain subject to licensing, barter deals with the former CMEA partners will be prolonged, energy export taxes will remain in place and so on. As an incentive to stimulate energy output, foreign-exchange retention quotas allowed to producers will be increased to a considerably higher level than existed in 1992.

1.3.7 Macroeconomic Performance

The tightening of fiscal and monetary policies to attain a reasonable degree of financial stability will cause a more moderate drop of total output in 1992–4 than is assumed under Scenario 1. The economy will turn around in 1995 as the positive effects of phased financial stabilisation and some initial effects of partial market reforms begin to be felt, even though the recovery will be weaker than in Scenario 1. With the establishment of a comprehensive set of functioning market institutions by around 2000, the conditions will be in place for sustained rapid growth of GDP in the following years (at an average 5 per cent per year between 2000 and 2005). While the short-term economic slump expected for the early 1990s will reduce domestic energy demand, matching at least the extent of GDP decline, the anticipated acceleration of growth associated with structural reforms will act in the opposite direction. The outcome in terms of net energy exports will then hinge upon the extent of supply-side adjustments in response to macroeconomic policies and partial market reforms.

1.4   SCENARIO 3: EXTENDED PERIOD OF REFORM IMPASSE

Failure to resolve issues relating to the distribution of authority among the various levels of government, interrepublican rivalries, and the inability to agree on the future course of economic reforms will perpetuate the profound political and economic crisis that the FSU experienced at the beginning of the 1990s. The economy will drift without direction as the old administrative system continues to crumble and the creation of a functioning market system is delayed. The much weakened central agencies will be unable to prevent worsening disorder in the established production and distribution systems. The downward drift of the disintegrating economy will steepen; and energy output and exports will drop sharply. By around 1996–7 the issues underlying the crisis are expected to be resolved in Russia and most of the other republics, and the FSU economy will begin to turn around and to grow, although from a lower GDP, on a track similar to that of Scenario 2. This will improve the prospect of reversing falling trends in energy exports through gradually expanding output and through advances in energy conservation. Only by the end of the projection period (2005) will net energy exports slightly exceed the already depressed 1991 level.

1.4.1   Management System

In the period of political and economic upheaval running until the mid-1990s, the old planning apparatus will continue to lose its effective control over the energy sector and the economy as a whole. Although the much-weakened ministries will continue to set prices and production targets in the form of state orders and issue regulations to control energy supplies, these may be increasingly ignored and rendered largely inoperative by the producing enterprises. In the absence of a functioning market mechanism the energy sector will act without clear signals to guide economic decisions, as will the rest of the economy. As subsidies decline rapidly in this period a large number of producing firms will face bankruptcy, resulting in a reduction in overall production. From 1995–6, with the resolution of conflicts over power and reform concepts, the lines of authority faced by energy enterprises are expected to become clear and, with the subsequent unfolding of gradual market reforms, producers will encounter a tightening of their budget constraints and financial accountability, as outlined in Scenario 2.

1.4.2 Supply System

Until 1995–6, with the breakdown of central administrative allocation of inputs, this scenario assumes severe disruptions in the established supply and distribution links of energy. The system of state orders and state distribution monopolies will increasingly be bypassed owing to the inability of authorities to enforce regulations. In the face of a possible disintegration of the former all-union market, various barriers to interrepublican energy trade can be envisaged. The tendency toward regional energy autarky is expected to be strengthened. With the partial or complete collapse of the formal distribution system, parallel energy markets will emerge in which mostly barter transactions are conducted. The shift toward barter deals is expected to be especially important as inflation gets out of control, shortages become more endemic and a multiplicity of republican currencies emerge. The diversion of supplies from the traditionally established distribution system is bound to affect energy production adversely as essential equipment and parts supplies may not be available in time or in sufficient quantity. After 1995–6 gradual progress will be made toward a functioning wholesale market in energy products, similar to the one described under Scenario 2.

1.4.3 Ownership Relations

Failure to resolve issues of property rights is one of the reasons behind the impasse characterising the first stage of this scenario. Although the much weakened central political and economic control will encourage 'spontaneous privatisation', it is expected that, in view of the large book value of energy companies, the latter will mainly remain in public ownership. But the exercising of ownership rights will shift to lower levels of government. Uncertainties, legal wrangles, inconsistent decrees and increasing labour unrest will prevent foreign investors from playing other than a marginal role in the privatisation of energy. Even when the period of reform impasse is over the privatisation process is expected to be very slow. Depending on administrative feasibility, most of the large energy companies will be converted into joint-stock companies in which ownership rights are exercised by state property funds (holding companies). In view of the improved overall political, legal and economic climate of the post-1995 period, foreign investors will be able to play a more significant role in the privatisation process.

1.4.4 Investment

Energy investment will be particularly hard hit by the overall economic disintegration and confusion associated with the first stage of this scenario. Energy investment will fall at a rapid rate under the combined influence of insufficient central allocations, shifting investment priorities (towards consumer goods, housing, infrastructure, high tech manufacturing and so on), the lack of commercial credits and inability to self-finance. Foreign investment will be put on hold. In these circumstances the energy industry's resources will be insufficient even for capital maintenance and repair, let alone large new investments. Consequently the sector's technical parameters and productivity will rapidly deteriorate. With the 1996–7 turnaround in the economy the conditions for an upswing in investment activity will be gradually established: higher domestic energy prices will improve self-financing, commercial credits will become available, higher foreign-exchange retention quotas will make it easier to import equipment, and the pressing foreign-exchange needs felt at different levels of government will give some measure of priority to state-funded energy investment. Also the more consolidated post-1996 period of predictable moves towards a market economy and a more stable political and legal environment will start to attract substantial foreign investment in oil and gas.

1.4.5 Prices

During the crisis-ridden stage of this scenario the authorities will continue to fix energy prices. But owing to rapid inflation and the disintegration of formal distribution ties, these prices will be largely ignored and thus will lose much of their operational significance. A multiplicity of prices will emerge in the various sectors of the non-traditional energy markets (barter market, commodity exchanges, direct cash transactions among enterprises at contract prices and so on); prices in these markets are expected to exceed 'official prices' by a considerable margin and will tend to converge quickly toward market-clearing levels. It is reasonable to assume that, within a few years, freely contracted prices in these markets will roughly reflect the export prices obtained in energy sales abroad. Thus by the time the acute crisis is over, around 1996–7, and the country begins to move toward market reforms in an orderly fashion, energy prices will probably need little further correction.

1.4.6 External Relations

In the early stage of this scenario the chaotic economic conditions, severe inflationary pressures and widespread shortages will not allow even limited internal convertibility for the ruble. It is doubtful whether any other republican currency within the FSU will fare better. The discrepancy between the commercial rate and those registered in the parallel currency markets will be large. Formally, state orders for energy exports will remain in effect, but the authorities will find it hard to enforce them. In order to generate the foreign exchange required for servicing external debt and financing essential imports, the authorities will create stronger incentives for energy exporters, mainly in the form of retention quotas that are much higher than those presently in place. Even with these incentives the share of 'illegal' energy exports (that is, exports without license) may increase appreciably. With the stabilisation of the economy, the unification of the exchange rate and the institution of market mechanisms on a wider scale, conditions for full convertibility will be able to be met, but no sooner than 1997.

1.4.7 Macroeconomic Performance

Failure to stabilise the economy, collapse of the established lines of economic authority, runaway inflation, interrepublican obstacles to trade, widespread labour unrest, shortages and production interruptions, all characteristics of the early period of this scenario, will pull the economy into an extended period of decline. From 1992–5, the average annual rate of GDP decline will hover around 9–10 per cent. Although such a steep decline in economic activity will reduce energy demand by at least the same amount, potentially freeing energy for immediate export, the danger is that the contraction of energy output could be even greater. The net result could well be a fall in the exportable energy surplus. The economy will begin slowly to turn around in 1996–7, and the conditions will be put in place for sustained and relatively rapid growth thereafter. In the 1996–2005 period, GDP is assumed to grow at an average 3–4 per cent per year.

1.5   SCENARIO 4: REFORM IMPASSE AND INTERNAL WAR

In broad terms this scenario is identical with Scenario 3, except that in addition, as a result of unresolved political and territorial conflicts, an internal war is assumed to break out in the first half of the 1990s and to last for about a year. Vital economic functions such as transport will be crippled or completely paralysed while the war lasts. Total output will fall sharply, as the management system disintegrates, and because vital inputs will not be able to be obtained final products will not reach their ultimate destinations. There will be widespread damage to production and transport installations in energy and other industrial sectors.

As in Scenario 3 the reform impasse will continue through to 1995–6, after which the civil war will end. But the subsequent turnaround will occur from a lower level of GDP. The rate of recovery will not exceed that posited in the preceding scenario. A substantial cost will be incurred over several subsequent years in restoring the physical capital installations lost in the war. Hence the level of GDP will remain below that of the other scenarios throughout the time span considered.

Prewar exports of energy in this scenario will equal those of Scenario 3. During the war, virtually all export capability will break down. Energy output will recover quickly after the war has ended, but only up to the level permitted by the undamaged production and transport installations. This lower level may be needed in its entirety to satisfy domestic needs. Export capability will emerge only slowly, as damaged installations are rebuilt.

Table 1.1 Anticipated impact on the energy sector of long-term direction of policy and systemic change assumed in Scenarios 1–3

	Scenario 1 (radical)			Scenario 2 (gradualism)			Scenario 3 (reform impasse)		
	Supply	Demand	Exports	Supply	Demand	Exports	Supply	Demand	Exports
Management system	+++	---	+++	++	-	++	+	-	+
Supply system	++		++	+		+	+		+
Ownership	++	-	++	+	-	+	+	-	+
Investment	+++		+++	++		++	+		+
Prices	+++	---	+++	++	-	++	+	--	+
External relations	+++		++	++		++	+		+
Macroeconomic performance		+++	---		++	-		+	-
Overall	+++	---	+++	++	-	++	+	-	+

Key: + small increase; ++ moderate increase, +++ large increase
     - small reduction, -- moderate reduction, --- large reduction

2 Production Constraints and Prospects

This chapter deals with the problems, constraints and economic prospects of the FSU's fuel supplies. The analysis is restricted to the three major fuels, with the main emphasis on oil and natural gas. We pursue the inquiry in the following order: Section one examines the physical and technological constraints on fuel extraction. This section also establishes the linkage between these constraints and the cost of and prospects for future extraction. Section two deals with the economics of FSU fuel production, projects the probable shifts in costs and relates them to our scenarios. Section three places the issues into the institutional and socio-political context. Fuel production under the different scenarios will be subject to constraints and disturbances of a socio-economic nature. It will also be influenced heavily by perceptions of national interest.

In the first two sections the three fuels are examined in turn because they are subject to very different and uneven limitations of the geological base, geographic environment and available technology. In Section 2 we find it essential to treat the export dimension separately in the case of natural gas. The technological and geographic rigidity of gas exports, the very high up-front investment required in the case of distant gas supplies, and the long-term commitment that these factors imply explain that special treatment.

2.1 PHYSICAL–TECHNOLOGICAL CONSTRAINTS

Given the time horizon of the year 2005, these constraints are shaped by (a) the volume, area distribution and geographic accessibility of proved recoverable reserves; (b) the quality of those reserves and the reservoirs that hold them; (c) addition to reserves in new fields accessible for development by 2005. Cumulative past production by province, and the extent, volume and character of the sediment are also relevant since they affect the distribution of remaining reserves by field size and well flows, both critical components for lead times, investment needs and future costs.

Geology and geography severely affect oil and coal extraction. For natural gas no reserve bottleneck exists. However the effects of reserve degradation from rash production practices have emerged even in the case of gas, while new gas fields will be more difficult to exploit. The physical constraints on the gas industry operate chiefly via transport and distribution costs, investment requirements and lead times.

It is impossible to construct a neat table of physically determined ceilings on output levels for the three fuels. Yet some broad quantitative statements can be made concerning feasible, but not necessarily economic, levels of extraction. These estimates are hazarded at the outset for each fuel.

2.1.1 Crude Oil

2.1.1.1 *Estimated Physical 'Ceiling' on Oil Extraction: 550 million tons*

The feasible level of oil production in the FSU up to 2005 'permitted' by the resource base may be gauged from the following physical–technical indicators: (a) a time series of four decades of well flow, and forecasts by Russian experts beyond 2000; (b) depletion of 62 per cent of high flow reserves in Russia's producing fields; (c) the size distribution of Russia's discovered deposits, 90 per cent of which held initial reserves of less than 30 million tons, with almost 80 per cent falling below 10 million tons. Soon after 2000, average well yields in the FSU will be no more than four tons per day.[1] A 550 million tons yearly extraction level would demand almost a tripling of the well stock early next century, and in far more scattered locations than in 1990. In that year one fifth of all wells were located in just five fields.[2] Significantly the latest Soviet oil minister claims that FSU reserves *could* make possible this level of extraction (Churilov, 1991, p. 4).

2.1.1.2 *Reserves: Geographic Distribution and Size*

Ninety-four per cent of cumulative extraction in the FSU has taken place in the European regions, the Caucasus and West Siberia (Map 2.1).[3] Per square kilometer of sedimentary basins, two thirds more oil was produced from these provinces than from those of the US, including onshore Alaska. Similarly West Siberia, which had no oil industry until the mid-1960s, produced two thirds more per square kilometer of sedimentary deposits than did continental US.[4] Extraction on such a massive scale has drastically affected the size distribution of the remaining reserves and well yields in petroleum reservoirs.

Map 2.1 Hydrocarbon basins of the FSU

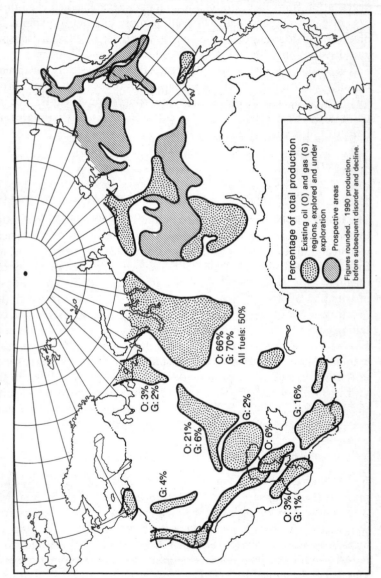

Percentage of total production

Existing oil (O) and gas (G) regions, explored and under exploration

Prospective areas

Figures rounded. 1990 production, before subsequent disorder and decline.

O: 66%
G: 70%
All fuels: 50%

O: 3%
G: 2%

O: 21%
G: 6%

G: 2%

G: 16%

O: 6%

G: 4%

O: 3%
G: 1%

Tables 2.1–2.3 give the distribution of proven plus probable reserves in the FSU.[5] These reserves are broken down according to geography, producing and undeveloped fields, and two crucial categories of quality. In addition Table 2.4 shows the remaining recoverable reserves for 29 producing West-Siberian deposits, together with their levels of depletion.

Eighty-six per cent of all proven and probable reserves of the FSU are in Russia, with West Siberia accounting for a dominant proportion of the total. The historic provinces of the Volgo-Urals, Azerbayjan and the North Caucasus account for only about one tenth of the FSU's petroleum reserves. Here the big fields are all 70–90 per cent depleted. Many small deposits do remain, but they contribute negligibly to aggregate reserves. For example, 98.6 per cent of all pools in Tatarstan hold less than one million tons of oil (Maksimov, 1989, vol. I, p. 47; Khalimov *et al.*, 1990, p. 106). Apart from Russia, only Kazakhstan has significant reserves in the proven plus probable categories.

Table 2.1   Proven plus probable reserves of oil in the FSU and republics in 1991 (million tons)

	Million Tons	*% of FSU total*	*% of reserves withdrawn from producing fields*
All fields			
FSU	22505	100.0	
Russia	19354	86.0	
of which:			
West Siberia	15999	71.1	
Other FSU	3150	14.0	
of which:			
Kazakhstan	2025	9.0	
Azerbayjan	518	2.3	
Turkmenistan	450	2.0	
Producing fields			
FSU	16338	100.0	49.4
Russia	11632	71.2	51.8
of which:			
West Siberia	8440	51.7	39.6

Note: For definition of reserves, see Note 5.
Sources: Computed from data obtained from Russian petroleum specialists. Supplemented by data contained in *Ekonomika i zhizn'*, no. 9 (February 1992), pp. 4–5.

Table 2.2 Proven plus probable oil reserves of Russia

	In all discovered fields		In producing fields		Reserves in producing fields as % of those in all fields	Percentage of initial produceable reserves extracted	Production (million tons)	Reserve production ratio in producing fields
	(million tons)	(% of total active vs others)	(million tons)	(million (% of total active vs others))				
	1	2	3	4	5	6	7	8
1976:								
Active	11229	76.2	8681	85.0	77.3	33.3	386	22.5
Hard-to-produce	3507	23.8	1532	15.0	43.7	16.4	17	90.7
1981:								
Active	10771	64.5	7618	80.3	70.7	46.7	506	15.0
Hard-to-produce	5928	35.5	1369	19.7	23.1	18.6	30	46.1
1986:								
Active	11251	59.8	6825	69.7	60.7	57.4	470	14.5
Hard-to-produce	7563	40.2	2967	30.3	39.2	18.3	58	51.1
1988:								
Active	11551	58.5	7854	66.9	68.0	56.2	465	16.9
Hard-to-produce	8861	46.0	5043	42.4	56.9	19.7	103	49.1
1991:								
Active	10316	53.3	6479	55.9	62.8	62.9	383	16.9
Hard-to-produce	9038	46.7	5152	44.1	57.1	22.4	117	43.9

Note: For definition of reserves see Note 5.
Source: Computed from data obtained from Russian petroleum specialists.

Table 2.3 Proven plus probable oil reserves of West Siberia

	In all discovered fields		In producing fields		Reserves in producing fields as % of those in all fields	Percentage of initial produceable reserves extracted	Production (million tons)	Reserve production ratio in producing fields
	(million tons)	(% of total active vs others)	(million tons)	(% of total active vs others)				
	1	2	3	4	5	6	7	8
1976:								
Active	6439	77.9	4758	91.1	78.9	10.1	148	32.2
Hard-to-produce	1826	22.1	464	8.9	25.4	0.3	0	1549.7
1981:								
Active	7331	63.9	4638	88.1	63.3	27.5	303	15.3
Hard-to-produce	4142	36.1	626	11.9	15.1	2.4	6	113.9
1986:								
Active	8339	59.4	4683	74.2	56.2	42.5	332	14.1
Hard-to-produce	5700	46.6	1628	25.8	28.6	5.8	27	60.8
1988:								
Active	8663	58.2	5938	70.3	68.6	41.2	342	17.4
Hard-to-produce	6222	41.8	2509	29.7	40.3	7.1	51	49.5
1990:								
Active	7883	54.4	5202	60.8	66.0	47.9	328	15.6
Hard-to-produce	6346	44.6	3353	39.2	52.8	10.2	65	51.9
1991:								
Active	9343	53.6	4929	58.4	52.8	50.6	286	17.2
Hard-to-produce	6655	46.4	3511	41.6	52.8	11.9	78	44.8

Note: For definition of reserves see Note 5.

Table 2.4   Reserves in producing oil fields in West Siberia and per cent of initial reserves withdrawn, 1990

Fields	Remaining recoverable reserves (million tons)	% of initial reserves extracted
Samotlor	1336	59
Fedorovskoe	415	45
Mamontovskoe	219	63
Tallinskoe	209*	20
Pravdinskoe	201**	9
Dovkhovskoe	194	6
Povkhovskoe	120	37
South-Surgut (Yuzhno)	109	49
Var'yega	109	59
Tarasovskoe	105	18
Sutorminskoe	95	29
Pokachevskoe	88	62
West Surgut (Zapadno)	87 (109)*	55
Sovetskoe	87	55
Vatinskoe	66	58
Vyngaiakhskoe	64	5
Yaunlorkskoe	62	38
Potochnoe	62	22
North Var'yega	59	36
Tagrinskoe	59	40
North-Pokurskoe	58	39
Ur'yevskoe	55	42
Danilovskoe	50	19
Lokosovskoe	43	60
Malorechenskoe	39	0
Karamovskoe	22	52
Barsukovskoe	22	35
Ombinskoe	17	0
Central Balyk	11	55
Total of above	4063	
Total for all West-Siberian producing fields	8441	39.6

* The larger figure for West Surgut is that of the Ministry of Oil Industry, now abolished. The smaller one is by the Hermes Corporation of Russia, which recently concluded a project of reassessing Russian oil reserves. In the light of this reassessment and the known difficulties with recoverability at the Tallinskoe field, reserves claimed for the latter are almost certainly too high.
** Only $B + C_1$ reserves were supplied. Because production takes place overwhelmingly from A reserves, cumulative output to date was used as a surrogate for that reserve category.
Sources: For eight of the fields, reserves were made public for the first time (in a somewhat oblique fashion) in *Ekonomika i zhizn'*, December 1991, special issue, pp. 8–9, by V. Neverov and A. Igolkin of Hermes Corporation of Russia. Data for the other fields were obtained from Russian petroleum specialists.

Producing fields contain the bulk of FSU reserves. The share of these reserves is less for Russia as a whole and for its key West-Siberian province, reflecting both a shorter history and worsening accessibility (Table 2.1). 55 per cent of FSU reserves and 52 per cent of those of Russia are in declining stages of output (Churilov, 1991–2, p. 4; Neverov and Igolkin, 1991, p. 8; see also Table 2.5). This in itself suggests that production will decrease in the immediate future, but size, accessibility and depletion rates worsen the outlook.

In Russia more than 60 per cent of the high-flow reserves of all producing fields had been depleted by January 1991 (Figure 2.1 and Tables 2.2–2.3). The situation was somewhat similar in the largest 20 deposits (Churilov, 1991, p. 4). These giants contained 60 per cent of all the recoverable reserves ever discovered in the FSU. The pressure on the best fields also points to an inevitable decline.

Most of the remaining deposits are quite small. Eighty per cent of Russia's 1586 oil fields, for example, held initial reserves of less than ten million tons, with the median size being well under five million. Such fields can produce only a few hundred thousand tons of oil in a year during their plateau phase, and less through most of their lifecycle. In West Siberia the average size of fields discovered during the 1980s was still double that of the FSU as a whole, but with a precipitously falling trend (Zolotov and Salmanov, 1992, p. 6).

Annual reserve depletion from mature reservoirs has fluctuated around 100 million tons for half a decade (Neverov and Igolkin, 1991, pp. 8–9; and Filimonov, 1990b, p. 4). Reserve replacement from fields of under 10 million tons of initial reserves is physically impossible. The entire known stock of deposits of that size would be withdrawn for reserve replacement in four years simply to maintain output at 400–450 million tons.

Maps 2.1 and 2.2 show the location of the FSU's petroleum provinces and outline West Siberia and its sub-regions, which account for 71 per cent of total oil reserves. The size of West Siberia's reserves and their location just east of the Urals made the province accessible to exploitation on a scale found only around the Arabian/Persian Gulf. Three decades of exploration, however, have also established the geological limitations on oil accumulation, which precludes the province from containing recoverable reserves of a magnitude similar to that of the Arabian/Persian Gulf.

More than two fifths of the area around the rim of the basin is quite shallow and lacks the high ratios of organic matter in the source rocks that are so prominent in the inner part of the province. The periphery

Table 2.5 Oil production according to well yields, percentage of reserves produced and dynamics of output, Russia and West Sibera (per cent of total production)

Characteristics	Russia					West Siberia				
	1981	1986	1988	1990	1991	1981	1986	1988	1990	1991
According to volume of output from wells, tons per day										
More than 100 tons/day	31.9	0.3	1.6	0.1	0.5	55.3	–	1.8	–	–
50–100	20.0	21.8	10.1	8.6	3.5	31.6	32.9	13.8	9.4	4.1
25–50	10.8	33.1	36.3	34.4	9.8	12.2	45.4	46.6	44.7	12.9
5–25	31.0	36.2	43.2	45.5	73.8	0.7	21.6	37.7	45.9	82.0
Less than 5 tons/day	6.3	8.6	8.8	11.4	11.4	0.2	0.1	0.1	0	1.0
Depletion of initial reserves in fields										
less than 20%	52.6	48.9	52.9	54.8	51.9	63.1	55.0	59.1	60.2	56.8
20–50%	25.1	26.4	26.7	23.1	23.3	26.8	27.5	27.7	22.4	23.0
50–80%	20.0	17.2	14.0	16.3	17.8	9.9	15.2	11.0	15.2	17.1
More than 80%	2.3	7.5	6.4	5.8	7.0	0.2	2.3	2.2	2.2	3.1
Dynamics of output from remaining recoverable reserves										
Increasing output	40.8	43.2	43.3*	30.2	30.9	49.6	56.3	52.9	30.0	31.2
Stable output	26.2	7.0	9.0*	12.0	15.7	39.4	5.7	18.9	12.6	16.6
Falling output	32.0	48.7	46.8*	56.6	51.8	11.0	38.0	28.2	57.4	52.2
At end of lifecycle	1.0	1.1	0.9*	1.2	1.6	–	–	–	–	–

* Data for 1989.
Source: Computed from data obtained from Russian petroleum specialists.

Figure 2.1   Percentage of 'active' reserves extracted in producing fields, Russia and West Siberia

Note: For a definition of reserves see Note 5.
Source: Tables 2.2 and 2.3.

has also been flushed with water, leaving behind mostly dry structures. In addition the subsidence and thermal history of West Siberia all but rule out the existence of massive oil deposits in the northern third of the basin (north of 65° latitude), and in a much larger proportion if offshore areas are added. That same geological history, however, has endowed the north of the province with the largest accumulation of gas reserves in the world (Grace and Hart, 1983; Yermakov and Skorobogatov, 1984; Shirkovskiy, 1992).

Oil accumulation in West Siberia is overwhelmingly concentrated south of 65° latitude, in the Middle Ob' core region and in the adjacent parts of neighbouring districts. Most oilfields here with more than ten million tons of recoverable reserves were being exploited by 1992 (Map 2.3). The majority of deposits not yet in production have highly problematic reservoir properties, as have a number of fields already worked. Complications also characterise the few oil fields in the northern third of the province (Mukhametzianov and Sonin, 1992, pp. 40–42).[6]

Map 2.2 The West-Siberian oil and gas province with subregions

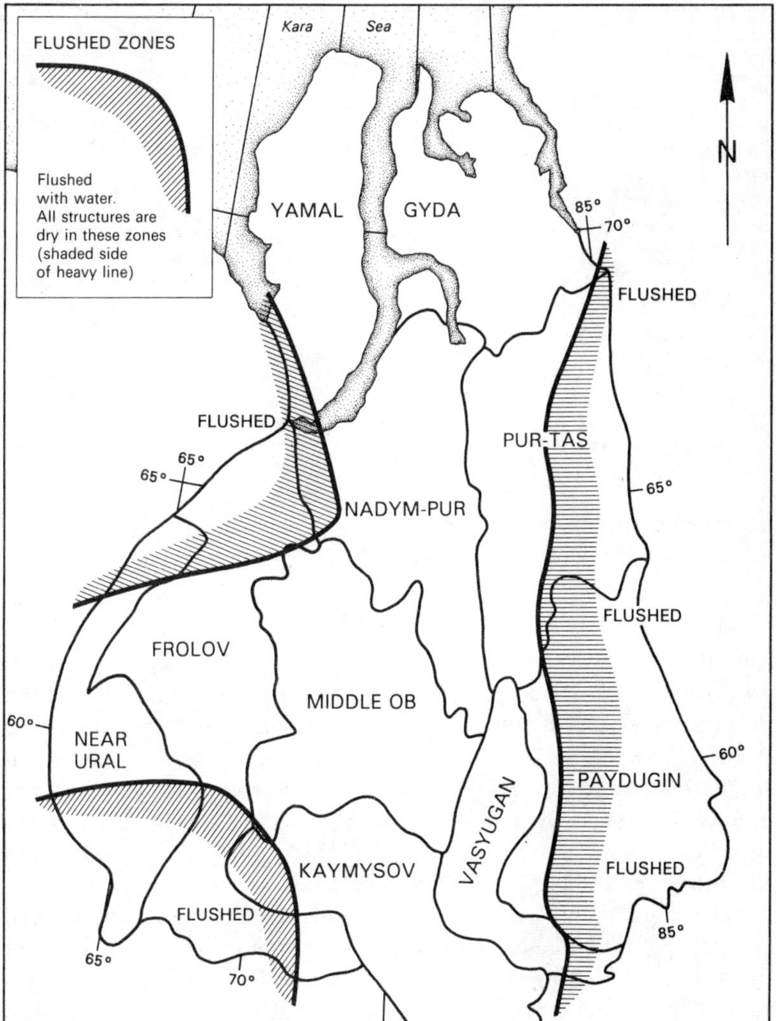
FLUSHED ZONES
Flushed
with water.
All structures are
dry in these zones
(shaded side
of heavy line)
Kara
Sea
N
YAMAL
GYDA
85°
70°
FLUSHED
FLUSHED
PUR-TAS
65°
65°
65°
NADYM-PUR
FLUSHED
FROLOV
MIDDLE OB
60°
NEAR
URAL
60°
VASYUGAN
PAYDUGIN
KAYMYSOV
FLUSHED
FLUSHED
85°
65°
70°
55°
55°
75°
80°
0
500
KILOMETERS

Map 2.3   Oilfields of the Middle Ob' petroleum region (after Maksimov)

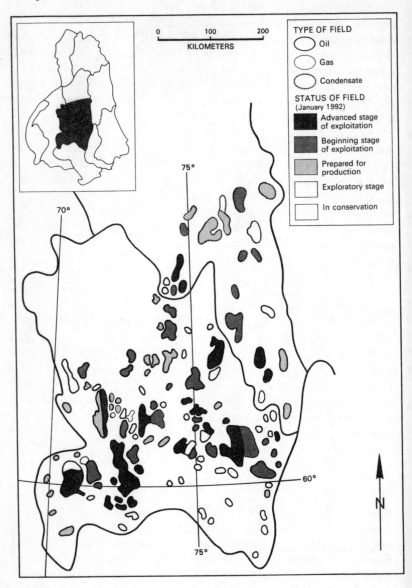

From the Yenisei river to the Pacific Ocean, which makes up almost half of the FSU, geographic remoteness and a harsh natural environment have severely limited exploration to date. All of East Siberia and the continental Far East, (excluding Sakhalin) count only some 45 deposits, most of them gas (Maksimov, 1989, vol. II, pp. 262–92). The East Siberian Platform presents a difficult terrain, where rivers provide the only means of surface transport. The geology is also extremely complex. Hydrocarbon reservoirs are mostly in rocks of extreme age (a very rare phenomenon), resulting in highly irregular reservoir properties. These deposits cannot be counted on to affect our projections in any significant fashion.[7]

The deposits of offshore Azerbayjan and those of Sakhalin will play a role in the time scale considered here. Their impact on aggregate FSU fuel supplies will be minor, but the output will be significant locally and for the participating foreign companies. Apart from those of Russia, the reserves of Kazakhstan, mostly in the North Caspian Province, are the only ones large enough to make a major impact (Map 2.1). This deep salt basin abuts European Russia, its western extremities extending west of the Volga River. It is much more accessible geographically than others in Siberia and Central Asia.

Very large reserves have already been proven here and prospects are still greater. However the engineering constraints are serious. Geological conditions are highly diverse. The quality and flow characteristics of the crudes vary widely. All the rich payzones are at great depth, below thick salt layers, and yield very sulfurous crude (and gas). Drilling to such depths requires heavy rigs and much auxiliary work. Tenghiz is a supergiant with 1850 million tons of oil in place and the third largest recoverable reserves ever discovered in FSU. Its appraisal in the original Chevron–Soviet Protocol (1991) and the slightly earlier Soviet technical–economic plan (1987), assessed peak annual production at 36 million tons and 30 million tons, respectively, for 7–9 years (information from Russian petroleum specialists).

2.1.1.3 *Reservoir Characteristics and Reserve Quality*

Reservoir characteristics constitute a restriction on output of equal severity as field size, depth, and geography. FSU specialists divide reserves into two categories, so-called 'active' reserves, that is, high flow and otherwise attractive reserves, and 'hard-to-recover' ones (for definitions see Note 5). Tables 2.2–2.3 provide information about the current state of the FSU's oil reserves in these terms. The share of 'active' reserves in all deposits discovered in Russia has sharply decreased in recent years, but in absolute terms their quantity has remained little affected. In producing fields in Russia, however, the volume of 'active' reserves has shrunk by one fourth in the past 15 years. This easy oil has been worked out rapidly: in 1976 only a third of initial reserves in this category had been extracted, but by 1991 nearly two-thirds had been extracted (Table 2.2, Column 6).

In West Siberia the reserve situation is much better. Yet the depletion of 'active' reserves in the province's producing fields has been even faster than in Russia as a whole, and by 1991 one half of such reserves were drained (Figure 2.1 and Table 2.3). The extraction decline from such pools is irreversible. To stabilise the province's output, a large number of far-flung smaller deposits must be developed without delay. In addition, more recalcitrant reservoirs and 'hard-to-recover' oil would have to contribute more to the total.

Once a reservoir has produced half of its reserves an inevitable decline begins in the great majority of cases. This can be slowed, but rarely arrested, by expensive new investment. Reservoir damage brings forward the onset of decline, a serious problem in some West-Siberian oil fields. Yet the reserve–production ratio in Russia as a whole and in West Siberia would be quite satisfactory,[8] if the industry had prepared itself for more difficult reserves with respect to quality, size and geographic location.

Instead of such preparation, what took place was sheer *Raubwirtschaft* , that is, predatory exploitation. In the oil regions of West Siberia a single geological complex, the Neocomean, supplied 90 per cent of all cumulative output until 1989, that is close to five billion tons. More than 90 per cent of this was extracted from only half a dozen fields, *all in the span of two decades* (Khalimov *et al.*, p. 103; *Izvestiia*, June 16, 1989, p. 4 and Sagers, April 1991, pp. 257–9). The rest was largely produced at 8–9 smaller deposits where reserve workout by the end of the 1980s reached 45 per cent or more. These deposits are fairly close together in the Middle Ob' district of West Siberia.

Though the reservoirs of Samotlor held only 20–30 per cent as much recoverable oil as the biggest supergiants of the Arabian/Persian Gulf, it was forced to produce approximately as much as Burgan or Ghawar within two decades. Most of Samotlor's high-flow oil is gone, and the remaining two fifths of its reserves (Table 2.4) will be far more difficult and costly to extract (Riva, 1991, p. 67; Nehring, 1978, p. 14; Brilliant, 1989, pp. 35–8).

The consequences of *Raubwirtschaft* are highlighted by Figures 2.2 and 2.3 and Table 2.5. During the 1980s the contribution of reserves with well yields of more than 25 tons per day fell dramatically, both in Russia and in West Siberia. In 1991 more than half of West-Siberian reserves had declining production compared with only one tenth a decade earlier. The problem is magnified by the fast rise in the share of hard-to-recover oil in total reserves, both in Russia as a whole and in Western Siberia.[9] Reservoirs of anomalously high pressure add further engineering constraints.

Figure 2.2   Production in Russia according to well yield

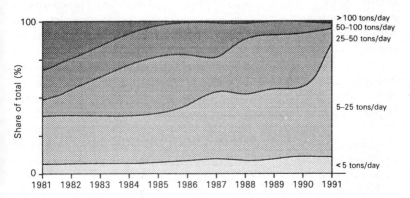

Source: Based on data obtained from Russian petroleum specialists.

Figure 2.3   Production in West Siberia according to well yield

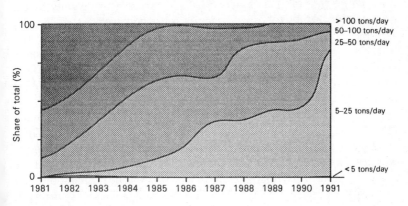

Source: Based on data obtained from Russian petroleum specialists.

Figure 2.4 attempts a breakdown of the extracted volume in the FSU between 1991 and 2000, according to Scenario 2. At a level of 370 million tons in 2000, only a third of Russian production would originate from wells operating in 1991, with the average yield from these slumping to only 3–4 tons per day. The wells drilled during the rest of the 1990s must account for 75 per cent of output by 2000, to reach the forecast volumes.[10] Crude oil outside Russia and gas condensate will still account for only a fifth of all the FSU's production in that year. Scenario 1, with a more elevated Russian output in 2000, attributes an even higher share of the total to new wells.

Given the accelerated deterioration of conditions in the oil industry, we assign a low probability to the extraction levels projected in Scenario 1. The probability of output in Scenario 2 will depend on developments in 1993–1995.

Figure 2.4   Sources of oil production for Scenario 2 (million tons)

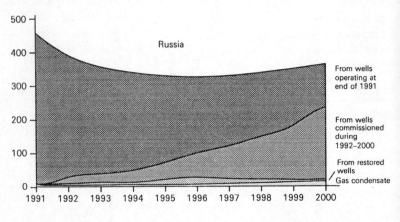

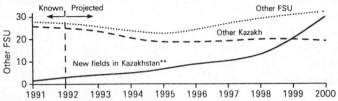

* Russian oil production will be at least 10 million tons lower than originally projected for Scenario 2.

** Tenghiz, Karachaganak, Kumkol.

Damaged fields, bypassed oil, complex reservoirs and enhanced recovery
The geological–technological limits on our production series are strongly influenced by the destructive production practices of the past. Especially in West Siberia, large quantities of bypassed oil remain in damaged reservoirs. Better recovery techniques, fine-tuned to the particular needs of individual fields, could have produced much of that oil. In addition recovery from a number of Russian geological formations, to which great hopes had been attached, has been disappointing. Specialists have become more pessimistic about future volumes of recovery than they were during the 1970s and early 1980s. The most recent advances in drilling and recovery techniques, however, *do* give access to some bypassed oil. They can also increase oil flow or steady erratic well yields from complex reservoirs.

Gauging the distribution and recoverability of bypassed oil and oil in complex formations adds an original contribution to our study. For this purpose we collated and examined some 900 reservoirs in more than 300 West-Siberian oil fields. From this total, a sample of 204 were subjected to a linear analysis of physical and geometric reservoir properties and to a model of multidimensional scaling (MDS).[11] Similar exercises on a smaller scale were carried out for the Pechora and Caspian provinces and the Ufa-Orenburg and Lower Volga regions

In order to estimate the location and volume of such oil, statistical correlations were computed between geological and engineering descriptor variables from all tabulated West-Siberian oil fields and their reported oil yields. The variables most strongly linked with oil yield are, in order of importance: permeability, initial gas–oil ratio, porosity, absolute height, overall formation thickness and reservoir height. The statistical results are readily interpretable in terms of standard reservoir engineering concepts. Collectively these descriptors are highly useful for predictions of theoretical productivity and for analytical comparisons with actual oil yields. Brief notes in Appendix 2.1 provide further detail on the methodological approaches. The geological analysis was conducted at the Kansas Geological Survey. Full details of the reservoirs and those that appear as seriously underperforming, together with the regression equations, the resulting scattergrams and the methodological notes, are held by the author of this chapter.[12]

We reached a number of conclusions from the quantitative analysis of reservoir data. These conclusions were supplemented by qualitative assessments, based on published sources and consultation in Moscow.

(1) 33 reservoirs in producing fields were significantly underperforming in the mid-1980s when the data was collected, including some in the second- and third-largest fields of West Siberia. In more than half the cases (though not in the case of Samotlor) they lie immediately below or above those which have been worked very intensively under the pressure of plan fulfillment. These reservoirs almost certainly suffered damage. Their indicated potential, therefore, may never be reached. The additional volume of theoretically recoverable oil from these reservoirs is very difficult to estimate, but it is crucial to note that the reference is not to the total amount of oil in place. By applying the per centage of underperformance to cumulative production from the relevant geological strata listed under the scattergrams, we came up with about 50 million tons of unproduced oil from these reservoirs.[13] More recoverable oil certainly exists also in reservoirs that could not be included in the regression equation. However only a proportion of all this oil could be recovered in the immediate future, though perhaps most of it by early 2000.

(2) In a far larger number of cases, however, severe underperformance simply reflects extreme geological complexity, resulting in erratic, unpredictable reservoir behaviour and well flow. Disappointing performance cannot be attributed to engineering errors, irresponsibility or even the pressure of plan performance in the past. Almost all these reservoirs are associated with three geological complexes: (a) the Bazhenov Formation, (b) the Achimov Succession and (c) the Middle and Lower Jurassic, with sometimes the Upper Jurassic added. Two decades of study and experimentation with (a) has confirmed the view that high well yields in the early years, and sometimes only months, are followed by a virtual collapse of well flows, resulting in an extremely wasteful use of fixed assets.[14] Reservoirs of (b) and (c) have so disappointed Russian specialists that by the early 1990s, they rate recoverability of reserves in (b) as 15–20 per cent and in (c) as ranging erratically from 0 to 25 per cent (Pliakov *et al.*, 1992, p. 38; A. I. Shirkovskiy, 1992)[15].

Significant underperformance also characterised the Pechora province, particularly its limestone reservoirs. Almost two thirds of the latter produced lower than predicted yields, 55 per cent very significantly so (Appendix 2:1). However the volumes left behind were small compared with those in West Siberia. Only 21 fields are in production (from 74 discovered), and cumulative extraction from the province amounts to less than 5 per cent of that from West Siberia

(Leonidov *et al.*, 1992, pp. 5–7). Underperformance in the Ufa-Orenburg and Lower Volga regions is less prominent.

Enhanced recovery methods (EOR), which include the injection of steam, natural gas or CO_2, and chemical miscibles, can augment the flow from such recalcitrant strata and also bring heavy oil to the surface. In 1990, EOR provided only 11.6 million tons of total FSU oil and 41.4 million *cumulatively* during 1986–90. Russia produced almost three-fourths of that and West Siberia more than one third. Oil-ministry specialists have estimated possible EOR contribution for each region and claim that by 2000 Russia could extract 17.3 million tons, and 23.2 million by 2005. World-market prices for oil and vigorous Western investment would augment production by an additional cumulative 10 million tons or more. New technologies, such as horizontal wells, are likely to have a significant impact on future EOR projects, especially in West Siberia where the bulk of the prospects are concentrated.

Enhanced recovery could rise gradually and attain 30 million additional tons annually by 2005. Until 2000 this flow is shown in the 'flow from wells operating in 1991' in Figure 2.4. The feasible additions to output from enhanced recovery must nonetheless be put into context. In the time-frame of our study the fate of Russian and FSU oil production will for all practical purposes continue to be decided by extraction from new wells and 'active' reserves.

2.1.1.4 Restoring Idle Wells

Old wells may stand idle for need of repair or restoration. Or they may be in the process of changing over from free flow to pumps. New wells need to be connected to oil-gathering systems, and they may be inoperative due to delays in connecting them. They may also be inoperative due to damage to or repair being carried out on gathering lines.

For these reasons a small per centage of wells will stand idle in any producing country, even when no capacity is shut in to influence supplies. In the FSU, however, and above all in West Siberia, the number of idle wells has risen enormously because of supply break-downs and the flight of skilled specialists. Lack of repair and a deteriorating physical stock is doubtless the main reason for the fact that a fifth of all West Siberia's oil wells and more than 12 per cent of all FSU's wells were standing idle by mid-1991. The proportions were even larger in 1992, with a total of 20000 wells idle in Russia and 22000 in the FSU (Ikonnikov and Fayzullin, 1991, pp. 3–4; *EBE*, April 1992, p. 4).

Well restoration is not a remedy for the longer term and has only a modest pay-off in very mature provinces. In West Siberia, however, that pay-off is still substantial. While well yields are decreasing precipitously (to one tenth of what they were 15 years ago; Table 2.5), they are still three to four times that in the old provinces of the Middle Volga, and ten times that in Azerbayjan (or the US).

Well restoration, combined with reservoir stimulation, thus represents one clear area for action, including Western investment. While the payoff is modest compared with what may be expected from the exploitation of attractive new deposits, much quicker financial returns could be anticipated. In addition the Russian government supports foreign involvement in this area, which promises immediate cash rewards without the political complexities associated with developing untapped deposits. However, given the predatory production practices of the past and the resulting damage to reserves, investment in mature fields presents substantial risks and will be economically attractive only for a fraction of West Siberia's fields and pools.

In our well-flow analysis, 30 per cent of the reservoirs studied had appreciably lower yields than predicted by the regression equations and the MDS model. Assuming that a similar per centage holds for the reservoirs of the 110–115 West-Siberian fields *in production* during 1991/2, we estimate that about 100 reservoirs would have lower than predicted well yields, and more than 50 substantially so.

The volume of oil available from well restoration at a good financial return is substantial but should not be overestimated. Projecting the secular decline from new and old wells, one may estimate close to 70 million tons of *cumulative* availability from January 1993 through to the end of 1995 in West Siberia by restoring two thirds of the inoperative well stock. Timely well repair in some of the better fields of mature provinces may bring that cumulative total to perhaps 90 million tons. However this is only a possible amount and not necessarily an economically rational or even a feasible one. A Russian forecast projects only 15 million tons from presently idle wells in this decade (NIIEng figures).

Reaction to well restoration and reservoir stimulation is always fortuitous, but damaged reservoirs respond particularly erratically. Ignorance of the extent of such damage, as much as severe logistical problems, lie behind the financially disastrous experience of the

Phibro–White Nights joint venture in West Siberia (*PIW*, 11 May 1992, pp. 1–2). In addition the economy of well restoration declines more than proportionately across the well population from abundant to meager yields. And in any case, output from restored wells will again decrease rapidly a year or two later. It is thus essential that extensive data on the production history of each prospective candidate for bypassed oil or restoration be obtained and analysed before any investment decision in mature fields.

2.1.2 Natural Gas

2.1.2.1 Estimated Physical 'Ceiling' on Natural Gas Extraction and Delivery cannot be Determined

In theory the crude ratio of reserves to production could support an extraction level double the current output of roughly 800 BCM annually. Even from a purely geological point of view, however, any such statement is meaningless. The physical 'ceiling' of extraction level depends not only on the reserve–production ratio but equally on still unknown technological limits to production along very harsh geographical frontiers. In the case of gas, this margin shifts not incrementally but by large, discrete leaps. Lead times to extract the most northerly deposits in West Siberia (both on land and on the Arctic shelf) are still unknown, and this is true for most reserves of the Far East as well. As a consequence decisions taken in the 1990s about the 'geographic margin' of extraction will heavily influence output ceilings by 2000, and even more beyond.

2.1.2.2 Reserves: Size and Geography

The FSU boasts 45 per cent of the world's proven plus probable gas reserves, 88 per cent of which are in Russia and 72 per cent in West Siberia. But while 16 per cent of the FSU's reserves are fully proven, in West Siberia that share is less than 8 per cent (Table 2.6). This point is made not to diminish the vastness of West-Siberian gas reserves, but to underpin the following.

West-Siberian production, 27–28 per cent of the world's total, is being withdrawn mostly from a very restricted portion of two super-giant fields, Urengoy and Yamburg (Maps 2.2 and 2.4). In 1990 the two fields produced 61 per cent of Russia's and almost half of total FSU free gas (gas not associated with oil production) from less than 1700 wells. These wells were concentrated on the southern halves of the

Table 2.6　Natural gas reserves in the FSU and republics, 1988 (BCM)

	Proven[1]	Proven plus probable	Column 1 as % of column 2	Possible[2]	Prospective[3]
FSU	8190	49242	16.6	12608	27495
Land	8015	48578	16.5	11924	16756
European Russia	682	698	97.7	78	118
Ural-Volga	818			1995	1853
Ukraine-Belorussia	1412	1974	71.5	247	592
Caucasus (including offshore)	333			95	142
West Siberia	2751	35296	7.8	7367	11848
of which Yamal		9650		6900	
East Siberia and Far East	93	1494	6.2	7111	1193
of which Yakutia	13	779	0.2	267	54
Central Asia	1859	4656	39.9	1066	982
of which:					
Turkmenia[4]		2250			
Uzbekistan[4]		1000			
Kazakhstan	68	1394	4.5	367	28
Shelf	175	664	26.3	684	10739

Notes:
1. Fully proven, recoverable reserves, with production wells.
2. Discovered but not yet explored reserves.
3. Promising but undrilled structures in productive formations, or extension of structures in the possible reserves category.
4. 1990–1.
Sources: VNII ekonomiki gazovoi promyshlennosti, unpublished *Doklad*, Moscow, July 1989; *WGI*, February 1992, p. 6; and information from Russian specialists.

fields, tapping mostly the shallow Cenomanian horizons for about 90 per cent of the gas produced.[16] The extraction level that prevailed in the early 1990s will significantly reduce reserves in these giants by 2000. Their physical ability to produce will drop substantially.

Inadequate prospecting and preparation led to overestimation of reserves even at Urengoy, the world's largest on-shore deposit, according to the latest evidence of falling pressure. Ten per cent of estimated reserves for the whole field and 30 per cent in some parts of the field may be non-existent. No further increases in extraction are possible from Urengoy. The deposit will begin to decline as early as 1996, with sharp decreases in well productivity (Skobtsov and Chernova, 1992, p. 17). In order to manage an orderly phase out, considerable exploratory and development work will have to focus on the northern parts of the

Map 2.4 Natural gas in West Siberia. Deposits of the Nadym-Pur gas region – largest fields in production

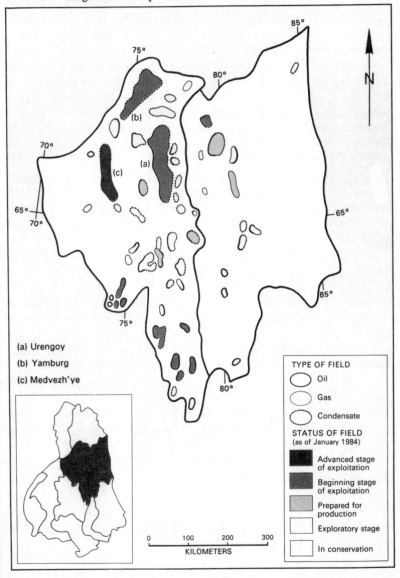

(a) Urengoy
(b) Yamburg
(c) Medvezh'ye

TYPE OF FIELD
Oil
Gas
Condensate

STATUS OF FIELD
(as of January 1984)
Advanced stage of exploitation
Beginning stage of exploitation
Prepared for production
Exploratory stage
In conservation

KILOMETERS
0   100   200   300

two fields, and on their 2200–3200 metres-deep Valanginian horizons. The latter reservoirs hold high concentrations of condensates, which will require additional compressor capacity to maximise output. The shallow horizons of Urengoy's southern half will also need compressors, or else their lifespan will be drastically shortened (Geresh, 1992, pp. 6–7). Yamburg can raise its output further, but only from its northern half and from deep horizons in the south.

Natural gas deposits are more resilient than oil fields. They need simpler equipment and fewer workers. Nevertheless some damage to Urengoy is already evident. Increasing water encroachment is causing problems and raising costs. It will require much new information and investment to fine-tune production and accommodate it to the irregular intrusion of water.[17] If Urengoy and Yamburg are forced to further augment production without very substantial prior investment and preparation, much of the history of the Siberian oil industry will repeat itself for natural gas. Additional large quantities can only originate from the Yamal Peninsula and the Zapol'yarnoe deposit further east, in environments for which neither Russian nor Western technology is yet prepared.

All our production scenarios envisage a fall in gas extraction through to 1995 and only moderate growth till the end of the decade. Given the enviable *aggregate* reserve situation, the chief limitation through the 1990s is on the consumption and distribution side. Nonetheless the geological and geographic constraints on extraction should not be ignored.

The physical constraints on West-Siberian gas are chiefly geographical (and environmental); such constraints are geological in Central Asia, the North Caspian Lowland, and the adjoining region of the Lower Volga. Payzones are 3500–5000 meters deep and under intense pressure, with extreme sulfur content and corrosive salt creating difficult technical problems. Nearly all reserves in the region contain very high proportions of condensates, increasing the value of the fields but adding to the already severe engineering problems of extraction and transport.

2.1.3 Coal

2.1.3.1 Estimated Physical 'Ceiling' on Coal Extraction and Delivery: 850 Million Tons or 360 MTOE

West of the Urals the physical constraints on coal are geological; east of the Urals they derive from location and quality. More than 60 per cent of the raw output would have to take place in the Asian regions of Russia and in Kazakhstan, and the bulk of that coal would need to be consumed there. Absence of transport and/or physical constraints on shipment affect coal extraction almost as much as that of natural gas.

2.1.3.2 Reserves: Location, Geology and Quality

Once location, geology and quality are taken into account, the FSU no longer appears coal-rich. The feasible level of extraction is far below that of the other fuels in equal energy content. The physical constraints cannot be loosened within the time-frame of this study. The conventional map of FSU coal fields, with their enormous expanse, is devoid of meaning. Areal extent has little to do with reserves and still less with their significance to the economy. The immense coal reserves east of the Yenisei River are essentially irrelevant, except for local use and some minor export from the Far East. Most of East Siberia's accessible reserves that are capable of expanded production are lignites. Distance and transport bottlenecks prevent even the Kuzbass and the coal fields of Kazakhstan from playing a major role in fuel supply west of the Urals.

The European regions of the FSU are like Western Europe, *not* the United States, with respect to coal resources. The Donbass (in Ukraine and adjoining Rostov Oblast' of Russia) has produced more coal than any other coal region in Europe. More than 100 mines reach below 800 meters (*Ugol' Ukrainy*, no. 6, [1990], pp. 2–4). Steam-coal seams of 75 cm are currently being worked, with even thinner seams for coking coal. Nowhere in the world is much coal extracted from permafrost, but output from the Pechora field north of the Arctic Circle is close to attaining one billion tons of cumulative output since its opening in the Second World War ('News Notes', *SG*, April issues).

Rapid decline in heat content, physical structure, and transportability has become a very serious problem. In the first eight years of the 1980s, gross mine output increased by 8 per cent, but it remained entirely stagnant in energy content (*Narkhoz. SSSR, v 1989 g.*, p. 377). By 1990 the average heat content of steam coal was no more than 4240 Kcal/kg (Rudenko and Makarov, 1990, p. 25). The rapid decline in quality affects not only surface mines but deep-mined coal as well. The heat content of coal itself may not fall, yet operations at narrow and deep seams will raise the share of ballast and increase the difference between gross mine output and marketable volume.

These physical limitations on supply, as much as capital costs and environmental concerns on the consumption side, have been responsible for the drastic fall in the share of coal in the fuel mix of thermal-power plants since 1970. While coal contributes 80 per cent of that mix in the US, this share was less than 30 per cent by 1990 in the whole of the FSU, and a mere 20 per cent west of the Urals (*Ekon. gazeta*, no. 6, 1992, p. 6).

A substantial expansion of coal capacity in a relatively short time-frame is physically possible only in East Siberia and, to a lesser extent, in the Kuzbass. Only giant coal-processing complexes could make East Siberian coal available to the whole Russian (and FSU) economy. The long lead times on the necessary investment for production, conversion and transport rule out this option for the time period examined in this study.

2.1.4 Western Technology and Its Expected Impact

The issue of Western participation and technology transfer must be raised briefly in advance of the economic, political and legal considerations brought up in the following sections. Western involvement will help to loosen the physical constraints in critical fields. Yet, apart from a few limited areas, the supply response will require significant lead times. In oil and gas production and transport, rapid response can be achieved in well workover and restoration, pipeline instrumentation and monitoring, and the furnishing of pumps and compressors. However, significant reserve additions through enhanced recovery and new development can be expected only at the end of the century and beyond.

Western technology cannot compensate for the severe geological deterioration in oil. The FSU's oil industry is so large that in the remainder of the 1990s foreign technology will not be able to substitute for the shortcomings and obsolescence of most of the domestic equipment. Seventy per cent of the FSU's drilling rigs, for example, date from the 1950–7 period and will take a long time to replace (Neverov and Igolkin, 1991–2, p. 9). Assimilation of the latest innovations by oil workers will also require years. For example, horizontal drilling has an even larger potential in the FSU than in the US (where it may double reserves over time). However the single most important factor affecting the success in that complex and delicate operation is *crew experience* (Von Flatern, 1991, pp. 16–22; Crouse, 1989, pp. 47–9). Only in the early 1990s has such experience begun to accumulate in the US; another five to seven years will be required before drillers in Russia, Kazakhstan and elsewhere in the FSU will assimilate the technology on a sufficient scale to make a large impact.

Nor can Western technology meet very quickly the serious engineering challenges faced by the gas industry. The difficulties faced in exploiting the gas reserves of Yamal, for example, are unique and have no analogue in the world so far.[18] So are the challenges facing would-be developers of the Shtokhmanskoe field in the Barents Sea and those of offshore Sakhalin. Both on Yamal and in ice-ridden offshore deposits, Western companies will be as much learners as the Russian gas and machinery industries. Such uncertainties are illustrated by the three-fold difference in cost estimates (from $200 to $600 million) for a single production platform, heavily reinforced against ice, on the Sakhalin shelf (Solomatin and Zhigarev, 1992, pp. 10–13). A major impact from foreign participation in the exploitation of these reserves can come only after 2000.

In regions of corrosive, sulfurous gas and oil, such as in Kazakhstan, however, all equipment is already supplied from abroad (Neverov and Igolkin, 1992, p. 4). This dependence will continue and will be crucial.

2.2 THE ECONOMICS OF FUEL SUPPLY IN THE FSU

The preceding section has provided some useful insights into the constraints imposed on production over time by the physical, geological and technological frontiers. Within the limits of these frontiers the study now moves into the economic realm.

The first objective is to establish the cost of marginal production at different levels of output, and to compare that cost with the price at which energy is sold. In an increasingly market oriented economy, production will be expanded only up to the level at which cost equals price. Since we are dealing with relatively extended time periods during which production capacity can vary, the relevant cost measure to compare with price will be the total cost of the marginal project.

Chapter 3 details the energy price paths in the FSU under alternative scenarios. It is assumed there that domestic ruble prices in real terms will rise in all cases until the international price level is attained. From about the turn of the century most domestic prices will have attained or will be approaching the international price levels. These price paths constitute one key element of the following analysis.

The second key element in our effort consists of projecting the future costs of average and marginal production at different points in time and at different levels of total output. This task raises formidable conceptual problems to which there are no ready solutions. Basically we see two alternative approaches to assessing the costs of the projects that will assure future output at the margin. Both have serious flaws.

The first one, which is popular with foreign analysts of the FSU scene, is explained by the general inaccessibility of costs and other relevant data, and by the perceived unreliability of whatever data that can be obtained. The basic approach is to seek maximum information on the geology and geography of future energy-production prospects, such as presented in the preceding section, and then to assess the cost of production and delivery from physically analogous prospects located in an industrialised market-economy environment, such as North America.

The main problem with this approach is that within our time horizon the costs in the FSU are likely to remain quite different from what they would have been in, for example, North America. Three factors are involved. First, the transformation of the FSU to a market economy is bound to be an extended and arduous process. Hence, even by the end of the century, there will be important pockets in the economy where prices and therefore costs will be determined in some measure by socialist principles and institutional politics rather than by market forces. Second, even in ten years' time the FSU will be a relatively poor economy, with per capita GDP only a small fraction of that in North America. For this reason, too, important cost differences will remain. For example, the absolute and relative cost of labour, even highly qualified labour, in the FSU is likely to remain quite low. Finally it is a well-known fact that purchasing-power parities and the underlying costs vary substantially even among the rich market-oriented economies. Hence cost assessments in one country based on the conditions in another can easily lead one astray.

The second approach to assessing future costs of energy supply in the FSU starts out from what is currently known about such costs and then projects these costs into the future, taking physical and technological constraints into account. The main problem here is that current costs have been established on the basis of social–political desiderata (and inertia) in a centralised economy. They may have limited relevance for the future. Hence, as the FSU is transformed into a market economy, both relative and absolute costs are bound to change, quite apart from physical and technological considerations.

The second approach has been adopted in the following pages, partly because earlier work has given us an exceptionally ample access to FSU cost data, but also because we feel that, however defective, these data provide insights into the particular circumstances of the FSU, without which projections of the future will not be meaningful.

We begin with a brief discussion of the ranges of uncertainty in marginal costs of FSU fuel production. There follow three sub-sections dealing with each of the fossil fuels in turn. Roughly the same format is employed in each case. We start by sketching the expected responses in supply to liberalised prices in the immediate future, and in the short and long term. We then examine the spread between average and marginal producers, identify their geographic location in 1990, and analyse expected developments in the cost of marginal output. In the next step we determine the average cost structure in 1987–90, project it forward until 2000 and relate it to the price assumptions. The forecast price and cost relationship suggests the levels of output, expected profitability and financial viability of the fuel industries through to the year 2000. Finally we provide a breakdown of the 1989–91 extraction of fuels by major Russian regions and FSU Republics, and project output for each until 2005 under the assumptions of Scenarios 1 to 3.

2.2.1 Marginal Costs and the Range of Uncertainty

In order to properly estimate long-term marginal costs, detailed knowledge of input requirements and costs for different output levels would be needed for a large number of deposits. Such information is highly incomplete. Moreover increased extraction from any deposit today affects costs in future years. For the oil and gas industries the technical-economic characteristics worsen at differential rates, creating a wide band of indeterminacy for marginal costs even with respect to already discovered fields (Eskin, 1991).

For natural gas this band of uncertainty is quite narrow in Russia. Russia encompasses such a vast proportion of the world gas reserves, and the reserve–production ratio at a handful of supergiants already tapped is so favorable that changes in the technical–economic parameters of extraction from these fields can be reliably assessed. Even for gas, however, marginal costs beyond 2000 remain elusive. These costs will be heavily affected by the rate of withdrawal from already producing deposits during the 1990s, and by the technical, economic and environmental uncertainties at new deposits, chiefly on the Yamal Peninsula.

In Kazakhstan and most of Central Asia the band of indeterminacy for long-term marginal costs is much wider. All gas is in condensate fields. Development of every large deposit therefore involves a number of by- and coproducts. Even short-term technological and investment choices remain unclear and need heavy foreign involvement. Alternative paths for supply increments and rates of return are yet to be subjected to thorough analysis. Short-term decisions on technology choices and by-product recovery bear heavily on long-term marginal costs. Such decisions also have environmental and political dimensions with a probable impact on costs.

Like that for gas in Russia, the band of indeterminacy is quite narrow for coal. The existing knowledge of the FSU's coal reserves and production technology leave few uncertainties, although since 1980 research on the industry has become rare. The main uncertainty about long-term marginal costs stems from the high labour intensity of coal production and the related socio-political impact of closing unprofitable mines.

The price assumptions in the three scenarios will play major roles in forecasting the quantities produced. The intersection of the price levels and the long-term supply curves will determine the volumes produced in most cases. Because fuel producers must soon generate all investment capital or borrow it from commercial banks, they will have to calibrate their investment strategies to the expected long-term marginal cost curves.

Long-term marginal costs for all three fuels will slope upward, at increasing steepness, with rising extraction levels. The upward slope, and the acceleration in steepness, as extraction rises, are considerably higher for oil than for gas.

2.2.2 Crude Oil

The supply response of the oil industry to liberalised prices differs greatly between the immediate future, the short term and the long term. In the immediate future (1993) the supply elasticity, theoretically, should be high. A part of the precipitous decline in oil production since late 1990 stems from the concealment of available capacity by production associations in anticipation of higher prices and export quotas and lower export taxes. The prospects for immediate response, however, must be deflated significantly because of the disintegration of the specialist workforce, particularly in West Siberia. In the short term of the next few years, the supply potential from shut-in wells also remains substantial. Yet this restored supply will be three times exceeded by declines in capacity due to depletion of 100–120 million tons per year (Section 2.1.1). Long-term elasticities (beyond 2000) basically depend on what happens in the current decade. Supplies in the long term must originate from new deposits, some of which are yet to be found.

Most of this section is devoted to the analysis of long-term cost developments at different levels of output, in order to gauge what level of production will be feasible and economical as oil prices attain international levels. To provide a further dimension to the issues facing the oil industry, we begin by gauging the magnitude of its investment needs.

2.2.2.1 *An Assessment of Total Investment Needs from 1993 to 2000*

We computed the necessary capital investment to reach certain critical levels of output in the 1993–2000 period with the help of the following combination of engineering and economic indices: (1) the cost of well completion and field preparation; (2) drilling costs and field development, including hook-ups to regional gathering systems; (3) two decades of yearly investment data, projected ahead to the mid-1990s by FSU experts, for the development of new capacity. These costs, which were obtained from published sources, employ the official price ratios (*smetnye stoimosti*) of 1988 that were used for investment and construction purposes. No new price ratios are available. At some risk, the deflator for material costs in industry is utilised to express the total in 1990 prices (Zoteev, 1991). The three derivations for the required investment are explained in Appendix 2.2. They lead to very similar results.

In order to extract 400 million tons of crude oil, *excluding gas condensates*, from 1993 to the end of 2000 annually, the FSU petroleum industry will need to invest 200 billion rubles (constant 1990 money), corresponding to $62–3 billion during that eight-year period, that is, $7.8 billion per year.

From 1988 to 1991 the yearly output of gas condensate in the FSU varied between 18.0 and 18.5 million tons (Sagers, 1991, p. 242). Scenarios 1 and 2 envisage 30–40 million tons of condensate production by 2000. This production would involve an additional investment of some 20 billion rubles, corresponding to $6.3 billion, or $0.8 billion per year.

The total annual sum, in excess of $8 billion, is a comprehensive figure. It includes well repair and restoration on producing reservoirs. The bulk of outlays, however, will have to be channelled into greenfield sites, especially in West Siberia. The smaller size, geographical dispersion and geological complexity of the new deposits is bound to result in rising investments per unit of output over time.

450 million tons of output, *again without gas condensates*, will require proportionally much more investment because the extra output will reduce average well yields. At levels of 500 million tons of yearly output and beyond, by the turn of the century the influence of diminishing returns will become prohibitive. The premised advantage of a marketising economy and technology inflow would be counterbalanced if crude-oil extraction were to be forced to such levels so quickly. Very substantial Western investment and the addition of gas condensates *could* lift the output of all liquids in the range of 520–50 million tons by 2005 but not before. The lower figure, corresponding to Scenario 2, is by far the more probable volume.

2.2.2.2 Current and Future Total Cost of Marginal Output

The marginal cost curve for oil in 1990 was quite flat because only a negligible proportion of FSU oil was extracted at the very high cost end. Less than 5 per cent of total FSU petroleum had costs 1.5 times or more than the industry's average (Birman, 1992). Ninety-five per cent of output came from increasingly scarce, relatively easy-to-produce reserves. The 5 per cent of marginal oil was extracted from very old, small fields. These have no relevance for long-term costs since they will soon be displaced by much larger, but also much costlier, deposits.

As West-Siberian output from 'active reserves' declines and most of the Volga fields go out of production, FSU production totals will be determined mainly by the rate at which reserves in the North Caspian Lowland are brought on-stream. Offshore production in the deep Caspian and, after 2000, in the Far East and perhaps the Barents Sea will also come into play, and East Siberia may contribute to total output. Substantial supplies of oil from low-permeability reservoirs could be available. These new sources will cost far more than did supplies from marginal fields in 1990. These new sources will define costs at the margin of production in the latter part of the decade and after 2000.

The data we have available allow the estimation of anticipated long-term costs around the margin in two different ways: (a) by taking the most critical province, West Siberia, which has entered the stage of long-term decline, and estimate the cost of the last million tons of oil on that downward slope with the help of some technical indicator, such as drilling, which drives marginal costs; and (b) by using the latest investment projections required for different levels of crude-oil extraction and applying a discount rate to this data.

Figure 2.5 presents putative increases in the total cost of marginal output in West Siberia, understood here as the cost per ton to effect a shift from a steeper to a more moderately sloping decline curve in petroleum output. The data comes from an unpublished 1989 study of the former oil ministry's economic research institute. The results were derived by applying to the projected 1990 production cost the per centage increase in the volume (metres) of developmental drilling required to move from the lower to the upper output curve at five-year intervals. The two lower curves present a pessimistic and a moderate decline in West-Siberian extraction, based essentially on domestic technology. The upper, optimistic, output curve assumes radical improvement in the efficiency of investment for the rest of the 1990s, continued after 2000. With such radical improvement, West-Siberian output would stay above 300 million tons until 2005, a prerequisite for the FSU to achieve the extraction levels projected in our Scenarios 1 and 2.

The pessimistic variant in Figure 2.5 foresees an extremely rapid rise in the cost of marginal output of West-Siberian oil. Extraction levels of 300 million tons become unfeasible between 2000 and 2005 because marginal cost would exceed the expected world price (about $160/ton). In the moderate variant this would not occur until after 2010. By mid-1992, the pessimistic variant moved close to reality. At that time internal oil-industry figures projected a doubling of investment per ton in West Siberia during the 1990s, even with output declining sharply to 230 million tons in 2000. Above that volume investment needs would rise at such rates that a production level of 300 million tons seemed highly improbable to specialists (NIIEng, 1992).

For the whole of Russia, we can project the total costs of marginal output from projected investment series, and by applying a conventional discount formula[19] (the investment estimates come from a Russian petroleum industry report; the ratio of capital to operating costs were assumed to remain constant). At a 30:1 ruble/dollar exchange rate (1992), the total cost of marginal supply at the wellhead will rise from $80 per ton in 1993 to $96 in 2000, *provided the level of production does not exceed 340 million tons* (Figure 2.6). At levels higher

68

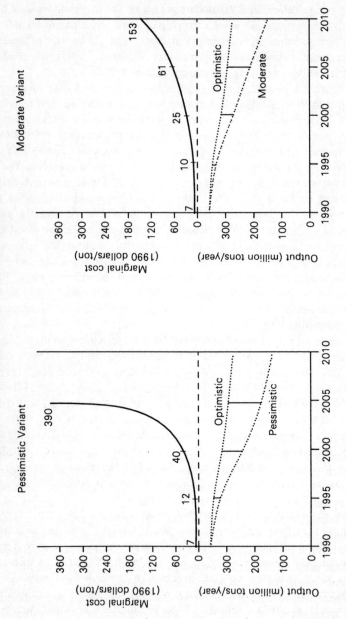

Figure 2.5   West Siberia: extraction levels and marginal costs

Source: See text.

Figure 2.6 Marginal cost of oil in Russia with a 10 per cent discount rate, 1993–2000 (1992 dollars per ton)

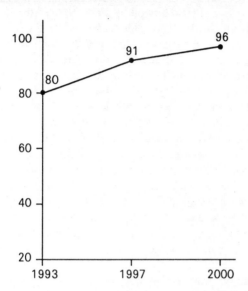

Assumptions: 1. Equilibrium exchange rate: $1 = 30 rubles.
2. Crude oil extraction in mid-1990s falls to 310–15 million tons, but not lower.
3. Crude oil extraction in 2000 will rise back to 340 million tons.
4. Operating costs are 35 per cent of total costs.

than that, wells operating in 1991 will be able to provide only a fraction of Russia's total output, shifting the slope of the curve sharply upward.

With a substantial contribution of gas condensates and vigorous growth of extraction in Kazakhstan, the figures indicate that Scenario 2 may still be realisable, and the cost of marginal output would remain well below the world price. But reaching the production level forecast in that scenario demands *immediate* investment and the start of large-scale foreign participation in FSU oil and condensate output. From the vantage point of late 1992, we assign only a very low probability to the volumes projected by Scenario 1 for 2000 and 2005.

Where will the margin of oil production be located geographically? The question is pertinent because investment must be targeted to specific projects.

Sakhalin has been frequently commented on in the press, but none of the experts interviewed in Moscow in the spring of 1992 believed that its offshore fields will yield any oil by 2000. Nine of the 21 reservoirs in the two main oilfields lie 1800–2800 meters below the ocean floor. One drilling season, which lasts only 2.5 months, will be insufficient to complete the deeper wells. Icebergs dragging over the shelf present drilling, production, and transport to shore with still unsolved technological problems (Maksimov, 1989, vol II, pp. 313–14; Konoplianik, 1992b; and Moldovanov, 1992, pp. 26–7). No one knows what the cost of output will be, and the latest estimates of Western and Japanese companies for a production platform that can withstand the ice vary by a factor of three (Solomatin and Zhigarev, 1992, pp. 10–13). The development of the two largest gasfields is reportedly unprofitable at current prices (*Hokkaido Shimbun*, 24 November 1992). The agreement the Russian government finally signed with the '3Ms' consortium is still only a protocol and not a final contract. The dispute between the Sakhalin government and Moscow also continues, delaying the start of the work (Konoplianik, 1992b; *EBE*, June 1992, pp. 9–10).

For *Tenghiz* we were able to consult a condensed version of the 1991 Chevron–USSR Protocol (now renegotiated with the government of Kazakhstan) and the original technical–economic project description drawn up in 1986–7 by the then Soviet oil ministry. The ratio of operating costs to capital outlays and the annual investment schedule required to reach peak capacity can be utilised for cost projections.

The initial Soviet development scheme for Tenghiz envisaged peak capacity by the tenth year after extraction began. This proved far too optimistic and Chevron has decided to go much slower. To reach peak capacity by 2005, however, Chevron and Kazakhstan must still spend two-thirds of the anticipated $20 billion investment, planned for the first 15 years, by the end of 2000. Given this large front-end investment, and at most 22 million tons of production in 2000, Tenghiz oil after desulfurisation and transport to a Black-Sea port would cost some 15 per cent more than the world price (assuming a 10 per cent discount rate on capital and the forecast international price of crude)[20]. The operation may be profitable by that time with the help of sulfur byproduct credits, but production costs will fall significantly and investments will be recouped only after 2000.

Even though quantitatively much less important, oil from the deep offshore Caspian will join the high-cost sources late in the 1990s. The cost of new wells in 1990 (mostly at the Azeri fields) was still only a fourth of that at Tenghiz. However, because of greater depth, well costs were rising in the offshore Caspian almost as fast as they were falling at Tenghiz with the gradual development of facilities there (Gorst, 1991, p. 26; Birman, 1992).

We must also have a notion of how expected production costs of so-called 'hard-to-recover' oil, especially from low permeability reservoirs, compare with anticipated costs at Tenghiz and offshore. Reserves of such oil are huge, especially in West Siberia (Tables 2.2 and 2.3), and the technology for its effective utilisation is well-established. The cost of new capacity for the remaining West-Siberian reserves has caught up with the FSU average and is rising faster. Yet for as much as two-fifths of that hard-to-recover oil, extraction costs most probably will be lower than at Tenghiz, even after the full development of that field and the consequent reduction in its cost of production. Thus it appears that at the turn of the century the most expensive Tenghiz wells will define marginal cost in the FSU.[21]

2.2.2.3 *Average Costs, Composition and Trends*

During the 1980s production costs, in real terms, in the FSU oil industry rose 2.4 times, or 9.5 per cent per year. Both capital costs and operating expenses rose as a consequence of worsening geological and technical conditions and shifting geographic location.

This is a capital-intensive industry, and depreciation accounts for by far the largest proportion of the cost of extraction. In 1987 it accounted for 68 per cent of all costs. Energy is the second-largest item in the cost structure (18 per cent in 1987). Indirect energy costs, embodied in equipment and structures, are much larger than direct energy expenditures.

The direct and indirect use of energy (embodied in equipment and capital installations) increases much more than proportionately as output rises. It is noteworthy that in 1992 Russian specialists assessed 500–550 million tons of extraction as being the transition zone beyond which the industry produces little *net* energy (interview in VNIIKTEP, April 1992).

Forecast trends in average costs juxtaposed with prices will define profitability for the industry as a whole during the time period under consideration. The industry's ability to generate investment capital internally and to borrow commercially will depend on its profitability. The development of average cost, however, depends critically on the expected price changes in crucial cost components.

Table 2.7 makes an heroic attempt to assess costs and determine levels of profitability in the FSU oil industry until the end of the century.[22] (Analogous material for the gas industry is contained in Table 2.8.) The original cost ratios were derived largely from coefficients of the 1987 input–output table and from more aggregate data for the 1990 cost structure of the still centralised Soviet economy. The figures assume that basic technology in the fuel industries will remain virtually unaltered until 1995, and that there will be only limited change even by 2000. Price ratios are in a state of flux, and direct energy inputs, a major component in total costs, will rise sharply in line with the energy-price increases postulated in our scenarios. The labour component of construction will remain a fraction of that on the world market even at the end of the 1990s. Domestic price developments for equipment and machinery, the share of Western inputs, and depreciation are the most uncertain parts of the changing cost function, and the study must live with this uncertainty.[23] We also assume that between the benchmark years of 1992, 1995, and 2000, capital investments will proceed in a reasonably smooth fashion. The original constant (1990) ruble figures are converted into dollars at the rate of 3.2 rubles per dollar, assumed to represent a realistic exchange rate in that year (see Introduction). A large part of the real-term cost increases projected for the 1990s, reflect the worsening physical–technological conditions in the fuel industries discussed in Section 2.1.

The oil-price path in Table 2.7 follows our second scenario. It is assumed that world levels will be reached only in 2000.

We present two variants for the 2000 forecast. Variant A assumes a continued modest decline in crude-oil production in the second half of the 1990s, easing the pressure on reserves. Accordingly the deterioration in the quality of reserves continues roughly at the same rate as in the 1980s. Variant B forces up extraction almost to the 1992 level, which sharply accelerates reserve deterioration. The table shows that from the mid-1990s until 2000, real-term increases in cost will be striking in both variants. We expect production costs to rise 2.5 times even if output declines. Nevertheless the low variant, coupled with world price levels by 2000, permits very healthy profits, but with output insufficient even for Scenario 3, let alone Scenarios 1 and 2.

An attempt to extract 450 million tons would increase expenditures about nine-fold in real terms, while the yearly volume of capital investment needed would almost triple.[24] Clearly, such an expansion for crude oil would be economically senseless at the assumed ruble/dollar exchange rate. The average cost of the marginal project would

Table 2.7   FSU crude oil: prices, extraction costs and transport costs to borders or major consumption centres (constant 1990 $/ton)

	1987	1992	1995	2000A	2000B
Volume extracted (MTOE)	624	466	390	380	450
Crude oil price	4.30	11.70	38	158	158
Extraction costs (excluding exploration):					
Energy	0.35	1.10	5.30	8.00	53.00
Machine building, metal working	0.15	0.45	0.70	1.50	10.00
All materials	0.45	2.20	7.15	10.70	71.50
Depreciation	1.30	4.60	10.80	13.85	25.00
Wage costs and administration	0.15	0.70	2.40	6.50	21.70
Total extraction costs	**2.00**	**7.90**	**12.40**	**31.00**	**115.00**
Plus transport costs	0.50	0.60	0.80	1.40	1.80
Sum of extraction and transport costs	**2.50**	**8.50**	**13.20**	**32.40**	**116.80**
Surplus of price minus extraction and transport costs	1.80	3.20	24.80	125.60	41.20
Memorandum items:					
Extraction: fixed capital stock	14.30	59.00	88.50	151.90	275.00
capital investment in year	3.65	14.75	20.35	28.90	52.20
Transport: fixed capital stock	0.70	3.00	4.50	7.65	10.40
capital investment in year	0.18	0.20	0.30	0.50	0.70
of which capital upgrading	0.12	0.15	0.20	0.40	0.50

Note: *Note*:   Constant 1990 rubles converted at 3.20 rubles per dollar. See text for further explanations.
Sources: Russian petroleum specialists; Birman, 1992.

well exceed the price even a few tons above 380 million tons. On the other hand, if the ruble/dollar exchange rate is doubled (6.4 rubles per dollar in constant 1990 money maintained through the decade) and the cost of marginal output increases exponentially (which it clearly does), the profitable level of output in 2000 rises to slightly above 400 million tons.[25] Scenario 2 demands crude production of *at least* that volume, with gas liquids contributing another 30–35 million tons.

This suggests that, within the limits set by geology and lead times, the economically rational level of output for the period of 1995–2005 will be very sensitive to exchange rates. To be economically justifiable, crude oil extraction levels suggested by Scenarios 1 and 2 will require ruble/dollar exchange rates well above the rate that we have established as 'realistic'. The 'realistic' exchange rate adopted for our analysis is, in fact, not static. It may well shift against the ruble, not least from the imperatives imposed by balance of payment considerations, in which the oil industry play such a critical role.

Transport costs represent a minor part of the delivered cost of oil (as opposed to that of gas), but they are rising rapidly, notwithstanding the decline in oil production and underutilised long-distance pipelines. A huge amount of repair and replacement will be necessary. Only 1.2 per cent of intrafield lines have inner anticorrosive coating, while trunklines have cut-off valves only every 30 miles (Kochnev, 1991, p. 2; *US News and World Report*, 1992, p. 43). In addition, the decreasing size of new fields requires many hundred kilometers of new pipelines, even if of smaller diameter.

The oil industry of the FSU is on a steep downward slope. Investment resources generated by price liberalisation and attractive terms for foreign companies must replace capital stock and infrastructure not merely on the margin but along the whole front. This will take years. So will the replacement of disbanded drilling brigades and other specialists. A return to the levels of the 1980s will not be feasible within the foreseeable future, even in a stable political climate and legal framework. A rebuilt, profitable industry with steady output, however, is possible well into the twenty-first century, but at significantly lower extraction levels. The production volumes of Scenario 1 have a very low probability. Scenario 2 still appears feasible, but only with foreign participation on a massive scale ($20–$25 billion in capital in Russia alone *before 2001*, and very significant product sharing). However such massive participation may not be feasible logistically, and politically, because all or most of the production *increment* until 2000 (and perhaps longer) will accrue to Western and Japanese companies (*Izvestiia*, 19 February 1992, p. 2). In Russia, at least, even the majority of reformers will oppose such a course (see Section 2.3).

2.2.3 Natural Gas

2.2.3.1 *The Shape of the Cost Curve in 1990*

Compared with oil, gas extraction is relatively simple. For instance, the gas industry requires a far smaller labour force per unit of output, and only one tenth as many components as the oil industry. The gas wells tapping giant deposits in the FSU, especially in Russia, produce at an enormous daily rate, and the reservoirs they tap have been drained to a much lesser extent than those that produce oil. In 1990 one fifth of the gas wells provided almost three-fifths of all natural gas. In the same year, a total of 9722 gas wells extracted about 13 per cent more energy than almost 150000 wells in the oil industry (VNIIE Gazprom, 1991, pp. 13, 33; Wilson, 1991, p. 8; Birman, 1992).

Even more than in the case of crude oil, the marginal cost curve for natural gas was very flat in 1990. Gas extraction was thoroughly dominated by very-low-cost producers, with those in the north of Tyumen' Oblast' and Central Asia supplying the cheapest gas. Ninety-four per cent of all output originated from deposits yielding gas at the wellhead at a cost of less than 1.5 times the mean, and almost 87 per cent of all gas was produced at less than 19 per cent above average cost (VNIIE Gazprom, 1991, pp. 32–4, 48).

What matters for natural gas, however, and far more than for crude oil, are not wellhead costs but delivered costs, both on the average and for the marginal output. In 1990 the average distance over which gas was transported within the FSU was 2500 km. This average distance is bound to increase in the future.

When the huge system of trunklines from Tyumen' was under development, average transportation costs to major load centres (at city gate) were more than twice as high as the cost of extraction. Depreciation per BCM transported multiplied five times during the 1970s and early 1980s (Tretyakova and Heinemeier, 1986, pp. 66–74). Once this system was largely completed by the mid-1980s, transport costs per BCM dropped to 75 per cent of wellhead production costs (VNIIE Gazprom, 1991, pp. 48, 175). The cost of capital repair is high, but it remains far below that of new construction.

2.2.3.2 Long-term Costs: Marginal and Average

The absolute dominance of the same supergiant fields will continue at least until the next century: nine tenths of all free gas will cost less than 1.5 times the average at wellhead, and the great bulk of it will differ from the mean by no more than 20 per cent. In the first decade after 2000, however, average and marginal costs at the wellhead will diverge more, as far more difficult frontier resources and deep, complex fields start to add substantial volumes to aggregate output. By that time, much of the easily tapped gas from the presently dominant supergiants will have been extracted, shifting their costs upward. This will moderate somewhat the difference between highest-cost and average-cost producers for the great bulk of gas even by 2005.

In the course of the 1990s the FSU gas industry will be attending to the following development areas: (a) the northern portions of Urengoy and Yamburg; (b) the deep Valaginian beds of these deposits for their condensates; (c) the Zapol'yarnoe field (in an environment almost as fragile as the Yamal Peninsula), earmarked to compensate for the decline of Urengoy; (d) substantial preparatory work on the Yamal deposits; and (e) a significant increase in extraction in the deep North Caspian Province. All this will demand very costly construction work, special equipment and auxiliary materials, and high energy inputs. Development will also face increasingly stiff environmental obstacles.

The future cost of new gas is difficult to estimate, both at the wellhead and when delivered to consumers 3–4000 kilometers downstream. The Yamal Peninsula will provide the bulk of new supplies beyond the turn of the century. In spring 1992 Yamal was still closed to energy ventures, with no agreement about the time when exploitation could begin. The development of Yamal requires new technologies, untested anywhere in the world. The Shtokmanskoe deposit in the Barents Sea could emerge as an addition or an alternative to Yamal in the early years of 2000. In March 1992 expert opinion in Russia held that FSU technology will be unable to cope with the Shtokmanskoe deposit until at least 2005. In the view of one specialist, domestic technology cannot bring that gas to consumers until 2015.

There is agreement on the North Caspian Lowland as the other main source of additional supply, but involving far smaller total quantities. Gas from the North Caspian Lowland, even at depths of 5–5500 metres, is expected to remain cheaper than from Yamal for wells not greatly different in daily yield. However all such comparisons are complicated by the range of by- and coproducts (condensate, ethane, sulfur) that the North-Caspian deposits will yield, and assumptions concerning their recovery.

Various Russian sources of the late 1980s and early 1990s suggest capital outlays per BCM on Yamal perhaps 3–4 times greater than the average for Urengoy and Yamburg. One Russian source claims that the first Yamal field (Bovanenko), with a maximum production of 160 BCM per year, will cost $56 billion (1990), including the necessary pipelines (one for export). To meet the extraction levels projected in Scenario 2 most of this sum would have to be spent by 2005. Scenario 1 would require other deposits to be on-stream as well, involving total investment costs of about $90 billion by that date (Konoplianik, 1992a, pp. 2–4; *Nezavisimaia gazeta*, 30 October 1991, p. 4; and *Ekon. gazeta*, no. 10 [March 1992], p. 11; *The Oil and Gas Journal*, 7 September 1992, pp. 17–20.)

Table 2.8 sketches anticipated developments in the average cost of gas until 2000.[26] To facilitate comparison with Table 2.7, where analogous data for oil are presented, the energy units are tons of oil equivalent (TOE – 1 TOE equals approximately 1200 cubic metres of gas or 40 million BTU.) As in the case of oil, the price assumption of Scenario 2 specifies that the world price ($120 TOE or $3/mm BTU) is reached by 2000.

Table 2.8   FSU natural gas: prices, extraction costs and transport costs to borders or major consumption centres (constant 1990 $/TOE)

		1987	1992	1995	2000A	2000B	2000C
Volume extracted:	BCM	687	784	744	790	852	1000
	MTOE	573	653	620	658	710	833
Gas prices at city gate		10.0	24.0	58	120	120	120
Costs:	Extraction	1.5	11.0	25	30	38	114
	Transportation	1.9	3.5	5	8	10	20
	Total	**3.4**	**14.5**	**30**	**38**	**48**	**134**
Surplus of price minus costs		6.6	9.5	28	82	72	– 14
Memorandum items:							
Capital invesment in year							
Extraction		4.2	7.9	27	32	37	64
Transportation		2.1	5.8	3	10	20	35

Note: Constant 1990 rubles converted at 3.20 rubles per dollar.
Source: Birman (1992)

We present three variants for output at the turn of the century. The ample reserves provide an array of options for the gas industry. These options are far more affected by exports, and the variables of transport and distribution than is true for oil.[27]

Variant 2000 A posits almost no growth in gas extraction beyond the level achieved in 1992, a situation that corresponds roughly to Scenario 2. This reduces the pressure for new investment, because only replacement capacity needs to be added in the extraction stage and the bulk of investment in transportation can also be devoted to capital repair. Energy expenditures per unit of output rise 3.5 times from 1992 to 2000 (as the gas industry itself copes with the effects of price liberalisation), but their share in average delivered cost changes only marginally. A more rapid increase in energy inputs at the extraction stage is counterbalanced by savings in the transport stage, following pipeline and compressor replacement and repair.

In this minimalist version the delivered cost of gas increases by 160 per cent between 1992 and 2000, while the price at city gate increases five-fold. As a result the industry can generate very healthy surpluses after the mid-1990s. By 2000 the surplus of price over total cost is more than twice as large as total investment needs.

Variant B projects moderate net growth in extraction, approximating that in Scenario 1. This net growth, however, requires an expansion from new reserves that is double that volume to compensate for declining output from mature fields. Consequently, investment requirement and costs of production are significantly greater, and the surpluses are reduced in consequence. In the transport stage, capital outlays are twice as large as in Variant A, and new investments significantly exceed this for capital repair.

The substantial difference between the two variants with respect to delivered volumes and unit costs raises the question of the economic equilibrium level of output in 2000. Will the total cost of marginal output at 710 MTOE (852 BCM) be lower than price? Most of the difference between Variants A and B in 2000 would end up as exports in our scenarios. The domestic versus foreign destination of shipment was of crucial importance in the era of administered prices and non-convertibility, but will not matter once prices on the two markets equalise.

At an output level of 710 MTOE (Variant B) the surplus generated by the industry would be $2.8 billion less than in Variant A. In moving from Variant A to B, the total average cost for the increase of output by 52 MTOE amounts to $175, which well exceeds the price. Hence, expansion according to Variant B would not be economically rational, given the subsumed 'realistic' exchange rate for the ruble. Such expansion becomes economical only if the ruble exchange rate is maintained at a 30 per cent lower level, or at 4.6 rubles per dollar in constant 1990 money, for at this rate the cost of marginal output at 710 MTOE will roughly equal price.

Variant C is hypothetical. It models a very sanguine growth in order to gauge the cost of a determined rapid push into very expensive new frontiers. With extraction raised to 1000 BCM by 2000, the average delivered cost per unit volume of output surpasses that for the no growth variant 3.5 times. Such an expansion would clearly be senseless because the huge volume of additional gas could not be marketed. Variant C is presented to show that the gas industry will encounter diminishing returns at an accelerated rate if production is expanded too rapidly.

By 2005, 1000 BCM would be less costly to reach, but would probably still be uneconomic, unless gas commands an 'environmental bonus' in Western Europe, or the prices of competing oil products rise significantly. A large part of reserves on the extremes of that geographical frontier may remain undeveloped for longer than 2005. This conclusion is supported by research undertaken by Russia's Institute for the Study of Complex Energy Problems on fuel supplies in the next 15 years. Modelling specialists at this institute conclude that the zone where gas production and delivery ceases to yield *any net* energy lies somewhere between 1100 and 1200 BCM. The limits of profitability will obviously occur at lower output levels (interview in April 1992).

With most trunk pipelines fully depreciated in the early 1990s, the transport costs are low and constitute a limited proportion of delivered price. This situation is likely to prevail until 2000, especially for Variant A, for in this variant there will be limited need for the laying of new pipelines.

Transport *fees*, however, are, and will be, set above these costs, given the rigidity of pipelines and little flexibility through storage. Monopolists will certainly attempt to impose much higher charges. The fees charged to the Baltic states in 1992 ranged from 22 per cent to 29 per cent of the ruble price of gas. In August 1992 Ukraine successfully set a fee of $0.66 per mmBTU for transit of Russian gas exported to Europe across 1500 km of its territory (*WGI*, July 1992, p. 2; August 1992, p. 13). This may roughly correspond to international gas-transport charges, but it is very high in the FSU context. If similar rates were to apply to the average transmission distance in the FSU, the transit fee per mmBTU would work out to $1.17 mmBTU, 48 per cent of the average interrepublic export price in mid-1992. Inside Russia, with wholesale prices of $1.32–1.92 per mmBTU, the Ukrainian level of fees would absorb a major share of the delivered price. With the Ukrainian rates applied all through 1992, FSU gas exports at the Slovak border would cost less than $1.60 per mmBTU after a 3000 km journey and $1.80 after a 3500 km journey. But the production cost is rising, and by 2000 the corresponding numbers will be roughly $2.10 and $2.30 per mmBTU (Variant A), even if transport charges remain the same. Transport fees from the Yamal Peninsula will certainly be higher, suggesting that a price of $3.00 per mmBTU in Western Europe may not be high enough for Yamal gas to be economically marketed there.

An important policy implication concludes our cost analysis. As noted, it is hard to establish the cost of marginal output in 2000. It is certain, however, that the cost curve will experience large discrete jumps as new areas are brought into production. Extreme environmental and technical obstacles at fields taking over the increment will guarantee that. For these developments to take place and be affordable, the expensive new supplies must be worked gradually into the price structure. Full long-term marginal cost pricing will be inappropriate, and in the earliest phase of these new deposits some cross-subsidisation will be necessary. The institutional arrangement for ownership and management will have to be tailored to that requirement.

2.2.3.3 Pipe, Compressor and Storage Requirement for the Rest of the 1990s and Beyond

A substantial proportion of the 220000 km trunk-lines (25 per cent of which are 1420 mm pipes and another 30 per cent consist of 1020–1220 mm pipes) was actually underutilised in the early 1990s (VNIIE Gazprom, 1991, p. 148). That slack is bound to grow significantly as the economy contracts, and as obsolete heavy industrial plants close rapidly under shock therapy and more slowly under gradual reform. Yet the cost advantage of that slack is quite limited, for future consumption growth is unlikely to tally with the pipeline system that is in place. The benefit of the slack is further diluted by the fact that in many regions the system is in a parlous shape. It operates with 29 different, poorly matching compressor types. Seventeen per cent of all accidents occur on lines less than five years old, with faulty welding a particularly frequent cause. Insulation on more than half of the pipelines lasts for less than the period of amortisation. A mere 30 per cent of the pipes are served with telemechanisation equipment, most of which is 1960s vintage technology. Twenty-one per cent of the pipes and 14 per cent of compressor capacity require immediate rebuilding or replacement.[28] While the pipelines from Siberia are only 5–15 years old, they were built in extreme haste and not always with sufficient care. Elsewhere, including many European regions, the pipeline network is much older (Vol'skiy, 1990, p. 2; Ivantsov, 1991, no. 11, p. 4, 1990, no. 4, p. 21; VNIIE Gazprom, 1991, p. 156).

Most of the underutilised capacity in the pipeline network is concentrated in a 1200–1300 km section from the two biggest West-

Siberian fields to the Urals (Map 2.5). Each year in the early 1990s as much as 340 BCM of gas flowed through that corridor, which has twenty 1440 mm pipelines laid a few metres apart. This Nadym–Punga pipeline corridor has the greatest concentration of energy flow anywhere in the world (Vol'skiy, 1992, p. 15). About 70 BCM more natural gas theoretically can be transmitted through these pipes, according to our calculation (confirmed in an interview in VNIIK-TEP, April, 1992). However 6000 kilometres of these pipes already need replacement or substantial repair. Russian experts are nervous about this extreme concentration of gas flow, and the dangers it presents.[29]

Table 2.9 presents assessments of future pipeline needs. By 2000 the FSU pipeline network will require an additional 6000 km of long-distance trunklines if the volume of extraction is to rise according to Scenario 1. It will need an additional 5–5500 km of new lines even if output for the rest of the 1990s increases only marginally (Scenario 2). Once existing bottlenecks are opened and hitherto slighted regions (particularly West Siberia's southern provinces) receive more transmission lines, the need for additional arteries will be dictated by the opening of new fields in North Tyumen' oblast, especially on the Yamal Peninsula. At some junctions, however, these can feed into the established network. Between 2000 and 2005, therefore, pipe requirement for new trunklines will reduce to 4500 km.

High-pressure distribution lines will account for two fifths of all demand for pipes by weight during the remainder of the 1990s. Scenarios 1 and 2 envisage a fall in gas demand by spatially concentrated heavy industries and an increase in gas usage by more widely dispersed consumers, which will require an expansion of the distribution network.

The need for pipes to renew gaslines, however, increases sharply from the middle of the 1990s, both absolutely and relative to total demand. Pipes for replacement constitute more than 40 per cent of pipe demand on trunklines from 1996 to 2000, but more than 60 per cent during the 2001–5 period. In the subsequent 10 years trunkline replacements will exceed new artery needs by more than three times. One-by-one all the 20 arteries transmitting gas from North-Tyumen' to European Russia will have to be replaced. The distribution network is in even greater need of renewal (*Moscow News*, no. 16, 1992, p. 10).

The five pipe-making mills of the FSU, when operating at full capacity, can provide only some 50 per cent of the pipes needed for the expansion sketched in Table 2.9. In the summer of 1992, these plants

82

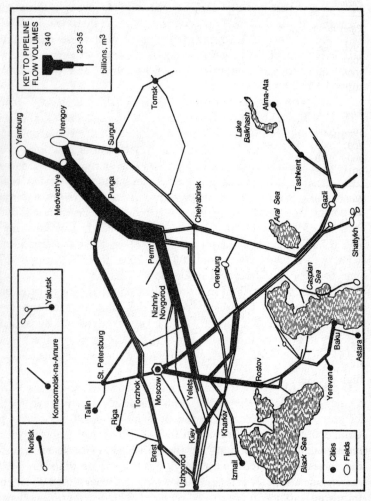

Map 2.5   Main gas pipelines and volumes transmitted

Table 2.9   Pipe requirement of the FSU gas industry

Period	Gas production at end of period (BCM)	Trunklines, weight (mill. tons)	Trunklines, length (km)	Distribution pipelines high-pressure, weight (mill. tons)	Total weight (mill. tons)
Pipes for New Gas Lines:					
1996–2000	860	3.7	6000	2.5	6.2
2001–2005	930	2.8	4540	1.8	4.6
2006–2010	1000	2.8	4540	1.8	4.6
2010–2015	1070	2.8	4540	1.8	4.6
Pipes to Renew Gas Lines:					
1996–2000	860	1.5	2430	5.8	7.3
2001–2005	930	2.0	3245	6.6	8.6
2006–2010	1000	9.2	14595	8.8	18.0
2011–2015	1070	9.2	14595	10.2	19.4

Note: The volumes of production are for Russia. For Russia alone, such volumes are not feasible. However they match closely the volumes for the FSU as a whole in Scenarios 1 and 2. By implication, therefore, they ought to suggest the rough magnitude of pipe requirements in the entire FSU.
Source: Adapted from tables and text in *Moscow News*, no. 16 (1992), p. 10.

operated at less than half capacity. The existing metallurgical industry of the FSU will be able to cope with the need for new trunklines in Scenario 2 (minimal increase in gas output till 2000), but it cannot cope with a significant increase in gas extraction without a large expansion of capacity, or heavy reliance on imports. In either case it is hard to see how the FSU gas industry will be able to avoid severe shortages of high-pressure distribution lines.

2.2.3.4   Gas Exports through the 1990s and Beyond

Until 2000 any theoretical gas surplus in the FSU will be a function of reduced demand much more than a function of increased supply. Given the forecasts for reduced domestic consumption in our scenarios, increased exports will be critical if production expands at all. Increased exports, however, are crucial, not only for the disposal of gas, but also to assure the foreign investment involvement that is needed to maintain the gas industry in reasonable health. With the inevitable decline of Urengoy, and the cost increases associated with severe water incursion, both at this deposit and in the older

Medvezh'ye, Gazprom must be well prepared for the new Yamal frontiers by the latter part of the 1990s. Meanwhile it must upgrade the industry on a broad front. Yet the collapse of investment since 1988 to less than one half of the level for that year has already hurt the industry (Baranovskiy, 1992, p. 11). The spectre of collapsing oil production haunts Russian officials. Only long-term collaboration with Western partners can guarantee that the degree of modernisation will be sufficient. As one Russian source puts it, 'The West European market is a question of life and death for Gazprom', but a crash of Gazprom, along the line experienced by the oil industry, would 'deliver a heavy blow to the economies of Western Europe' (Skobtsov and Chernova, 1992, p. 17). Whether this is true or not, that theme was brought up a number of times in our interviews.

Under the assumptions of Scenario 1 a significant difference exists through the rest of the 1990s between what can be produced for export and what can be actually delivered, given the constraints of the transport system and foreign demand. By 2000 that difference is eliminated. In Scenario 2, transport and marketing bottlenecks do not constrain exports, because the exportable surplus is far smaller, given the higher domestic consumption.

In order to export safely and reliably 95 per cent of the theoretical surplus foreseen in Scenario 1, and even of the much smaller surplus of Scenario 2, very significant replacement and improvement of the existing pipeline network is needed. In early 1992 Wintershall's president, H. Detharding, made the extraordinary claim that Russia could double its European export capacity to more than 200 BCM a year without laying another kilometre of pipe (*WGI*, March 1992, p. 2). This claim is contradicted by Russian data. Safe and reliable delivery for FSU and Western consumers will demand appreciable capital outlays, even if domestic consumption declines substantially. Such investment needs will be still larger if by 2000 Russian and FSU demand returns to the levels of the early 1990s.

Substantial new investment is also needed to expand storage capacity. Far more variable demand characterises both new domestic users and foreign customers than is true of the largely base-load steam turbines, metallurgical, chemical, and cement plants that currently burn the bulk of gas. Investment in storage capacity has contracted sharply since 1988 in line with the collapse of all investment (VNIIE Gazprom, 1991, pp. 17, 162, 236). Capital outlays to double that capacity by 2000 would run to about $1 billion.

Our estimates of the FSU's export capabilities and corresponding investment requirement are set out in Table 2.10. In estimating the cost of new pipelines, we assume that all construction and engineering work for pipeline installation would employ Russian labour at Russian wages. Imported pipes, compressors and other equipment, with transport charges added, define the upper limit of the range. Russian-made pipes and equipment define the lower limit. We use published Russian cost data from 1990 and the late 1980s and cost information from Japanese sources in our computations. The derivation is explained in Appendix 2.3.

We computed the approximate upper limit for the 3000 km and 4000 km export pipelines as $4 billion and $5.4 billion respectively. The lower limits are $1.7 billion and $2.4 billion. The lower limit seems unduly low because in 1989–90, the year for which such data could be gathered, Soviet capital-goods industries were heavily subsidised. Successful reforms will eliminate most of these subsidies, but movements in exchange rates could still keep the floor of the range very low by Western standards. New pipeline projects at such favourable construction costs may nevertheless be unattainable because of insufficient domestic production capacity, most of which will be tied up with repair and replacement work.

Until the mid-1990s, improvement and pipe replacement on key sections of the existing network, and the addition of relatively short loops to open up bottlenecks, will constitute suitable investment projects for Western firms. For less than $1 billion close to 30 BCM of additional exports (that is, an expansion from the current level of 105 BCM to 135 BCM) can be secured annually through many of the remaining years of the 1990s. In the second half of the decade a new export pipeline from the western slopes of the Urals represents another plausible investment project. This pipeline, costing $2–4 billion, could transmit a further 28–30 BCM. However an increase of yearly exports to a reliable 160–165 BCM would require additional investment, amounting to perhaps another $3 billion, to overhaul other parts of the network and expand storage capacity.

In all scenarios export volumes exceeding 135 BCM by 1995 require expanded production. Investments in extraction need to rise substantially, to attain such export levels. Beyond the mid-1990s, investment outlays for extraction must also include expensive preparations for development on the Yamal Peninsula and of the Zapol'yarnoe field east of Urengoy.

Table 2.10   FSU natural gas: potential exports and estimated investment requirements (BCM and billion 1990 dollars.)[1]

	Scenario 1			Scenario 2		
	1995	2000	2005	1995	2000	2005
Production forecasts (BCM)	673	824	928	719	766	882
Potential exports (surplus of production over consumption) (BCM)	133	186	174	116	139	139
Potential exports minus 1992 exports[2] (BCM)	30	83	71	13	36	36
Investment costs:						
Pipelines and storage from Jan 1992 to end of respective year, to permit domestic delivery and potential exports (billion dollars)[3]	2.0	6.5	8.5	2.0	4.0	8.0
Extraction, including gas treatment facilities (billion dollars)						
1992–1995[4]	4.0			5.0		
1992–2000[5]		12.0			10.0	
of which: North Tyumen' (excluding Yamal)		6.0			5.5	
Caspian Lowland		6.0			4.5	
Preparation for Yamal and Barents Sea development		2.5			2.0	
Development of Yamal and Zapol'yarnoe fields[6]			40.0			38.0
Total investment costs	6.0	21.0	48.5	7.0	16.0	46.0

Note:
1. The investment estimates were .derived from Russian sources, using constant 1990 rubles. Dollar values were obtained by employing a 3.20 rubles per dollar ratio. FSU pipe and equipment prices were used. Hence the cost figures must be considered as minimums.
2. 1992 export estimates from *PlanEcon. Business Report*, 1 April 1992.
3. For 1995 the investments comprise replacement and repair of about 12–14000 km of pipelines and 1.7–2.0 million kw of compressor capacity plus substantial expansion of storage capacity. For 2000 and 2005 we assume the replacement of at least 35000 km of major pipelines and five million kw of compressor capacity. We also assume a tripling of active storage capacity and usage and two new export pipelines of 1420 mm, one from Yamburg, the other from the north-eastern edge of European Russia.
4. Investment in production is assumed to decline more in Scenario 1 than in Scenario 2 (VNIIE Gazprom, 1991, pp. 236–8).

5. Investment figures for north Tyumen' (excluding Yamal) were estimated from capital outlays and increments achieved from Urengoy and Yamburg during 1981–90. Data about investment per 1000 BCM of new capacity from Urengoy's Cenomanean vs Valanginian beds were also used (VNIIE Gazprom, 1991, pp. 33, 243–4; VNIIKTEP, *Toplivno-energeticheskii kompleks*, 1989, pp. 64–5; Goskomstat SSSR, *Kapital'noe stroitel'stvo SSSR*, Moscow, 1988, pp. 65–7; Sagers, 1991, p. 266; and Shchenkov, 1988, p. 51). Investment requirements in gas production and treatment facilities in the North Caspian Lowland were estimated from outlays for wells and desulfurisation plants at the Astrakhan' gas complex and Karachaganak (VNIIE Gazprom, pp. 33, 42, 45, 245; Turevskiy *et al.*, 1990, p. 105; Istomin, 1991, pp. 1–2).

6. Assumed production of 115 BCM in Scenario 1 and 110 BCM in Scenario 2. These numbers are extremely uncertain. Scattered Russian sources suggest outlays three to four times greater than the average for Urengoy and Yamburg per BCM. One source claims that the development of Yamal deposits will require investments in pipes, which alone will exceed $25 billion (Skobtsov and Chernova, 1992, p. 17; *Ekon gazeta*, no. 10 (March 1992), p. 11).

In this section we argued that at the end of the century the gas industry would be much more profitable if it accepted only modest growth in output. Exports could still grow significantly and could be managed without building a new export pipeline, although significant investment would be required for pipeline replacement and repair and expansion of storage capacity. The rise in both average and marginal costs would also be smaller if no preparation were made for Yamal and Barents-Sea reserves during the 1990s and if all growth in export came out of reduced consumption. In that case, however, a much steeper upward shift in the cost curve would occur soon after 2000, as heavy investment in fast-maturing Siberian gas fields would coincide with the even larger outlays required by an unavoidable leap to mobilise Yamal.

2.2.4 Coal

Less information exists on the economics of the coal industry in recent years than on the economics of the other fuels. This fuel faded from the scene of economic and policy analysis during the first half of the 1980s. We deal with coal in the aggregate and concentrate on steam coal.

2.2.4.1 The Range and Geography of Production Costs

About 60 production associations extracted coal in 1988 at widely varying costs. The marginal cost curve was far more sharply sloping than for gas or oil. In equal energy units, 15 per cent of output cost little more than 20 per cent of the FSU average, while the highest-cost 15 per cent had cost levels 50 per cent above that average. Geological conditions (deep mines, narrow and sloping seams) essentially determined the margin (Figure 2.7).

The cheapest producers are all physically capable of large-scale expansion. Yet they have increased extraction only modestly since 1975, and not at all since 1986, because of geographic remoteness from the main centres of energy demand. West of the Urals, geological constraints have overwhelmed the advantages of favourable location, and coal production was declining even before the recent disintegration of the energy-supply system. East of the Urals the geographical constraints of remoteness checked the advantages of geology.

The FSU coal market will be geographically fragmented even more than before economic transformation, when producers did not have to take the added transport charges fully into account. As a result the cost of coal supply will differ noticeably among at least four geographic zones: the FSU west of the Urals; Kazakhstan and the south of West Siberia; the Yenisei–Baykal region of East Siberia; the settled portion of the Russian Far East.

Within each zone the cost of marginal output will diverge sharply in the short term and very significantly even in the long term. The Yenisei–Baykal zone, followed by Kazakhstan and South-West Siberia have by far the lowest costs of marginal output for steam coal and will retain this advantage. The European FSU west of the Volga and the Russian Far East, in contrast, will have to live with much more elevated cost levels.

2.2.4.2   Viability and restructuring needs

Coal is a labour-intensive industry. Wages, bonuses and social insurance form the largest components of the costs. Between 1987 and 1992 large wage increases raised the labour component from 23 per cent to more than half of total cost per ton.

The former Soviet coal ministry employed a total of 2.4 million persons in 1990. 900000 persons worked in coal production directly, a number larger than in any country except China, and all but 7.4 per cent of them toiled underground (TsNIEI Ugol', 1991). Output per worker in coal production is very low: in 1990 it was only 330 TOE, less than a quarter of the figure in the oil industry and only 2 per cent of the

89

Figure 2.7 Selected coal producers by volume and cost

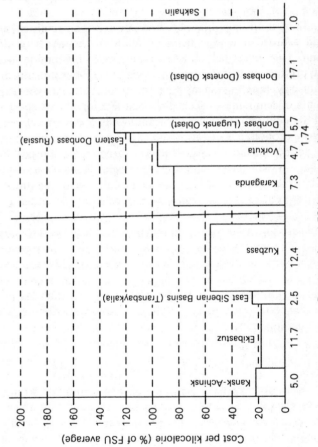

Source: USSR Goskomstat statistics, 1988.

Note:

energy output per employee in gas. (*Trud*, 12 December 1990, p. 1; Rudenko and Makarov, 1990, p. 29). Output per worker is only 8 per cent of that in the US and one-third of that in the UK (TsNIEI Ugol', 1991).

The obverse of very high labour intensity is the declining share of machinery. Inputs from the machine-building industries declined sharply during 1987–92.

Existing facilities are quite old. A yearly average of only 4.1 million tons new capacity was put into production in the FSU between 1981 and 1990. Almost 70 per cent of existing underground mines were put into operation before 1960 (*Narkhoz SSSR v 1990 g.*, p. 566; Khrilev and Makarov, 1991, pp. 62–4). In 1992 the coal industry was in as bad a shape as the oil industry. There is little prospect of reversing its decline within our time horizon, whatever happens to prices and to domestic and export demand.

As with oil and gas, we projected forward the ruble cost of coal production from its 1987 and 1990 structure. However a meaningful conversion to dollars proved unsuccessful, given the huge wage increases and erratic price changes for the industry's material inputs in recent years. It is clear that when valued at world prices, the FSU's coal industry has been hugely unprofitable, both in the late 1980s and even more in 1992. This conclusion is supported by other recent studies using the 1987 Soviet input–output table. When its major inputs and its output were calibrated in world prices, the coal industry showed negative value added and large losses (Hughes and Hare, 1991; Duchene and Senik-Leygonie, 1991). Coal production in Ukraine and the adjoining Russian part of the Donbass has become particularly unprofitable, given that labour productivity is 60 per cent below the FSU average. A number of producers in the Urals, Georgia, and Central Asia were no better off (TsNIEI Ugol', 1991).

The industry's options until 2000, and probably beyond, are unenviable. It is in need of comprehensive restructuring and rationalisation, which the enterprises cannot finance.

Projecting from the industry's cost structure and value of fixed capital in 1987 and 1990, we estimate that to be fully capitalised the coal industry would need to increase its fixed capital almost tenfold, relative to the early 1990 level. Capital investment would need to rise even more to compensate for the replacement of retired assets.

Official steam-coal prices were 550 rubles per ton in mid-1992. A mere doubling, in constant money, is needed to bring them up to the international price level at our 'realistic' exchange rate. Even at that higher price the industry will be unable to finance the recapitalisation indicated above.

The need for very substantial mine consolidation is obvious. Average daily capacity of FSU coal mines is only 40 per cent of that of British mines. Seams are on average 10–14 per cent thinner than in Britain or Germany, and almost a third thinner than in Poland, with still worse conditions in the Donbass (TsNIEI Ugol', 1991). Restoration of the coal industry to financial health implies massive closures which dwarf anything experienced in Western Europe. We estimate that achievement of profitability and self-financing will require coal extraction to plunge to 60 per cent of the 1989 output, or to some 190 MTOE. This is far less than the energy produced from the single gas field of Urengoy in the early 1990s. With such a reduced level of production the investment needs per ton of capacity will fall much more than proportionately.

The drop in extraction envisaged here requires that about two thirds of all mines in Ukraine and European Russia, half of those in Karaganda (Kazakhstan), and a fifth of those in the Kuzbass would have to close. Out of a total of 0.9 million miners, 0.5–0.6 million would have to be laid off. In Scenario 1, 0.5 million would lose their jobs as early as 1995.

Such magnitudes of mine closures in the course of the 1990s appear to us entirely unrealistic on political and social grounds. With family members included, eight to nine million people are directly dependent on coal extraction (Rudenko and Makarov, 1990, p. 29). In 1990, 54 per cent of all miners lived in Ukraine, 37 per cent in Russia and 6 per cent in Kazakhstan (TsNIEI Ugol', 1991). The social and political dimension will play a crucial role in determining the coal industry's prospects in the 1990s.

Closure of mines will also be constrained by the role played by coal in power generation. In the mid-1980s this fuel generated almost 90 per cent of all electric power in Kazakhstan, and 50 per cent in Siberia and the Far East (estimated from 1975–80 trend and share of thermal power in total. Nekrasov and Troitskiy, 1981, pp 200–32). In 1992 coal still represented 31 per cent of all power generation in Ukraine (*Vechernyi Kiev*, 19 May 1992, p 3). The recent shut-down of nuclear reactors and subsequent power crisis in Ukraine and elsewhere points to the serious problems that would be encountered by a rapid decline of the FSU coal industry.

2.2.5   Geographic Breakdown of Fuel Production

The volume of fuels produced in the 1990s and beyond will depend to a great extent on geology and economics, but also on the course of the reform process. Our scenarios formulated possible alternative paths for that process and sketched their assumed contours for the FSU as a whole. However we recognise that economic transformation will not proceed at a uniform rate among the new states. Intra-FSU variations in the speed and success of the economic transformation will thus affect the geographic breakdown of future production.

A formal analysis of the linkages between fuel output and the differential pace of reforms at the republican level is simply impossible within the realms of this study, if at all. Economic forecasts for Russia lack reliability, while the forecasts for the new Moslem states are no more than guesses. The geographic breakdown of the extraction forecasts that follow is anchored to qualitative assessments of political progress and its impact on energy output, supported by knowledge of the energy-production base in each of the individual republics.

Table 2.11 provides a republican subdivision of current and forecast total fuel production. In 1991 Russia produced 78 per cent of all FSU fuels. It dominated oil and gas extraction with an 84 per cent combined share, but accounted for only some 54 per cent of all coal. Apart from Russia, Kazakhstan is the only state with strong potential for the production of all three fuels, although the volume of gas output is still modest. The overwhelming dominance of Russia is destined to last. For individual fuels, however, we can expect greater relative shifts, both on account of the size, quality, and accessibility of reserves and the state of the capital stock, and because of the differential impact of the reform scenarios on the three fuels across the republics.

2.2.5.1   *Russian Production under Alternative Scenarios*

Oil. By 2000 Russia's share in FSU oil extraction will drop somewhat in all scenarios. In absolute volumes, 1991 production levels cannot be reached again until, at best, 2005 and then only if gas liquids nearly triple their contribution. Production plunges profoundly in the mid-1990s in all three scenarios. The subsequent recovery is strongest in Scenario 1 (Tables 2.12 and 2.13).

Our forecast that oil extraction under shock therapy will not exceed that under gradual reform before 2000 seems to contradict the conventional wisdom. The forecast difference for 1995 output between

Table 2.11   Fuel production in the FSU, 1989–2005 (MTOE)

Year	Total	Russia	Ukraine	Kazakhstan	Central Asia	Transcaucasia
1989	1567	1214	118	94	118	23
1990	1523	1187	109	90	116	21
1991	1435	1116	92	91	117	19
Scenario 1:						
1995	1170	894	71	84	105	16
2000	1375	1050	62	114	129	20
2005	1550	1207	56	131	133	23
Scenario 2:						
1995	1235	948	79	83	108	17
2000	1330	1006	69	114	123	18
2005	1485	1150	56	128	130	21
Scenario 3:						
1995	1200	929	70	79	106	16
2000	1290	1005	56	97	118	14
2005	1385	1075	52	115	125	18

Note: The figures comprise oil with gas condensate, natural gas and coal. Production in Belarus (2 MTOE in 1991) and Baltic Republics not included. Central Asia comprises Kyrgyzstan, Tadjikistan, Turkmenia and Uzbekistan. Transcaucasia comprises Armenia, Azerbayjan and Georgia. Transcaucasian production consists almost exclusively of oil and gas. Virtually all of the output originates in Azerbayjan.

these two scenarios is entirely due to West Siberia, where the collapse of investment and the discontent and flight of specialists have been most severe. The shock scenario will initially add to ongoing disruption, and it will take the West-Siberian producers until the end of the decade to bring order to the industry. In the meantime production will suffer. The disorder will be less pronounced, and production will consequently be higher, under gradual reform.

The Far East and East Siberia continue to play a very small role in our forecasts. Historically only Sakhalin has been a producer, with 2–2.5 million tons of annual output. Very large foreign investment could raise Sakhalin's production to 10 million tons by 2005, that is to 2.5 per cent of Russian output. No other province of the Russian Far East could significantly supplement that volume in this century.

Table 2.12   Fuel production in Russia, 1989–2005 (MTOE)

Year	Total	Oil	Gas	Coal
1989	1214	555	495	164
1990	1187	516	515	156
1991	1116	461	517	138
Scenario 1:				
1995	894	335	463	96
2000	1050	380	560	110
2005	1207	460	632	115
Scenario 2:				
1995	948	340	498	110
2000	1006	370	521	115
2005	1150	440	595	115
Scenario 3:				
1995	929	332	492	105
2000	1005	370	530	105
2005	1075	420	555	100

Note: The oil figure includes gas condensate.

Gas. The gas industry in Russia is much younger than the oil industry. It is also younger than the gas industry in the rest of the FSU. The ability to maintain or even expand production, therefore, is reasonably robust. Demand, primarily domestic but also foreign, constitutes the major constraint to output (Table 2.14).

Domestic demand will contract most severely in Scenario 1 (see Chapter 3). Accordingly we project a 10 per cent drop in Russian gas extraction in 1995 relative to 1990. Scenario 2, which assumes less contraction of demand from heavy-industrial consumers, foresees a smaller fall in gas output. With the subsequent turnaround in consumption, prospects for expansion beyond the level reached in 1990–1 are quite plausible in both scenarios.

With a reform impasse and failure to reduce appreciably the energy intensity of the economy (Scenario 3), Russian gas production in 1995 will be as high as in Scenario 2, despite sharply declining gas industry investments, and by the turn of the century output will exceed the 1991 level. This forced expansion, however, would critically injure the gas industry and plunge it into a crisis, reflected by much lower output

Table 2.13 Oil production in Russia, 1989–2005 (million tons)

Year	Russia total	West Siberia	Volga-Urals	Other regions
1989	555 (18)	405	121	29
1990	516 (18)	375	114	27
1991	461 (18)	329	108	24
			All other regions	
Scenario 1:				
1995	335 (15)	232	103	
2000	380 (30)	274	106	
2005	460 (38)	325	135	
Scenario 2:				
1995	340 (15)	235	105	
2000	370 (30)	270	100	
2005	440 (38)	310	130	
Scenario 3:				
1995	332	230	102	
2000	370	265	105	
2005	420	295	125	

Note: Oil production figures include gas condensate. Total Russian gas condensate output is also shown separately in parentheses in MTOE.

levels in 2005 than in Scenarios 1 and 2. It should be added that the numbers projected in Scenario 3 are particularly uncertain, given that the possible variations in a continued reform impasse are manifold.

As is true of oil, the vast expanse east of the Yenisei River contributes a mere 0.5 per cent to Russia's extraction of natural gas (Sagers, 1992, p. 253). Large reserves do exist in northern Sakhalin and in widely separate locations far inland. By the end of our forecast horizon, reserves off Sakhalin may yield up to 15 BCM per year, with the Yakut-Sakha Republic yielding roughly the same amount. This prospect raises an interesting dilemma. There will be strong political pressure to reserve any production for the satisfaction of local needs in the first place. However, development of production hinges on massive foreign investments which are unlikely to occur unless large volumes can be exported. It is unclear whether the exportable surpluses would be large enough to motivate the construction of export pipelines (AN, IKARP SSSR, 1991; Konoplianik, 1992b, pp. 2–4; Dzhangirov *et al.*, 1991, p. 13).

Table 2.14   Natural gas production in Russia, 1989–2005 (MTOE; BCM in parentheses)

Year	Russia total	West Siberia	Urals-Lower Volga	Other regions	Oil-well gases
1989	495 (616)	(508)	(51)	(27)	(30)
1990	515 (641)	(537)	(49)	(23)	(32)
1991	517 (643)	(551)	(48)	(17)	(27)
Scenario 1:					
1995	463 (575)	(508)	(40)	(17)	(10)
2000	560 (695)	(602)	(45)	(30)	(18)
2005	632 (784)	(675)	(50)	(40)	(20)
Scenario 2:					
1995	498 (617)	(540)	(40)	(25)	(12)
2000	521 (646)	(548)	(46)	(32)	(20)
2005	595 (737)	(640)	(42)	(35)	(20)
				All other sources	
Scenario 3:					
1995	492 (610)	(525)		(85)	
2000	530 (657)	(560)		(97)	
2005	555 (688)	(600)		(88)	

Note: A conversion rate of approximately 1.24 BCM = 1 MTOE has been used.

Coal. Since the 1960s Russia has produced only some 55 per cent of FSU coal, by far the smallest share among the three fuels. Ukraine and Kazakhstan combined extracted not much less. Russia is much less dependent than the other two republics on coal as an energy material, and on the employment that the coal industry generates. Also coal mining in Russia is geographically more dispersed than in Ukraine or Kazakhstan.

We asserted in the preceding section that mine closure at a rate assumed by Scenario 1 will not be politically possible for the FSU. For the reasons just elaborated, however, such a decline might be somewhat more feasible in the case of Russia. We argue, therefore, that the deep recession of Scenario 1, reaching its limit in 1995, will affect coal extraction in Russia more severely than in Ukraine or Kazakhstan in all scenarios (Tables 2.15, 2.16 and 2.17). By 2000, however, with the least efficient mines already shut down, Russia will be able to capitalize

Table 2.15   Coal production in Russia, 1989–2005 (MTOE; gross mine tonnage in parentheses).

Year	Russia total	Kuzbass	Rest of Siberia and Far East	European Russia
1989	164 (410)	91 (170)	37 (160)	36 (80)
1990	156 (395)	86 (160)	36 (160)	34 (75)
1991	138 (353)	72 (133)	35 (150)	31 (70)
Scenario 1:				
1995	96	58	18	20
2000	110	65	25	20
2005	115	75	30	10
Scenario 2:				
1995	110	63	22	25
2000	115	70	25	20
2005	115	80	20	15
Scenario 3:				
1995	105	63	20	22
2000	105	64	19	22
2005	100	65	20	15

on its basins with favourable geology. A modernised industry would stabilise output, though on a level much below that of 1990 and 1991. Extraction may even increase somewhat after 2000 with new investment in clean-burning technologies for power generation.

2.2.5.2   Other FSU States

Compared with Russia, the other republics of the FSU are only minor contributors to aggregate fuel supply: with less than 320 MTOE in 1991 their combined output was only 29 per cent of Russia's (Table 2.11). Nevertheless some republics are major players in individual fuels: Turkmenia in the case of gas, Ukraine and Kazakhstan in coal. Kazakhstan is already an important oil producer, with much greater potential in the future. Uzbekistan is a large producer of natural gas, with minor oil and coal output. A recent discovery may augment substantially its petroleum potential. However, with a population of more than 21 million in 1992, Uzbekistan is also the fourth-largest fuel consumer among all FSU republics, so energy imports are needed to satisfy its needs. All three republics in Transcaucasia consume more fuel than they produce. Azerbayjan plans the development of new deep-water fields jointly with Aramco and the refurbishing of its century-old petroleum industry. Given its high quality oil and long tradition in the field, the new state could develop a modest international role. In the early 1990s, apart from Russia, only Turkmenia had a net energy surplus, while Kazakhstan produced enough for its own needs. Because of the large surplus of Turkmen gas, the whole of Central Asia shows up as a fuel surplus region.

Our treatment in what follows begins with Ukraine, hitherto the second-most important energy producer in the FSU, but also a large-scale importer of oil and gas from Russia. We continue with Kazakhstan, and then deal with Central Asia as a whole.

2.2.5.3   Ukraine

Until the early 1970s Ukraine was self-sufficient in energy. Sizable surpluses of coal and gas compensated for its deficit in oil. Depletion has dramatically reduced the volume of extraction and turned the republic to a fuel importer for 60 per cent of aggregate consumption. By 1991 gross fuel production in Ukraine was on a par with that in Kazakhstan. The difficulties and delays in tapping the vast gas deposits in Western Siberia, and in replacing that region's oil reserves, were instrumental in heavy over-working and premature peaking of Ukrainian hydrocarbon deposits in the 1970s. As a result, by the late 1980s the cost of marginal fuel supply in Ukraine was among the highest in the FSU (Dienes 1992, footnote 10). A rapid further decrease in output is inevitable, and all scenarios project such a course (Table 2.16).

The very large Ukrainian energy deficits are of high relevance for our investigation because imports of fuels from Russia and Turkmenia will affect the volume of exports beyond the FSU. In addition, adequate energy availability in Ukraine is critical for Russian and other FSU energy production. This is because Ukrainian factories supply key metallurgical and chemical products and machinery throughout the FSU, with the coal, petroleum and gas industries being important customers. Most FSU coal-mining equipment, and the bulk of steel pipes, for example, are produced in Ukraine.

The volume and terms of oil and gas supply from Russia to Ukraine, therefore, are critical components for the Russian energy sector. Paying world prices for oil and gas from Russia (124 MTOE in 1991) would

Table 2.16   Fuel production in Ukraine, 1989–2005 (MTOE)

Year	Total	Oil	Gas	Coal
1989	118	5	25	88 (180)
1990	109	6	23	80 (165)
1991	92	5	20	67 (136)
Scenario 1:				
1995	71	4	15	52 (106)
2000	62	6	12	44 (90)
2005	56	9	15	32 (70)
Scenario 2:				
1995	79	4	17	58 (115)
2000	69	5	11	53 (105)
2005	56	7	11	38 (75)
Scenario 3:				
1995	70	4	16	50 (106)
2000	56	6	11	39 (81)
2005	52	7	10	35 (73)

Note: Oil figures include gas condensate. Figures in parentheses in the coal column provide gross mine tonnage.

devastate Ukraine's economy, severely damaging that of Russia in turn. Price concessions to Ukraine in the next few years are therefore certain, although the volume of oil and gas exports will be significantly reduced. The depth of that cut will in turn play a major role in the availability of Russian exports beyond the FSU. The intergovernmental agreement between the two states specifies 40 million tons of oil for 1992, 66 per cent of the volume supplied in 1991. The forecast for government guaranteed deliveries in 1993, however, is a mere 13 million tons (*Vechernyi Kiyev*, 14 May 1992, pp. 3–4; *Neft' Priob'ia*, September, 1992, p. 2).

2.2.5.4   Kazakhstan

Coal. In 1991 coal accounted for two-thirds of Kazakhstan's aggregate fuel production in heat content (Table 2.17). Fifteen per cent of the output, almost nine MTOE, was exported, mostly to Russia. Yet coal will not enhance its role in the Kazakh energy sector. Coal-output originates from the Karaganda and Ekibastuz basins. The former produces very poor-quality coking coal. Coal from Ekibastuz is a very abrasive fuel and therefore hard to handle. We foresee a declining coal output in all scenarios, and a sharply reduced role for coal in the Kazakh energy balance as the output of oil and gas expands.

Oil and Gas. With two of the FSU's petroleum provinces, Kazakhstan has been producing oil since 1911 (Map 2.1). By the late 1960s exploration had shifted to the deep sub-salt layers of the North Caspian, from which the great bulk of the expansion in extraction is expected. Oil and gas in these provinces originate largely from the same deposits. Until 2005 expansion hinges on a mere four to five giant fields, of which Tenghiz (oil) and Karachaganak (gas, condensate and oil) are the largest.

Peak annual production of liquids from the two fields could eventually climb to 45 million tons. A few additional millions would come from other deposits to be developed. Given the extreme complexity of Tenghiz and Karachaganak, and their excessive sulfur content, we do not expect that peak before 2005 (*WGI*, November

Table 2.17   Fuel production in Kazakhstan, 1989–2005 (MTOE)

Year	Total	Oil	Gas	Coal
1989	94	26	5	63 (138)
1990	90	26	6	58 (132)
1991	91	27	6	58 (130)
Scenario 1:				
1995	84	30	6	48 (98)
2000	114	52	16	46 (95)
2005	131	60	26	45 (94)
Scenario 2:				
1995	83	27	6	50 (102)
2000	114	48	18	48 (90)
2005	128	58	22	48 (90)
Scenario 3:				
1995	79	26	6	47 (88)
2000	97	37	17	43 (84)
2005	115	51	23	41 (81)

Notes: Oil figures comprise gas condensate. Condensates are assumed to contribute 20–25 per cent to forecast oil production. Figures in parentheses in the coal column provide gross mine tonnage.

1991, pp. 16–17; and *EBE*, June 1992, p. 12). We project no more than 20–22 million tons of liquids from the two by 2000 in Scenario 1 and a little less in Scenario 2. This will allow Kazakhstan to roughly double its 1991 oil output by 2000 and raise it a bit further by 2005 in the event of radical reform. These large expansions in oil production are possible only with the massive foreign inputs envisaged in Scenarios 1 and 2. In Scenario 3 we expect substantially lower production, mostly because of an inability to assure secure pipeline transport through other republics for exported oil, and because of input-supply problems from Russia.

In the early 1990s Kazakhstan's gas production was quite small. From 1992 through to 2000 and 2005 we expect gas output to grow at very fast rates. Apart from the technological problems and lead times caused by great depth, complex geology and extreme sourness, much of the gas from Kazakh fields will have to be recycled to maximise condensate recovery since liquids represent the main attraction to Western companies. The proximity of the giant Karachaganak deposit to the sour-gas-processing centre of Orenburg in Russia, where the gas will be treated and the condensates recovered, adds significantly to its attraction for Western investors (*WGI*, November 1991, pp. 16–17; *EBE*, January 1992, p. 5; Grigor'yeva *et al.*, 1992, pp. 10–14).

2.2.5.5 Central Asia

The four republics of Central Asia (Uzbekistan, Turkmenia, Kyrgyzstan and Tadjikistan) are far less industrialised than Russia and Ukraine and their economies remain highly centralised. Energy production and consumption in Central Asia therefore will be much less influenced by the pace and nature of reform than the Slavic states. Only Turkmenia will be considered here. It is by far the largest energy producer among the four, and the only one with a sizable energy surplus.

Gas is the dominant fuel in Turkmenia. In the early 1990s it accounted for 93 per cent of total energy output. Turkmenia has been the second largest producer of gas in the FSU since the late 1970s and the only major exporter beside Russia. Most of its exports have gone to Ukraine and Russia, with small volumes to neighbouring Uzbekistan, Kazakhstan and (via Russia) Transcaucasia. In 1990–1, the republic was credited with a part of the overall FSU exports abroad (*WGI*, February 1992, pp. 5–6). As a consequence 11 per cent of Gazprom's total exports are to be credited to Turkmenia at world prices (*Financial Times, International Gas Report*, February 1992, p. 8).

Turkmenia has the lion's share of the Amu Dar'ya gas and oil province, which is predominantly gas-producing, though prospects for oil exploitation have improved in recent years. In addition the Central Caspian oil province of Azerbayjan extends to westernmost Turkmenia (Maksimov, vol. ii, pp. 69–71, 119–124).

The Turkmen gas industry faces difficulties in both production and marketing. Extraction encounters similar problems as in Kazakhstan (see above). In 1990 production costs were 20 per cent higher than in north-west Siberia (VNIIE Gazprom, 1991, p. 48). The Turkmen gas fields are far more isolated from consumption centres than those of Kazakhstan. Transport costs are therefore high. Turkmenia is not a partner in Gazprom. Much of the long transmission network to Russia and Ukraine, which was constructed from the mid-1960s to mid-1970s, is badly corroded and in urgent need of replacement. Transmission costs, which currently double the cost of Turkmen gas in Ukraine and Moscow, are therefore likely to rise (Fadeyev, 1987, pp. 2–5).

With the breakup of the USSR the price of gas delivered to Russia and Ukraine has become a critical issue. A key factor in this context is that gas consumption is falling throughout the FSU, and our scenarios project further declines. Turkmen gas has to be piped through the Russian pipeline network and must compete with Russian gas. Deliveries to Transcaucasia have been reduced. For seven months in 1992, Turkmen gas deliveries to Ukraine stopped altogether following a dispute over price. Many gas wells in Turkmenia were shut down, with shipments resuming only in October of that year (Nikolaev, 1992, p. 13; Sagers 1992, pp. 256–7; *EBE*, October 1992, p. 16).

Extraction in Turkmenia dipped by 6 per cent between 1989 and the end of 1991. Our scenarios anticipate further declines through the mid-1990s. However the fall in Central Asia as a whole will be smaller than in Turkmenia alone. The large Uzbek production will be less affected because the great bulk of Uzbek gas is consumed domestically.

The marketing difficulties for Turkmen gas should ease in the late 1990s because of recovered consumption in Russia and Ukraine, and possibly also because of an alternative outlet for export. Agreement on the construction of a new pipeline through Iran to Turkey, with a probable extension to Europe, might permit the transmission of 13 BCM to these new markets early next century. This growing outlet for gas could allow further increases in extraction by 2005 (Table 2.18 and *PlanEcon. Business Report*, April 29, 1992).

Turkmenia produced 5.4 million tons of oil in 1991, one third of the level attained in 1975. In the immediate future and through much of the

1990s, the Turkmen oil industry will expand only modestly. The potential reserves have not been proved up yet into better defined reserve categories. The infrastructure of oil production is weak. The rising level of the Caspian Sea has begun to flood industry structures and installations on the Cheleken Peninsula, while the rising water table onshore has damaged the water supply and sewage network, which are crucial to this desert region (*SG*, September 1991, p. 517). Almost all Turkmen production is from this peninsula. The higher sea level of the Caspian will affect petroleum production there for the 1990s and longer.

Longer-term production prospects are more optimistic since there are good possibilities of developing new oil deposits. Turkmen production could double by 2005. We project Central Asian output as a whole (nearly all from Turkmenia and Uzbekistan) to reach 18–20 million tons by that date in Scenarios 1 and 2. Production will be substantially less in Scenario 3 (Table 2.18).

Table 2.18   Fuel production in Central Asia, 1989–2005 (MTOE)

Year	Total	Oil	Gas	Coal
1989	118	9	105	4 (11)
1990	116	9	103	4 (11)
1991	117	10	103	4 (10)
Scenario 1:				
1995	105	10	92	3 (10)
2000	129	14	112	3 (9)
2005	133	18	115	0 (0)
Scenario 2:				
1995	108	9	96	3 (10)
2000	123	15	105	3 (9)
2005	130	17	111	2 (9)
Scenario 3:				
1995	106	8	95	3 (10)
2000	118	10	104	4 (11)
2005	125	13	108	4 (10)

Note: *Notes*: Central Asia comprises Kyrgyzstan, Tadjikistan, Turkmenia and Uzbekistan. Virtually all gas and 98% of oil are produced in Turkmenia and Uzbekistan. Uzbekistan and Kyrgyzstan mine 97% of all coal. Figures in parentheses in the coal column provide gross mine tonnage.

2.3   INSTITUTIONAL AND SOCIO-POLITICAL ISSUES IN ENERGY-SECTOR REFORM

So far in our assessment of FSU fuel production we have linked economic analysis to physical constraints. In this section we examine parts of the institutional structure of the fuel industries in mid-1992, and assess the influence of that structure on market reforms and levels of fuel output. In addition, we raise a few issues concerning the socio-political environment which affect the prospect of the energy sector in the 1990s and beyond.

2.3.1   The Institutional Structure of Fuel Production in 1992

The political disintegration of the USSR in late 1991 brought with it the dissolution of the centralised energy ministries. The successor states continue to exert control over fuel production, but to different degrees. In Russia and to some extent Ukraine, this control varies significantly among the three major fuels and through the successive stages from exploration to final-product delivery. The evolving institutional pattern exerts a strong influence on the prospects of energy production both in the short and the longer term. Given the weight of Russia, its institutional arrangements are examined separately.

The governments of Kazakhstan, Azerbayjan and those of Central Asia continue to maintain tight control over all aspects of the fuel industries. Hydrocarbon production in Azerbayjan is a century old, and this republic also possesses a developed scientific infrastructure of petroleum geology and engineering. Corresponding infrastructures are less developed in Kazakhstan and are highly rudimentary in Turkmenia and Uzbekistan. The modernisation of the energy sector in these republics will proceed with strong central-government control, and with very little freedom of decision-making by local authorities. The political culture, the absence of managerial expertise and the great technological difficulties involved in oil and gas production, provide a justification for continued strong control by the central authorities.

Of necessity, the political leaderships in the Moslem republics appear hospitable to foreign investment in exploration and development. Only oil and gas is of interest to the foreigners. None of the states has export outlets, except through Russia. Developing alternative export routes will be expensive and risky. The relative isolation will increase the cost of fuel production and marketing for multinationals and will slow down the introduction of Western technology. Before 2000 the impact of these republics on the world energy market will be imperceptible. It will be very minor even by 2005.

2.3.2 Institutional Arrangements in the Russian Fuel Industries

In Russia the institutional structure of the oil industry is complex and in a state of flux. This stems partly from the large number of oil enterprises, but also from the complexity of interdependent technological stages in the production process. A great number of enterprises produce coal too, but the technology of the industry is far simpler. In contrast gas extraction in Russia is dominated by a few giant producers and the transmission stage remains highly centralised through Gazprom, an interrepublican corporation. Russia does not have centralised ministries for each fuel as did the USSR. Instead there is an overarching fuel ministry, with committees for the production of the individual fuels as well as oil refining, but the functions of targeted output and guaranteed supplies are gone.

2.3.2.1 *The Structure of the Russian Oil Industry*

By 1992 the Russian oil industry had assumed a fluid structure over which Moscow no longer had much control. Within that structure government committees, pseudo-market state corporations, integrated 'independent state companies', and true commercial organizations (shareholding corporations, investment funds, commodity markets) jockeyed for position, resources and hard currency. The absence of a clear structure of petroleum legislation contributed to the institutional fluidity. In that environment contractual linkages were poorly developed and a financial infrastructure barely existed, while the lines of authority and accountability had become tangled in the extreme. Figure 2.8 illustrates that organisational tangle and its ambiguity.

Most extraction is carried on by about 30 regional production associations plus Gazprom, which in addition to its gas business also extracts some crude oil. These associations are state owned, most of them grouped into Rosneftegaz (Russian State Oil and Gas Corporation), whose downstream subsidiaries act as monopolists for refining and product distribution. The production associations are no longer controlled or even supervised by the Ministry of Fuel and Energy, and Rosneftegaz itself has no legal authority of enforcement (it was abolished in 1993). Relations between the ministry and oil-field managers have become increasingly strained. The temporary appointment of Viktor Chernomyrdin (former gas minister, then chairman of

Gazprom) as minister of fuels and energy in the first half of 1992, marked an attempt by Moscow to regain some influence with producing associations. However the Ministry of Fuel and Energy itself may face reorganisation and fragmentation (*FSRC News*, 1 June 1992; *PIW*, 8 June 1992, pp. 1–2).

A number of producing enterprises have tried to bypass Rosneftegaz and its monopolistic downstream concerns. For this purpose the producers established state companies, such as Lukoil and Yunos, both in West Siberia, to develop alternative links with refineries. A number of regional groupings for the independent distribution of products have appeared. The managers of these independent state companies have had to battle officials of both the fuel ministry and Rosneftegaz. Upstream a new Ministry of Natural Resource Use and Ecology (replacing the old USSR Ministry of Geology) is formally responsible for most exploration and prospecting. At the same time several geophysical associations are trying to move into production.

The managements of most producing associations are dominated by the old government and party bureaucracy that assumed *de facto* ownership rights without corresponding accountability to government, shareholders or the financial market. The result is irresponsible 'rent seeking and asset stripping' (Ericson, 1991, p. 3). Newspaper articles report deplorable stewardship of oil resources by this local bureaucracy. Revenue is misappropriated, and geological information is sold to foreign companies for personal enrichment. Thirty-one oil fields were reportedly given to SINCA, a newly formed company with no experience in oil extraction (interview with Tyumen' officials, September 1992; *Kommersant*, no. 18 [1992], p. 2).

Legitimate as well as shadier commercial bodies provide another layer of this chaotic structure. A number of joint-stock companies have been set up at the initiative of the local political elite and include members of Rosneftegaz, independent producers, marketing associations and other concerns. Some of these are claimed to misappropriate revenues on a large scale.

The institutional instability is further aggravated by the conflict between local authorities and Moscow over revenues. In the autumn of 1992 a presidential decree slapped an 18 per cent surcharge on all sales by producers with lower than average costs, with all revenue to accrue to the Russian government. The decree caused consternation in Tyumen', where specialists predicted a strongly adverse effect on production (*Tiumenskie izvestiia*, 24 September 1992, p. 3, and interview with Tyumen' officials, September 1992).

The most damaging long-term consequence of the unstable institutional structure is a collapse of exploration. Producers are expected to sign contracts for exploration with the various geological committees in the Ministry of Natural Resource Use. However most production associations find further prospecting unprofitable under prevailing conditions (interview with a Tyumen' official, *EBE*, April, 1992, p. 10). The geological committees themselves are also reaching out and trying to form joint exploration-cum-production companies with foreigners, but with very modest success so far. Yet another presidential decree issued in the second half of 1992 imposed restrictions on privatisation, the formation of joint-stock companies and foreign participation in the energy industries, reserving to the president all such decision-making rights. This implies that Rosneftegaz's earlier offer of several oil fields to foreign companies on some participatory basis has no legal standing (*Kommersant*, 1 September 1992, p. 24; *EBE*, September 1992, pp. 2–4).

2.3.3 Effects of Intra-FSU Political Tensions

Political tensions among members of the FSU and even regions of Russia affect interindustry supplies, which are already strained by the monetary crisis. Oil and coal production have suffered the most, but the gas industry has also been affected.

The extreme monopolisation of key equipment and machinery production is worsening the situation. Baku and Groznyy (Chechen-Ingushetia) hold a virtual monopoly on oil-well equipment. Azerbayjan manufactures two fifths of the equipment used in oil extraction. All shipment from there to Tyumen' had reportedly ceased in the summer of 1992 (interview with Tyumen' officials. September 1992). Seventy-two per cent of all drilling rigs are made in Russia's Uralmash factory. Most coal-mining machinery comes from Ukraine and so does the bulk of steel pipes. The forest regions of Russia supply the pit-props for Ukrainian and Kazakh mines (*Ekonomika i zhizn'*, no. 25 [June, 1992], p. 10; *EBE*, June 1992, p. 14). Trade in such inputs, which is indispensable for the maintenance of fuel production, is endangered by existing interrepublican and interregional tensions.

Political tensions also pose complications for fuel exports beyond the FSU. For example, it is doubtful whether the construction of the pipeline to carry Tenghiz oil through the Caucasus to the Black Sea will get under way until relations with and inside Georgia have stabilised, and the constitutional issues between Russia and Chechen-Ingushetia

108

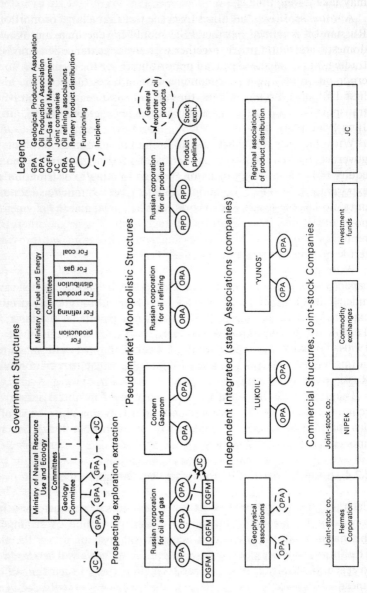

Figure 2.8   Institutional structure of the oil industry of the Russian Federation, 1992

Government Structures

Legend

GPA Geological Production Association
OPA Oil Production Association
OGFM Oil-Gas Field Management
JC   Joint companies
ORA Oil refining associations
RPD Refinery product distribution

Functioning
Incipient

Ministry of Natural Resource Use and Ecology
Committees
Geology Committee

Prospecting, exploration, extraction

Ministry of Fuel and Energy
Committees
For production | For refining | For product distribution | For gas | For coal

'Pseudomarket' Monopolistic Structures

Russian corporation for oil and gas

Concern Gazprom

Russian corporation for oil refining

Russian corporation for oil products

General exporter of oil products

Independent Integrated (state) Associations (companies)

Geophysical associations

'LUKOIL'

'YUNOS'

Regional associations of product distribution

Commercial Structures, Joint-stock Companies

Joint-stock co.
Hermes Corporation

Joint-stock co.
NIPEK

Commodity exchanges

Investment funds

JC

have been settled (*EBE*, August 1992, p. 6; *PIW*, Nov 1992, p. 6). This may take a long time.

Another sensitive issue arises from the fact that a large proportion of Russian oil is refined in other FSU republics. The huge gap between domestic and world prices, together with the appearance of commodity trading, has created widespread opportunities for the illicit diversion of crude oil on its way across republican boundaries to refineries. In the first half of 1992 ten million tons of oil disappeared in intra-FSU transport between producers and refineries (*Ekonomika i zhizn'*, no. 26, June 1992. p. 4)

With the new republics controlling their resources but not yet governed by market prices, the terms of fuel/energy supply and the equity of linkages from extraction through refining to distribution and exports have become contentious political issues as much as economic ones. So has the security of exports, transit rights, and the payment of port and transit fees. Exports of fuel from Russia to other FSU republics require a license, increasing political friction and providing fertile ground for corruption.

With the breakup of the USSR only 42 per cent of FSU tanker-port capacity has remained in Russia, which now depends on its newly independent neighbours for a substantial part of its crude and product export (Yershov, 1992, p. 17). Almost all gas exports from Russia and Turkmenia, some 100 BCM per year, transited Ukraine in the early 1990s. The energy crunch affecting Ukraine, and its strategic position in this regard, explains Ukraine's tough stand in the negotiations with Russia over transit fees.

The resolution of such political tensions and their underlying economic conflicts of interest is bound to take a long time. The disruptions and uncertainties that will prevail in the meantime will impact negatively on fuel supply.

2.3.4 Socio-Economic Constraints to Fuel Output in Scenario 1

Each of the scenarios has its own unquantifiable socio-political constraints. We end the chapter by considering some constraints of this nature that may surface in Scenario 1, involving shock therapy. The optimistic energy-output forecasts in this scenario will be very hard to reach, especially early on in our forecast period, if such constraints emerge with force.

Scenario 1 assumes very fast price increases for oil and gas in the FSU, so that world price levels are reached by 1995. This is bound to have a very strong multiplier effect through the economy, with sharp increases in the cost of electric power, agricultural produce and construction (A. Tretyakova, US Bureau of the Census, Center for International Research. Personal communication). The pace and extent of such repercussions is hard to gauge. The 1987 I–O coefficients (the latest that are available) give only limited guidance for the 1990s. A Russian specialist claimed a 50–60 per cent indirect feedback on the cost of energy from the price hikes in fuels during 1992 (*Ekon. gazeta*, no.41 [October 1992], p. 16).

The rapid restructuring of industry envisaged by Scenario 1 will be seriously hampered by the low sectoral and geographic mobility of the labour force. Given the age structure of the working population and the very severe housing shortage, a rapid increase in that mobility is not a realistic hope through most of the FSU.

A possibility exists that the very swift and painful structural transformation will engender disorder in sectors that furnish the energy industries with essential inputs. This, in turn, would impose constraints on the growth of fuel extraction, at least in the early years of our forecast horizon.

The differential labour intensities of the main extractive industries and the unequal impact of restructuring in our scenarios will impose divergent social and political constraints. We argued earlier in the chapter that even in the shock treatment scenario, the coal industry could not return to profitability during the present century because of employment considerations.

The labour factor looms much more importantly for the future of oil than of natural gas. Only about 110000 persons work in the extraction, treatment and transport of FSU gas. Employment in oil in the late 1980s totalled 1100000, and 600000 in West Siberia alone (*SG*, 1989, pp. 432–3; *PIW*, 27 January 1992, pp. 6–7). Feeding and supplying the Siberian oil workforce has involved difficult logistical problems. The flight of labour from the Tyumen' oil fields has had a detrimental impact on production. At least in the early years of market reforms, whether through shock therapy or more gradual change, oil extraction in Siberia will continue to suffer from that ill effect.

Scenario 1 is assumed to create the most attractive climate for vigorous foreign involvement and infusion of technology. Such an infusion will occur only if a clear legal framework is quickly put in place and foreign investment gains widespread acceptance. Both provisos are under considerable doubt. In Russia which will continue to dominate total FSU fuel output, the political constraints to large scale foreign involvement are manifest in three ways: (a) the ruble/ dollar exchange rates, which in 1992 were far below any reasonable equilibrium level, make foreign ownership participation in energy politically impossible; (b) the Russian government and the major foreign oil companies appear to have different priorities; and (c) the goals of the national and local levels are also frequently in conflict.

Russian attitudes and policies vis-à-vis foreign investors have been highly confusing. In October 1992 two leading liberal figures called for a two-to-three-year ban on foreign firms holding shares in the oil industry. A month later, following a contentious debate, the Russian parliament passed a decree concerning the privatisation of oil-producing enterprises, reportedly permitting foreigners to hold an interest. However the decree appears to restrict the foreign share to 15 per cent and stipulates that a special (not yet announced) exchange rate will be applied for the purpose of asset acquisition by foreigners (Neverov and Igolkin 1992, p. 5; Radio Free Europe/Radio Liberty, *Daily Report*, 13 November 1992).

Apart from the restoration of idle wells, Moscow's main offers to Western companies through 1992 have concerned high-risk, difficult fields, often with disputed reserve potential and little infrastructure. This has considerably cooled foreign interest since the international oil companies normally focus on large, geographically accessible fields and accept serious geological complexity only when reserves are massive. Only four of the oil fields that Rosneftegaz was offering to foreign companies have reserves larger than 40 million tons, and these reserve figures may be overstated (*EBE*, September 1992, pp. 2–4) . Rosneftegaz itself was abolished in 1993.

Local authorities, especially in Siberia and the Far East, have historically chafed under a perceived subordinate, colonial status. For them, long-term concessions and resource exploitation by multinationals appear not as a selling of their patrimony but as a means of developing desperately needed infrastructure and improving consumer-goods supply. For Moscow, on the other hand, the most sensitive issues are precisely the degree of foreign control over natural resources and perceived curtailment of national sovereignty.

Our discussions with non-governmental specialists also revealed the following view: resource projects in hard-to-access geographic locations, with which Russian technology is unable to cope, ought to be offered for long-term concessions to foreign companies. These companies should be allowed full freedom in planning and exercising management control, providing adequate measures are taken to protect the environment. The deposits of offshore Sakhalin, the Barents and the Kara Sea were given as examples. For all other resources Russian control over the pace and scale of development should not be compromised.

The above discussion makes it very clear that both legislation and attitudes must undergo a substantial change to permit foreign-investment inflows into the energy sector on the scale and with a speed envisaged in Scenario 1 and even in Scenario 2. It is unclear how much time will be needed for such change to occur.

APPENDIX 2.1   ASSESSING THE DISTRIBUTION AND RECOVERABILITY OF BYPASSED OIL

A2.1.1   Regression Models of Oil Production

The productivity of petroleum reservoirs is related to numerous factors, many of which may be unique to individual oil accumulation. Certain geological properties, however, have a logical consistent relation to production and can be used to assess reservoir yield. Among these are the basic constituents of volume, which are reservoir height, area of closure and porosity. From these, the area of void space that potentially could be filled with oil can be calculated. If, in addition, the initial oil saturation and gas/oil ratio are known, the proportion of void space that is filled with oil can be determined and the volume of initial oil in place estimated.

Producibility is an expression of the amount of oil that can be recovered from a reservoir as a function of time and reflects not only the volume of oil in place, but also the physical characteristics of the reservoir fluids and rocks, as well as the environment of the reservoir. Permeability is a response of the nature of the network of pores that contain the oil and other reservoir fluids. Temperature and pressure, both related to depth of burial, alter the viscosities of the fluids and hence the rate at which they can be extracted from the pore network. A reservoir may contain a large volume of oil but may produce only a small amount if the factors affecting productivity are adverse or if the reservoir has been damaged by poor production techniques. Our studies are designed to pinpoint those reservoirs which seem, from the available data, to be under-producing for whatever reasons.

Unfortunately not all of the critical properties of reservoirs needed to perform such an analysis are contained in the available data. A critical property is some measure of lateral reservoir extent, such as reservoir area. Without such a measure, or a surrogate such as the number of production wells (assuming a more or less consistent development spacing), gross reservoir volume cannot be estimated. However there is a weak, positive correlation between the height of an oil pool and the area it covers, so measures of reservoir height or thickness also reflect area and hence volume. Other important variables are in the data base, but none are complete. Some variables are partially redundant and others are deterministically correlated. It is fortunate that such redundancies exist between the variables because the data are incomplete for most reservoirs, and this allows us to pick and choose among the variables to obtain the most complete set of reservoirs for each analysis. Because it is necessary to use a slightly different set of variables for each analysis, direct comparisons between different petroleum regions are not possible. Each analysis should be regarded as relative assessments of the reservoirs within that set, and not as expression of absolute volumes of unrealised production.

The composition of the reservoir host rock greatly influences the pore structure and fluid characteristics in a complex manner. Following standard industry practice, therefore, we have analysed reservoir properties separately for the major lithologies identified in the database (sandstone, limestone and reef rock). It is also common practice to distinguish reservoirs on the basis of drive mechanism (gas cap, solution gas, water drive and so on), but the necessary information is not given in the data tables.

Two forms of statistical assessment have been made. The first is a more conventional multiple regression of oil yields on reservoir properties, which embodies the assumption of a linear relationship between reservoir properties and yield. The second employs the logarithm of oil yield as a dependent variable. The rationale for the latter is experience elsewhere which suggests that volume may increase in a greater-than-proportional manner within the largest field-size classes (given that the distribution of field volume is highly skewed).

In a conventional application, using a large number of predictor (independent) variables in the regression equation results in better predictions. Yet the statistical significance of a regression based on many variables may be no greater, and may even be less, than the significance of a simpler model. That is so because more degrees of freedom are required for a model as the number of parameters to be estimated is increased. This effect is exaggerated if values are missing in the data, since fewer reservoirs will have all of the necessary measurements needed for a complicated model. Consequently selecting an appropriate regression model is a trial-and-error process, balancing the better predictions produced by a larger model against the greater sample size available if a smaller model is used. For this reason the regression model differs from one data set to another.

The regression analysis by the Kansas Geological Survey (KGS) produced four scattergrams for subregions of West Siberia and seven for the Timan-Pechora, Ufa-Orenburg, and Lower Volga regions. The reservoir units whose characteristics indicate that they are under-producing were identified by name and/or number from the full KGS file. The figures contrast actual oil production with that predicted by the regression model. Those that most clearly underperform fall below the line of the 95 per cent significance curve. The reason(s) why a specific reservoir unit fails to produce as expected, however, cannot be deduced from this analysis. Beside inappropriate extraction technology, geological factors not considered by the equation or simply incorrect reporting may lower yields. The regression model flags those reservoirs that may be most amenable for enhancing production, but cannot predict the amount of oil that might be produced.

The North Caspian Province differs significantly from all other regions studied. Although the distribution of the reservoir properties appear similar to distribution from other regions, and interrelations between variables seem to follow patterns observed elsewhere, it was not possible to find a linear combination of any of the reservoir properties that would provide an estimate of oil yield. Very great differences in crude composition, the presence of large gas caps and condensate volumes (reducing the contained amount of oil without a commensurate reduction in measures of thickness and porosity), and a great variety of trapping mechanisms that can produce extreme structural configurations characterise the North Caspian Province. Any of these circumstances may result in a heterogeneous mixture of population of oil-field types that, when combined, show no consistent relationships between field properties and field yield.

A2.1.2   Multidimensional Scaling Model of Oil Production

In the second approach to the analysis of reservoir data, a multidimensional scaling (MDS) was applied to map apparent similarity of individual reservoirs, based on their geological characteristics keyed to production. As with the regression analysis, the lack of clear measures of areal dimension in the database was a significant limitation.

In the MDS approach, the matrix of interreservoir similarities was used as the input data for the two-dimensional MDS 'map'. On these maps the distances between reservoirs is the best possible representation of the reservoirs' similarities. By the use of monotonic regression the method 'maps' the reservoirs in a non-metric manner so that the most similar reservoirs are closest together and the least similar are farthest apart. Similarity is predicated on geological characteristics most strongly tied to oil production. The similarities were computed as a weighted composite of the variables that were the most effective in the prediction of total oil yield. The weighing coefficients were Spearman rank correlation coefficients between variables and oil yield.

The MDS classification is based on both numerical and categorical measures of all available geological and reservoir engineering parameters. No standard equation, therefore, can be given. The classification process is controlled by intrinsic reservoir variability, based on aggregate observable reservoir measurement instead of interpretation of genesis. Although the input reservoir-classification variables are mixed quantitative and qualitative data, output from the classification is numerical so predictions may be linked explicitly with quantitative measures of producibility.

The size of a bubble in the MDS 'maps' produced at KGS reflects the total oil yield of the reservoir. The potential for increased production is suggested for those reservoirs that are significantly smaller than neighbouring reservoirs. The analysis indicates that they have a similar mix of geological characteristics which appear to be linked with production. In coordination with the results of the regression analysis, the plots should be considered as a reconnaissance device to flag reservoirs that have a potential for increased production. Indeed we find excellent correspondence between the list of under-performing reservoirs produced by the regression equations and the MDS modelling. The conclusions must be tempered by the additional consideration of areal size, since smaller reservoirs would be expected to have lower total yields. Hopefully, some indication of reservoir area has been captured through implicit correlation with vertical measures of size.

APPENDIX 2.2   THREE METHODS TO COMPUTE REQUIRED
INVESTMENT IN THE FSU'S OIL INDUSTRY BETWEEN 1993
AND 2000

A2.2.1   Investment Cost via Well Completion

From time series on well yields, average well output by 1996–7 is
projected to be no more than 4.5 tons per day. Capital investment per
well (average for the FSU) increased between 1985 and 1990 from
695000 to 969000 (1990) rubles. An average yearly output of 400
million tons up to the end of 2000 will require 243500 operating wells at
the latter date. In January 1991 the number of production wells was
almost 150000. That number may have risen to perhaps 155000 in
1992. The required *increase* by the end of 2000 therefore amounts to
88500. With 2 per cent replacement of the existing well stock per year,
this means that almost 120000 production wells will need to be drilled.
We must add one third as many injection wells and thus arrive at a
total of 179000. With 1990 well costs, the necessary investment will
amount to 174 billion 1990 rubles.

In 1985 well completion represented 87 per cent of total investment
on the oil fields. With a roughly similar ratio, aggregate investment
from January 1993 to the end of 2000, therefore, will total just under
200 billion 1990 rubles, or close to 25 billion per year.[30]

A2.2.2   Investment Cost via Drilling

In 1989, 67 metres of operation drilling were completed for the
production of 1000 tons of crude oil. In 1990, 64 metres of operation
drilling were completed for the production of 1000 tons of crude oil.
Cost per metre in 1989 was 143 rubles (fact). Cost per metre in 1990
reached about 148 rubles (extrapolated from trend), that is, 9598 rubles
per 1000 tons in 1989 (fact), and 9472 rubles per 1000 tons in 1990
(extrapolation). Here a cost of 9500 rubles per 1000 tons is used for
investment estimation. The cost of operation drilling in 1990 prices rose
by 2.03 per cent per annum during 1981–89, and will continue to rise by
2 per cent per year to reach 11115 rubles in 1990 money by the end of
2000.

The relative cost of field development (*obustroistvo*) declined steadily
from being twice that of operation drilling in the 1970s (when the West-
Siberian petroleum province was virgin territory) to 1.45 that of
operation drilling in 1988–90. We expect a ratio of 1.4:1 to hold until

2000. Therefore, in order to extract more or less steadily an annual average of 400 million tons of crude oil until the end of year 2000, the cumulative cost of operation drilling and field development will have to approximate 44 billion and 61 billion respectively in 1990 rubles, or 105 billion combined.

In 1989–90 the cost of exploration by all ministries amounted to almost 43 rubles per 1000 tons of oil produced, and with 400 million tons of annual production would total 137 billion rubles during the eight years. Exploration, however, has been technologically and organisationally inefficient, with too many unnecessary wells drilled. Assuming improved seismic technology and a 30 per cent reduction in the cost of exploration, the aggregate cost of prospecting and exploration would amount to about 96 billion rubles in 1990 money. The grand total of investment for an average yearly output of 400 million tons from 1 January 1993 to the end of 2000 would thus amount to about 200 billion rubles in 1990 money.[31]

A2.2.3 Investment Cost via Preparation of New Reserve Capacity

New capacity in the FSU oil industry in recent years has been *compensatory* capacity, that is, it simply replaces the oil extracted. In 1990 the decrease from the carry over well inventory was claimed to be 100 million tons; in 1991 the decrease was assessed at 100–120 million tons.

Capital investment in constant 1990 rubles per ton of new capacity rose between 1985 and 1990 from 62 to 130 rubles, or by almost 16 per cent per year. Assuming similar rates of increase due to deterioration in reserve quality and location, cost per ton would rise to 365 rubles by 1997, the mid-point of the period under consideration. A yearly average of 400 million tons output, however, amounts to only two thirds of the 1988 and 1989 volume of crude oil extracted, with a consequent easing of pressure on reserves. Cost per ton of new reserves, therefore, may rise to only 245 rubles. Replacing 100 to 105 million tons per year, that is, cumulatively some 820 million tons from the beginning of 1993 to the end of 2000, would therefore require a total of 200 billion rubles. The annual average of outlays would be 24–25 billion rubles.[32]

All three methods of calculation apply to crude-oil production only and ignore investment in associated gas and gas liquids. In the cost structure of the oil ministry, the latter accounted for 9 per cent in 1987 and seems to have increased somewhat since. Raising capital outlays by 10 per cent for these by-products would bring aggregate oil industry investment in the FSU to about 220 billion cumulatively for the eight years, or 27.5 billion rubles annually in 1990 money.

It is unlikely that market forces (coherently functioning only after 1995 in the very best of circumstances) and Western technology could reduce this sum significantly in the present decade. First, the degree of disintegration of the capital stock, infrastructure and skilled labour force in mid-1992 was much greater than in 1990. Second the great bulk of new wells will have to be drilled on a far larger number of scattered deposits than hitherto. The extra cost, which could not be incorporated in the investment estimates, will more than counter-balance any savings from technology improvement and Western investment in the present decade.

APPENDIX 2.3   DERIVATION OF INVESTMENT COSTS FOR A GAS EXPORT PIPELINE

The 3000 km line would run entirely in the European FSU, the 4000 km line would originate from the Yamburg area.

The cost of a 1440 mm pipeline on permafrost is given in a 1990 source as one million rubles per kilometre, with the pipes and equipment representing 60 per cent of the total. Another source of the late 1970s provides a range of 274000–306000 rubles per kilometre for construction cost alone, while a third gives adjustment factors for construction over different terrain (Ivantsov, 1990, p. 39; Yufin, 1978, pp. 238–41; Semenov, 1977, p. 72).

Using these data for Russian/FSU construction costs, we estimate the labour component of building a 3000 km export pipeline from the western slopes of the Urals to the Slovak border as approximately one billion rubles in 1990. Each of the West Siberia–European FSU trunklines, however, experienced a 30 per cent cost escalation compared with the previous line (Albychev *et al.*, 1989, p. 22). Because this line avoids permafrost and transits mostly inhabited regions, we apply only a 15 per cent cost escalation for an estimate of 1.15 billion rubles in 1990. The cost of constructing a 4000 km pipeline all the way from Yamburg, which does run on permafrost and over the steep northern Urals, amounts to 1.3–1.4 billion rubles in 1990 and 1.7 billion if the 30 per cent escalation coefficient is applied. Converted to dollars at a 3.20:1 rubles/dollar exchange rate (1990) yields $360 million and $530 million respectively for the construction part of the two pipelines.

As the upper limit for equipment, we assume that the 1440 mm seamless pipes are imported from Japan. An official of a Japanese company exporting such pipes to Russia quoted us a price of $660–700 per ton, plus a freight cost of $50–75, with pipes of 1440 mm diameter being at the upper end of the range. Indeed, the Japanese trade journal, *Chousa Geppou Rosia Touou Bouekikai* (June 1992, pp. 20–1), records the sale of 7248 tons of such seamless pipes during January–April 1992 at an average price of $730 a ton, probably CIF at a Russian port. The port cost of Japanese pipes for a 3000 km pipeline therefore amounts to $1.3 billion; a 4000 km pipeline of the same specification amounts to $1.8 billion (Special thanks to Ms Wajima, Mr Nobuo Arai, and Mr Shigeru Wada).

Throughput on gas pipelines is determined by diameter, the installed compressor capacity and its pacing. Russian sources provide these data for a number of the 1440 mm trunklines. They claim 28–36 BCM of throughput under a pressure of 75 atmospheres, with compressor station intervals of 110–125 km (Yeremenko and Vorob'ev, 1989, pp. 25–112). Western experts, however, consider the upper limit excessive, with 30–33 BCM being a more realistic figure. About 10 per cent of the gas in transit is used up by the compressors themselves. Western compressors for such large capacity lines cost $1000 per HP ($736/kw); the cost of imported compressors, therefore, adds up to $1.3 and $1.7 billion for the 3000 km and 4000 km lines respectively, if they transmit 28 BCM. (With 36 BCM of throughput, their cost rises to $1.5 billion and $1.9 billion respectively.) Supplementary equipment, if imported, adds another $750 million and well over $1 billion for the respective lines. Such additional costs are particularly critical for the 4000 km line, which would traverse permafrost.

Summing these numbers yields an upper limit of about $4 billion for the 3000 km pipeline and $5.4 billion for the one of 4000 km. Pipelines originating in the Yamal Peninsula would be far more expensive.

The lower limit of our estimate assumes Russian supplies for everything, but data exist only for the costs of pipes and compressors in the late 1980s and 1990 (about 600000 rubles per km of pipe and 700 rubles per kw of compressor capacity. Ivantsov, 1990, p. 39; Tretyakova, 1986, p. 62). These add up to three billion rubles for a 3000 km line and to four billion rubles for a 4000 km line. Supplementary equipment, especially for cooling, increases these totals to 5 billion and more than 7 billion respectively. With a 3.20 ruble per dollar exchange rate for 1990, the lower limit of the two lines approximates $1.7 billion and $2.5 billion.

3 Prospects for FSU Energy Consumption

3.1 INTRODUCTION

The aim of this chapter is to explore the implications of the alternative scenarios for future patterns of energy consumption in the FSU. Given the large reservoir of untapped energy efficiency, it is reasonable to assume that market reforms will generate substantial savings relatively soon after their introduction. For some time changes in export performance may be predominantly shaped by these demand-side improvements.

The connection between domestic consumption and energy export prospects in the FSU is strong. In the past, unchecked consumption growth acted as an important constraint on the FSU's exportable energy surplus. In future, energy exports, based on energy savings, will be able to experience a considerable increase even when one allows for the possibility of a weak and slow production response to the emerging market incentives.

This chapter intends to provide the quantitative dimensions of plausible future changes in energy consumption. Those forecasts, in conjunction with those obtained for the production side (Chapter 2), can then be used for sizing up future FSU capability in energy exports under the alternative scenarios (Chapter 4).

The analysis of consumption proceeds as follows. First, it is necessary to present the key characteristics of recent Soviet and FSU consumption patterns, with a focus on energy efficiency. Examination of current conditions provides a background against which the scope and direction of future consumption trends can be gauged.

An important aim of the market reforms is to raise domestic energy prices to world price levels. To provide a perspective to this task, the second part of this chapter assesses the structure of energy prices at the outset of the reform programmes. For mid-1992 an estimate is provided for the difference between international energy prices and the prices in Russia, the predominant producer and consumer of energy in the FSU.

Knowledge of the degree of distortion between the two price levels is crucial for determining the extent of necessary price adjustment.

The third part offers projections for the consumption of three major tradable fuels (oil, natural gas and coal) in the FSU as a whole and in major republics, for the period 1992–2005.

3.2 ENERGY USE PATTERNS IN THE FSU

The aggregate energy consumption in the FSU grew briskly during the 1970s (4.1 per cent per year), in sharp contrast with the OECD countries where consumption growth slowed to 1.9 per cent a year (Figures 3.1 and 3.2). The growth rate of total consumption began to drop appreciably only in the early 1980s, a half-decade later than in the West. Yet in the 1980s Soviet growth in consumption (1.8 per cent a year) was still almost twice the average rate (1.0 per cent) for the developed market economies. With the subsequently unfolding economic crisis there was a sharp break with the historical pattern. Growth in energy consumption stalled in 1989, declined 2.1 per cent in 1990, 2.3 per cent in 1991 and an estimated 8 per cent in 1992.

The fuel-by-fuel analysis shows sharply contrasting patterns in consumption trends (Figure 3.1). Coal use has been in steady decline since the late 1970s. The fall became precipitous after 1988, partly reflecting shrinking production. Thus consumption of coal fell by 3.5 per cent in 1989, 5.7 per cent in 1990 and 9.7 per cent in 1991. For 1992 the decline is estimated at only 2.5 per cent owing to a strong effort by Russia and Ukraine to rely more heavily on domestic coal so as to free more gas and oil for exports (in the case of Russia) and to offset the reduced supply of Russian oil and gas (in the case of Ukraine).

Oil consumption shows particularly varied behaviour over time. After rapid growth in the 1970s, consumption levelled off for most of the 1980s. A falling trend marks recent years (1989 −2.7 per cent; 1990 −4.8 per cent; 1991 −1.2 per cent; 1992 an estimated −15 per cent). Apart from 1992, this slide in refined-product consumption was more moderate than the reduction in crude-oil output, which suggests a deliberate policy of forcing the export sector to absorb most of the fall in crude production. There is evidence, however, that the recent decline in consumption may be seriously understated. Analysts assert that the increasingly decentralised exports of refined products are under-reported to avoid high export duties and export licenses (PlanEcon, February 1992).

Figure 3.1 Energy consumption in the FSU, 1971–91 (MTOE)

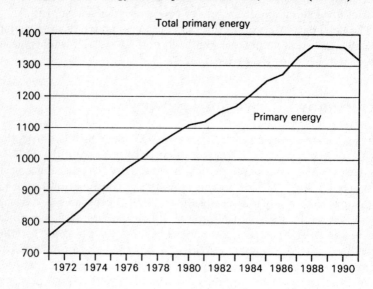

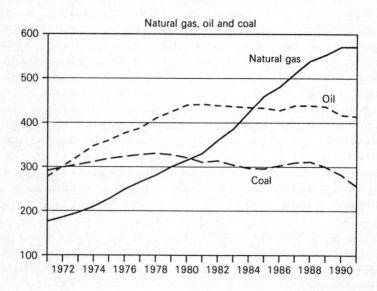

Figure 3.2   Total primary energy consumption in the FSU and the OECD

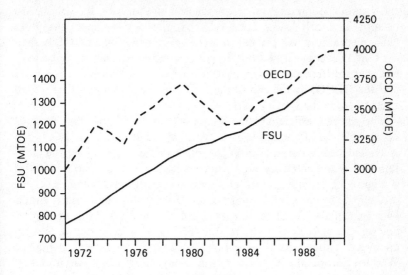

Natural gas has been an exceptionally dynamic component of FSU energy consumption, expanding at 5.5 per cent annually even during the 1980s. By as early as 1980 gas had become the dominant source of energy in the FSU, accounting for 41.5 per cent of total primary consumption, an exceptional figure in an international comparison. Gas has become the most important fuel, meeting the entire incremental demand for energy over the past decade and providing the flexibility needed for overcoming mounting supply bottlenecks in other fuels. In the most recent years gas too has experienced a sharp change in its consumption trend. The increase in gas use in the FSU was down to 2.4 per cent in 1990 and 0.5 per cent in 1991 while in 1992, consumption fell by an estimated 4 per cent. During these years, natural gas continued to expand its share in the power-station fuel market (52 per cent in 1989) as it had to make up for the large drop in coal output (residual fuel oil has been another, though less important, substitute for coal in electricity generation).

3.2.1   Trends in Energy Efficiency

Trends in energy efficiency (measured by energy intensity, defined as tons of oil equivalent per million dollars GDP), appear in Figures 3.3

and 3.4. Energy intensity in the FSU was significantly higher than in the market economies even before the first oil shock. In the early 1970s, despite its much lower level of economic development, the FSU consumed almost 40 per cent more energy per dollar of GDP than the OECD average, and about 80 per cent more than Japan. Because of the sharp differences in the post-oil-shock developments in the FSU and the OECD, by the end of the 1980s the FSU energy intensity had risen to twice the OECD level.

The energy efficiency gap between the FSU and the West is observable for all sources of energy. As shown in Figure 3.4, the steep and steady rise in natural gas intensity more than offset the long-term fall in coal intensity and the more recent downturn in oil intensity.

Figure 3.5 provides a further indication for the energy-intensity bias of the FSU by comparing total primary energy consumption per capita with that of the OECD countries. If one ignores the US as an outlier among the industrial nations, the FSU's overuse becomes clearly apparent. Though its per capita GDP was less than half of that in Western Europe, the FSU's energy use per person in 1989 was about 50 per cent higher. When compared with countries with a similar per-capita income, such as Greece and Portugal, the FSU's per-capita overuse works out as high as 150 per cent.

Figure 3.3   Energy intensity of GDP in the FSU and the OECD

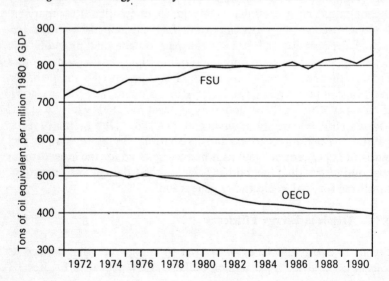

Figure 3.4 Energy intensity in the FSU

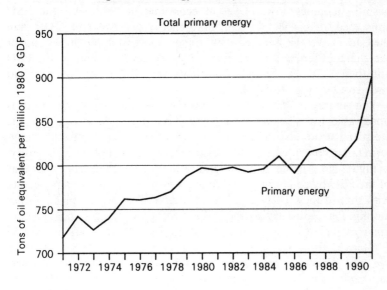

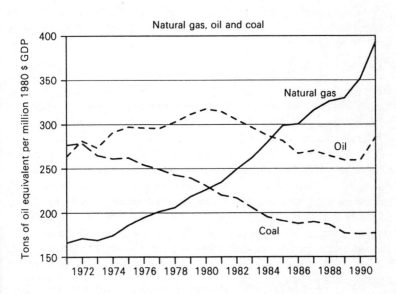

Figure 3.5   Primary energy consumption per capita

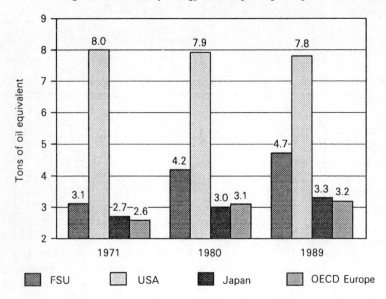

The overuse is equally apparent when final (as distinct from primary) energy consumption is considered. In 1980 FSU final energy intensity was 70 per cent higher than in the OECD. By 1990 the difference had risen to 100 per cent.

In 1990 and 1991 energy consumption in the FSU showed a surprisingly modest fall in relation to the severity of the slumping GDP. This implied a drastic further worsening in energy efficiency, with energy intensity rising by 2.6 per cent in 1990 and 8.6 per cent in 1991. This recent deterioration could have several explanations. Both official Russian statistics and Western sources may have overestimated the fall in GDP. Energy use too, may have been overestimated, due to disguised exports of oil products and unreported stock-building in response to expectations of massive price increases. A very high share of electricity consumption is of a fixed nature, not varying with the level of output. Finally, because of very rapid general inflation, real official energy prices rose only marginally in the first half of 1992, and the low level of real prices has prolonged the energy waste (IEA 1991c; PlanEcon, April 1992).

The reasons for the high energy intensity in the FSU are varied but, in the final analysis appear to be predominantly 'systemic', that is caused by the structure of incentives, institutions and decision-making specific to the command economy.

3.2.1.1 The Energy Sector's Deteriorating Ability for Releasing Final Energy

Between 1971 and 1990 total primary energy consumption grew at an annual rate of 3.0 per cent while final energy consumption grew at only 2.7 per cent. In 1990, 6.5 per cent more fuel was needed per unit of final energy than in 1971. This indicates a reduced efficiency in producing and delivering end-use energy. The negative process unfolded especially rapidly during the 1980s. It is not entirely clear which factors underlie this worsening trend. The own use of the energy sector rose from 4.2 per cent in 1971 to 6.2 per cent in 1990. The combined share of own-use and distribution losses went up from 7.0 per cent in 1971 to 8.9 per cent in 1990 compared with the 3.9 per cent OECD average in the latter year. In 1990, in the natural gas sector, own-use and distribution losses were as high as 74 MTOE or 13 per cent of total domestic gas supply compared with 8.8 per cent in 1971, partly because of increasing distances of gas transport (Chapter 2). The worsening geological conditions facing the oil industry led to an increase in its electricity use per ton of output between 1980 and 1989. FSU sources (Narkhoz, 1990) report a marked slowdown followed by virtual stagnation in improvements of fuel rates in electricity and heat generation. The advantages from rapid penetration of high-efficiency natural gas were apparently counterbalanced by the deteriorating quality of coal burned in power plants and the growing stock of inefficient boilers and furnaces.[1]

3.2.1.2 Skewed Sectoral Composition of Final Consumption

The structure of final energy consumption in the FSU is quite different from that in market economies (Table 3.1). The FSU stands out in the following respects: the very high share of energy absorbed by industry (47 per cent in 1990 compared with 34 per cent in OECD countries), especially in branches of heavy industry, such as ferrous and non-ferrous metallurgy and machine building;[2] the extremely high share of agriculture (almost six times the OECD average); the low shares used by the transport sector (about half that of a typical market economy), and by the residential sector. Clearly the skewed pattern of energy end-use reflects decades of economic planning favouring energy-intensive heavy industries.

Table 3.1 Sectoral distribution of final energy consumption in the FSU, the US and OECD Europe (per cent of total final energy use)

	FSU		US		OECD Europe	
	1980	1989	1980	1989	1980	1989
Total industry	53.1	46.2	35.1	30.1	37.2	33.9
Iron and steel	14.5	10.4	–	–	7.6	6.0
Chemicals	11.1	9.5	–	–	10.6	11.0
Non-ferrous metals	2.9	3.0	–	–	1.4	1.3
Non-metallic minerals	5.6	5.8	–	–	4.2	3.5
Machine building	8.3	8.5	–	–	2.6	2.5
Food and tobacco	3.6	3.0	–	–	2.5	2.3
Paper, pulp, print	0.1	0.1	–	–	2.5	2.4
Forest products	1.4	1.3	–	–	0.4	0.4
Construction	2.6	2.6	–	–	0.5	0.5
Transport	15.6	15.4	31.7	35.1	22.7	25.6
Other sectors	27.3	33.7	30.2	30.9	37.1	38.0
Agriculture	5.8	9.6	1.0	1.1	2.0	2.3
Trade and public services	9.0	9.7	10.8	11.5	9.1	9.9
Residential	8.9	13.8	18.0	17.9	22.4	23.8
Non-energy use	4.0	4.7	4.3	4.1	3.0	3.1

Note: Industry breakdown for the US is not available.
Source: IEA, 1989, 1991b, 1991d.

Since industry is generally more energy-intensive than the rest of the economy, its large share in total energy use in the FSU contributes importantly to the high energy intensity of total output. This tendency has been compounded by two additional factors. First, the 'frozen' nature of the sectoral composition of total output in the 1980s (very few structural shifts were noticeable even at lower levels of disaggregation) denied the FSU the opportunity to save energy by reducing the share of energy-intensive industrial activities. The second factor was a surprisingly weak ability to generate direct energy-efficiency gains (by lowering the energy use per unit of output) at the level of individual industries, especially if consideration is given to the large amount of inherent conservation potential.

Figure 3.6 provides data for the final energy use per unit of value added for the major economic sectors and several industrial subsectors. Among the major sectors, transportation stands out with an annual 2.6 per cent decrease in the energy use per unit of value added between 1971 and 1987. Energy intensity in the industrial sector shows a decline

Figure 3.6 The FSU: energy intensity of end-use sectors

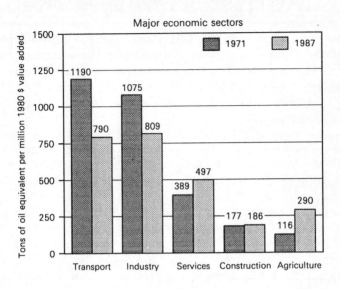

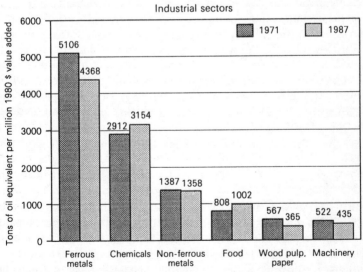

Sources: GDP data are from Directorate of Intelligence (CIA), Handbook of Economic Statistics, various issues and Joint Economic Committee, US Congress, Measure of Soviet Gross National Product in 1982 Prices (Washington, DC, 1990). Energy-concumption data are from IEA.

of 1.8 per cent a year, while the other major sectors' energy/value-added ratios trended upward (at a remarkably high rate for services and agriculture).

The efficiency performance of the most energy-intensive industry sectors during the same period is disappointing. The energy intensity of ferrous metallurgy, which accounts for almost one-quarter of industrial energy use, dropped by only 1.0 per cent a year, the chemical sector's energy intensity actually increased, and that of non-ferrous metals remained unchanged.

To place these developments in perspective, Table 3.2 compares the energy-efficiency performance of the major economic sectors of the FSU with that of three OECD countries for the period 1980–8. Despite its much higher level of specific energy use in 1980, industry's efficiency improvement in the FSU lagged behind that of Japan and Germany, and was similar to that of the US. As a result, by 1988 the FSU's use of energy per unit of value added stood at a level more than four times the German level and more than three times the Japanese level; the difference was 70 per cent vis-à-vis US industry. Agriculture, a large end-user in the FSU, displayed a massive increase in energy intensity from an already elevated initial level in 1980.[3] Although the agricultural sector's energy-efficiency record also showed a worsening trend in the US and Japan, its impact on aggregate energy efficiency in these countries was marginal, owing to the sector's small share of energy use. The efficiency improvement in the FSU service sector was unimpressive, if account is taken of the large reservoir of untapped energy efficiency (extremely wasteful space heating, lack of metering and underpricing of heat and hot water are some of the causes of the prevailing inefficiency). Transportation was the only major sector where the FSU appears to have performed reasonably well.

3.2.1.3 Technological Lags

Relative technological backwardness is a significant factor behind inefficient energy consumption in the FSU. Available evidence suggests that technological advance slowed markedly during the 1980s. This period saw an accelerated fall in total factor productivity in industry, a proxy measure for the pace of technological change.[4] The possibility of raising the energy efficiency of the capital stock was seriously hampered by the slowdown in new investment and declining imports of modern equipment from the West. The slowness in adopting advanced energy-efficient technologies resulted in a widening of the

Table 3.2 End-use energy intensity by sector in the FSU, the US, Japan and Germany in 1980 and 1988 (tons of oil equivalent per million 1980 $ GDP)

	FSU		US		Japan		Germany	
	1980	*1988*	*1980*	*1988*	*1980*	*1988*	*1980*	*1988*
GDP	633	573	491	398	235	184	243	203
Industry	1017	809	592	478	366	254	256	195
Construction	209	186	NA	NA	37	38	NA	NA
Agriculture	185	290	171	237	83	124	137	130
Transport	1092	790	2592	2330	1103	728	844	838
Trade and other services	566	497	248	188	87	78	92	132

Sources:
GDP data for the FSU are from Directorate of Intelligence, various issues; for the other countries they are from the World Bank, *World Tables*, various issues; data for the sectoral composition of GDP of the three OECD countries are from UNCTAD, 1991.

'energy technology gap' vis-à-vis the West. This gap probably explains a large part of the difference in unit energy requirements between the FSU and the advanced market economies.

Based on a comprehensive inventory and a technological assessment of fixed assets conducted in 1986, Table 3.3 highlights the large share of worn-out and obsolete energy equipment. On average the share of modern energy equipment matching best-practice world levels was less than 10 per cent, while the ratio of obsolete equipment requiring immediate replacement was close to 50 per cent. Investment growth slowed in the second half of the 1980s and turned negative thereafter. Hence the technological level and age structure of the capital stock in the early 1990s must look worse than in 1986.

For ferrous metallurgy, a major user of energy, the proportion of modern equipment was only 14 per cent, while worn-out facilities represented 29 per cent of the total. In steel-making the FSU continued to rely heavily on energy-inefficient open-hearth furnaces. In 1989, the combined share of the more energy-efficient basic oxygen and electric furnaces was only 48 per cent, compared with 99 per cent in the major market economies. The proportion of steel continuously cast was only 17 per cent. In the market economies continuous casting represented 85 per cent of the total (*Narkhoz*, 1990).

Table 3.3 Technological and vintage characteristics of equipment in the former USSR (official inventory, 1 April 1986)

	Technological level			Age composition			
	Best world standard[1]	National standard[2]	Obsolete[3]	Below 5 years	6–10 years	11–20 years	Over 20 years
Energy equipment							
Steam boilers	10.5	52.9	36.6	26.1	26.8	31.3	15.8
Waste-heat boilers	5.7	48.5	45.8	19.2	22.2	35.4	23.2
Steam turbines	2.6	36.6	60.8	8.6	13.2	28.6	49.6
Gas turbines	5.2	76.3	18.5	23.7	46.4	29.9	–
Hydro turbines	2.0	21.5	76.5	4.7	6.3	17.4	71.6
Diesel engines[4]	6.7	52.3	41.0	31.0	32.8	23.4	12.8
Electrothermal equipment							
Electric arc furnaces	4.9	38.6	56.5	18.6	16.2	31.1	34.1
Metal treating furnaces	7.8	47.4	44.8	34.0	24.8	23.4	17.8
Induction melting and heating equipment	9.8	51.5	39.1	30.4	25.0	30.4	14.2
Electric welding equipment							
Open-arc welding machine	12.2	50.0	37.8	43.2	33.8	18.9	4.1
Contact welding machine	7.1	44.7	48.2	27.9	27.8	33.8	10.5
Total industry	16.0	55.9	28.1	32.0	27.1	26.2	14.7
Energy industry	14.0	59.8	26.1	36.3	23.7	23.6	16.4
Iron and steel	14.3	56.6	29.1	28.2	24.0	26.4	21.4
Chemicals	16.0	53.1	30.9	28.9	29.4	25.6	16.1
Machinery	19.9	54.1	26.0	32.0	28.3	29.8	9.9
Food industry	14.6	53.1	26.9	28.4	32.6	29.4	9.6
Construction	10.7	58.5	38.8	29.1	27.7	26.3	16.9

Notes to Table 3.3
1. Best-practice world standard or higher.
2. Currently accepted national standard but requiring modernisation in the near future.
3. Outdated and should be replaced.
4. Other than automobiles and tractors.
Source: Based on Gosudarstvennii Komitet, 1988.

The share of obsolete equipment in the chemical industry as a whole was one third, but it was probably much higher in the aging oil-refinery sector, the bulk of which is technologically obsolete by world standards. The depth of refining is low. Catalytic cracking accounts for only 9 per cent of distillation capacity and 12.5 per cent of secondary processing (compared with 23 per cent and more than 50 per cent, respectively, for the OECD countries). The share of medium and light products is only 52 per cent compared with 75 per cent in the OECD (IMF *et al.*, 1991). The unsophisticated nature of the refinery sector leads to substantial losses in the value of output. In turn the large volume of heavy fuel oil resulting from the outdated refinery processes is used inefficiently in power generation.

The highly energy-intensive cement industry represents a clear case of technological backwardness inducing an overuse of energy. In the most cement-intensive economy of the world, the bulk of cement is still produced using the older 'wet' process (83 per cent, compared with the average 25 per cent for the US, Japan and Germany), which requires one-third more energy per unit of output than the more advanced 'dry' process. Despite its obvious advantage, the share of the dry process in the FSU rose only by 3 per centage points between 1970 and 1990 (*Narkhoz*, 1990).

3.2.2 Behavioural Factors behind Inefficient Energy Use and the Magnitude of Systemic Wastage

The serious shortcomings of the centrally planned FSU economic system include traditional preoccupation with gross output as opposed to profitability, weak managerial incentives to minimise costs, an anti-innovation bias associated with a profoundly non-competitive and permissive economic system; an extensive safety net provided by the state to all enterprises and gross underpricing of energy resources. All this created fertile ground for excessive use of all productive inputs, including energy. Although the lack of a 'market for energy efficiency' contributed to the FSU's tendency to overuse energy compared with market economies, it is an open question what proportion of the recorded overconsumption (that is, the higher energy intensity of GDP) is attributable to 'systemic waste'. Once it is quantified, the size of the systemic waste can be taken as a rough indicator of the magnitude of savings potentially realisable under a market-based economic regime.

Determining the relative weight of the 'systemic factors' in energy overuse is no simple task because the economic system is only one of numerous determinants of energy intensity. Unit energy requirements display considerable variation even among market economies.

We have chosen a straightforward statistical technique to estimate the systemic effect on the level of energy use in the FSU. For 1980 (the year for which the estimate was made for data reasons) this technique first econometrically estimates the relationship between energy consumption and a set of explanatory variables for a reference group of market economies which, in order to account for the variation in the level of development, includes both developed and semi-developed countries.[5] The model was then used to predict the hypothetical 'market economy' level of FSU consumption. This works out to 708 MTOE. Actual consumption in that year was 1116 million tons, implying that the FSU used 58 per cent more energy than it would have done if it had behaved like a typical market economy, after accounting for the size of the GDP, the structure of the economy, the pattern of fuel consumption and the domestic resource base in energy. At the 'market-economy' level of energy consumption, the 1980 FSU energy/GDP ratio works out to 508 tons oil equivalent per million dollars GDP, about the same as the average OECD ratio that year. The actual FSU value was 800 tons.

Assuming that the 58 per cent degree of system-induced over-consumption has remained constant up to the present (given the divergent energy/GDP trends between the FSU and the OECD countries, this margin has probably widened), for 1990 the magnitude of excess consumption works out to roughly 500 MTOE, a staggering quantity by any standard. It corresponds to 6.4 per cent of current world consumption of primary energy, it is equivalent to 40 per cent of total oil production by OPEC, and it is almost twice the 1989 level of FSU fuel exports. In 1990 FSU energy intensity was twice as high as in the OECD. Without systemic overuse, the intensity works out to be only 30 per cent higher than the OECD average. This implies that almost three-quarters of the apparent overconsumption is attributable to systemic forces; other conditions (such as the favourable resource base, the large size of the country and so on) account for the remainder of the discrepancy.

The above estimate for systemic overuse of energy comes surprisingly close to that obtained through a different approach in a large-scale FSU research project, which for 1990 calculated the hypothetical level of energy consumption by assuming the full adoption of the world's best-practice technologies. The detailed fuel-by-fuel and sector-by-sector assessment put the magnitude of potential energy savings at 515 MTOE (Table 3.4). After adjusting for that project's 8 per cent overprediction of total energy consumption for 1990, the corrected estimate is around 480 MTOE.

Although the FSU study terms this amount 'technological savings', it clearly reflects the effects of a host of systemic factors conditioning the large lags in FSU technology. These include the familiar anti-innovation bias under central planning, the artificially low energy prices which make the application of energy-saving technologies uneconomic, the lack of competition to force enterprises to minimise costs and the difficult access to energy-efficient equipment, owing to the lack of a functioning domestic market in capital goods and the state monopoly of foreign trade. Thus the suggested savings potential appears to be comparable to our estimate and lends a measure of credibility to its relative accuracy.[6]

While the measure of aggregate energy waste is of considerable policy interest, knowledge of the sectoral origins of the waste is equally important for determining the focus of future energy-saving activities. The breakdown of potential energy savings by user-sector shown in Table 3.4 may serve as a rough guide for locating the areas with the largest misuse of energy. Not surprisingly the worst performance is revealed by those sectors which also display a poor record of energy efficiency in a cross-country comparison. Industry stands out as by far the largest sector with underutilised savings potential, accounting for 66 per cent of the total (even without the energy sector, the industry share comes to 47 per cent). At a greater level of disaggregation, the metallurgical sector displays the most disappointing performance, closely followed by the energy sector. The two together account for a sizeable share in the industry aggregate. The residential/municipal sector should also be mentioned as a large area of untapped energy efficiency, accounting for more than one-fifth of the total conservation potential of the FSU.

Table 3.4   Magnitude of energy savings potential in the FSU by sector, 1990 (MTOE)[1]

	Actual consumption[2]	*Estimated consumption with best-practice world standard technologies*	*Savings potential*
Electricity, total	150	106	44
Motive power	91	70	21
Lighting	15	7	8
Electrothermal use	15	8	7
Electrolysis	7	6	1
Other	8	6	2
Grid losses	14	9	5
Steam and hot water, total	299	203	96
Residential/municipal heating and hot water	73	41	26
Space heating in production	67	45	22
Technological needs	128	98	30
Network losses	31	13	18
Direct consumption, total	669	445	224
Metallurgy	109	53	56
Other industry (exc. energy)	130	98	32
Residential/municipal	149	95	54
Agriculture	68	42	26
Transport	130	94	36
Non-energy use and raw materials	112	91	21
Conversion losses, total	234	109	125
Electricity	181	77	104
Heat	53	33	20
Own-use and losses in production, processing and transport	91	66	25
Total	1443	928	515

Notes:
1. All data are converted from million tons of 'standard fuel' in the original source to MTOE by multiplying by 0.697.
2. 'Actual consumption' figures in the original source are predicted values. Actual total consumption turned out to be 8 per cent less than the predictions. Hence the aggregate savings appearing in the table should also be reduced by this percentage.

Source: Makarov and Chupiatov, 1990, p. 6.

3.3 STRUCTURE OF ENERGY PRICES AT THE BEGINNING OF MARKET REFORMS

Prices of energy and other natural resources in the FSU were systematically suppressed in relation to any rational base of comparison, such as the true national cost of production (including social cost), marginal costs and prices of manufactured goods, let alone world-market prices. Based on ideologically motivated principles, energy prices reflected the planned average cost of the given energy sector plus a normative profit markup, without fully incorporating differential resource rents, depletion allowances, the full cost of capital or environmental externalities. These prices failed to reflect relative resource scarcities or to assure supply and demand balance. The low price levels provided large-scale implicit subsidies to the energy-intensive industries and thus contributed to sectoral distortions in total output. They also stimulated wasteful utilisation and made energy-saving investment economically unattractive.

Although, with Russia's adoption of 'shock-therapy' reforms in January 1992, price controls have been lifted on most commodities, energy products continue to be subject to government control. With the emergence of parallel markets, a multitude of energy prices at different levels exists side by side. In 1992 five types of energy prices could be identified in Russia and other parts of the FSU (Tables 3.5 and 3.6).

3.3.1 State-controlled Prices

On 2 January 1992, while increasing the nominal energy prices considerably, the Russian government set the maximum level to which regulated prices were allowed to rise. On average, energy prices were raised by about 400 per cent. At the wholesale level,[7] the size of the maximum increase was crude oil 500 per cent, natural gas and steam coal 400 per cent, coking coal 700 per cent and electricity 300 per cent. At the retail level the maximum allowable increases were generally smaller: 300 per cent for gasoline; 200 per cent for diesel oil, kerosene, liquefied petroleum gas, central heating and electricity in urban areas (in rural areas the electricity tariff was raised 700 per cent); and 400 per cent for household fuels (coal, briquettes of peat or coal, heating oil and firewood) and pipeline gas. In addition to raising prices the Russian government imposed a 28 per cent value-added tax (to be reduced to 20 per cent in 1993) on most goods, including energy,

Table 3.5   Wholesale energy prices in Russia, June 1992 (rubles per ton)

	Official wholesale price[1]	Commodity exchange price[2] in sales with			*Interrepublican export price*
		No export license	*License to export to FSU states*	*License to export to non-FSU states*	
Crude oil	1800–2200	2600	6400	9000	2820[3]
Heavy fuel oil	2875	4645			3500[3] 4125
Diesel fuel	5480	7500			6600[3] 8800
Jet fuel	8905				
Leaded gasoline (76 octanes)	6333	9170	13380	17500	7500[3] 12500[4] 17500[4]
Leaded gasoline (93 octanes)	8750	8260			11500[4]
Natural gas (Rbl per thousand m³)	1100–1600	4200			2050[3] 3000[4]
Coking coal	1400				
Steam coal	550	1000			
Electricity (Rbl/kWh)					1.20[6] 0.24[5]

Notes:
1. Excluding VAT.
2. Average of June–July 1992 (exc. VAT).
3. Average of all exports to FSU republics.
4. Exports to Latvia.
5. Exports to three Baltic states.
6. For industry.

although its application shows some selectivity (for example household electricity is exempted from VAT).

All of the FSU republics, including the Baltic nations, followed Russia's lead in energy-price increases, although the extent of adjustment varied, leading in some cases to considerable price differences across the FSU. In the first quarter of 1992 the differences between gasoline prices were as large as thirtyfold (lowest in Russia and

Kazakhstan, highest in Estonia); in electric power the discrepancy in ruble prices was threefold, with Uzbekhistan and Turkmenia at the lower end, and Lithuania at the high extreme (*Komsomolskaya Pravda*, 26 March 1992). For some time the geographical differences in energy prices may remain relatively large, reflecting differing domestic supply conditions, administrative restrictions in interrepublican energy trade and some diversity in government pricing and fiscal policies. It is reasonable to predict that the increases in domestic energy prices will proceed faster in the energy-deficit countries, for the shipments from the major FSU exporters will soon reflect world-market prices.

The official wholesale prices apply to energy sold for satisfying 'state needs', a concept never clearly defined. In effect it appears to substitute for the former system of 'state orders' (*goszakazy*). In 1992 most of the energy sales in Russia and other FSU republics took place at state-controlled prices. In 1991 state-order shipments accounted for 94 per cent of Russia's oil output. For 1992 this share was expected to be between 75 and 85 per cent (*Ekonomika i zhizn'*, no. 38 [September], 1992). This means that the 27 Russian refineries still obtain the bulk of crude-oil shipments at the state-set price. But as a result of the ongoing partial liberalisation of energy marketing, the share of sales conducted at state prices is expected to fall in 1993 and beyond. A resolution taken on 4 January 1992 by the Russian government formally released from state price control up to 20 per cent of crude oil and natural gas production and up to 10 per cent of the output of oil products.

However producers can sell at unregulated prices only after the specified 'state needs' (which include exports) have been satisfied. In the case of the coal industry, all deliveries in excess of 'state needs' could be marketed at freely negotiated prices. This exceptional treatment of the coal sector is designed to improve its extremely depressed financial situation (see Chapter 2).

In March 1992, under mounting pressure from the financially struggling energy producers, the government raised to 40 per cent the share of crude oil, natural gas and oil products that can be sold at unregulated prices (again, after satisfying the state requirements).[8] As a result, by early 1992 an estimated one fifth of domestic energy trade was conducted at unregulated prices. It is important to note, however, that the government retains the right to lower the proportion of production allowed for sale on the open market should conditions require such modification.

To take effect on 18 May 1992, the Russian government established new wholesale prices for crude oil, oil products, natural gas and coal.

Crude-oil prices (excluding VAT) were allowed to move within a set range of 1800 and 2200 rubles per ton (an average 5.7-fold nominal increase relative to the 350 ruble state price introduced in January 1992). Natural-gas prices were allowed to move within the limits of 1100 and 1600 rubles per thousand cubic meters (an average 5.2-fold increase). In the first few months of this partial decontrol the government tried to keep prices within the range through a novel taxation scheme, which levies steeply rising taxes on sales prices exceeding the bounds of the set ranges. In the case of oil, the tax rate rises from 60 per cent in the range of 1801–1900 rubles per ton, to 90 per cent in the range of 2101–2200 rubles per ton. Similar rates apply to natural gas. Selling oil and gas at prices higher than the ceiling of the range has been considered a 'violation of the price discipline of the state' and has led to confiscation of the extra revenue and the imposition of fines. These harsh fiscal and administrative measures have been used to keep oil and gas prices at a lower level than the spot prices registered in early 1992. In fact the penalty tax has also been applied to transactions conducted on the commodity exchanges.

Actual wholesale prices moved quickly to the price ranges set in May. In June 1992 the average wholesale price of crude oil in Russia was reported to be 1940 rubles per ton, but this average concealed a fairly substantial geographical dispersion (*Ekonomika i zhizn'*, no. 35, [August], 1992). In early June 1992 the average price of natural gas

Table 3.6   State-set retail prices of energy in Russia, June 1992 (rubles per ton, including taxes)

Leaded gasoline (76 octanes)	7800
Leaded gasoline (93 octanes)	10140
Leaded gasoline (98 octanes)	11050
Diesel fuel	8080
Fuel oil	360
Lighting kerosene	800
Natural gas (Rbl per thousand m^3)	260
Liquefied gas (butane and propane)	1360
Electricity (Rbl/kWh)	0.21^1
	0.14^2
Heat (Rbl/Gcal)	17

Notes:
1. For urban customers
2. For rural customers
Source: Various issues of *Ekonomika i zhizn'* and private communication.

ranged from 1060 rubles per thousand cubic meters in the Saratov region to 1300 rubles in the Perm region (*Ekonomika i zhizn'*, no. 26 [June], 1992).

Despite the large nominal price increases effected in the first half of 1992, wholesale energy prices have not gone up so much in real terms. Because of the high rate of general inflation (industrial wholesale prices rose 14.6 times in the first half of 1992) the real price of crude oil rose only 90 per cent, while that of coal and natural gas went up by 67 per cent and 20 per cent, respectively. The real price of electricity charged to industry decreased by 14 per cent. (When calculating the real price increases, the average selling prices were compared with the state prices in place at the end of 1991.)

The price increases effected until mid-1992 were insufficient to close the gap between the regulated domestic prices and international prices. They were also inadequate to permit coverage of the rapidly escalating production-cost levels. As an example, in February 1992, the cost of crude oil output in the Tyumen' province, was estimated at 750 rubles per ton. The wholesale price at that time stood only at 350 rubles per ton. Owing to the continued rapid rise in input prices, the cost of production was predicted to reach 2800–3200 rubles per ton by the end of 1992 (*Komsomolskaya Pravda*, 5 March 1992), substantially above the permitted wholesale price range.

3.3.2 Commodity-Exchange Prices

A rising proportion of energy output produced in excess of state needs is sold on a spot basis, mainly through the dozen commodity exchanges that have emerged since May 1990. Futures sales are also conducted on some of these exchanges. In 1991 only about 1 per cent of the aggregate output of crude oil and refined products was sold on the spot markets. In 1992 the sales volume was projected to increase sixfold, as shown in Table 3.7.

However the projected volumes (in particular for crude oil) are open to question, given the effect of recent restrictions on the commodity exchanges involving a reduced number of export licenses and, as of 18 May 1992, extension of price controls. As a result, during the summer months of 1992 growth in the volume of open-market transactions in refined products slowed considerably, while in crude oil only a few deals were registered.

Prices on the exchanges have been rising sharply. By mid-1992 they had reached levels 1.4 times (crude oil) to 3.6 times (steam coal) higher

Table 3.7   Volume of energy products traded on the Russian commodity
exchanges (million tons)

	1991	1992 (forecast)
Crude oil	6.2	80.0
Gasoline	0.8	6.5
Diesel fuel	0.3	14.0
Heavy fuel oil	0.5	20.0

Source: *Kommersant*, No. 5, 1992, p. 15.

than the official wholesale prices. Open-market prices in sales with
license to export to other FSU republics tended to be 50 per cent
(gasoline) to 150 per cent (crude oil) higher than prices charged in
transactions without export license. With license to export outside the
FSU, the differences were 90 per cent to 250 per cent respectively
(Table 3.5). The large difference between prices with export licenses
and those without prevailed despite the imposition of high export
tariffs[9] on energy resources and the compulsory exchange of 40 per
cent of the hard currency revenues at an unfavourable rate (55 rubles to
the dollar). On 1 July 1992 the share of compulsory-exchange
submission was raised to 50 per cent and the special exchange rate
was replaced by the going commercial exchange rate, which is more
favourable to exporters.

3.3.3 Contract Prices

Contract or negotiated prices, too, apply to the output that is produced
in excess of state orders and sold outside the commodity exchanges in
arm's-length transactions between producers and buyers. Little is
known about the prices achieved in these transactions; what evidence
is available suggests that they tend to be below, but close to, the
commodity-exchange prices. As an example, during spring 1992 the
average price of crude oil in this sector of the market was estimated at
1500–2000 rubles per ton (*Kommersant*, 20–7 April 1992). Contract
prices and commodity-exchange prices are expected to converge over
time, as higher spot prices create an incentive to channel more output
through the commodity exchanges with a consequent downward
pressure on their prices.

3.3.4 Barter Prices

The highly inflationary climate of the FSU creates fertile ground for the widespread use of barter deals in energy. No reliable information is available on either the volumes or the average level of the implicit price in the barter transactions.

Scattered references in the Russian business literature suggest that implicit energy prices in domestic barter deals are considerably below the commodity-exchange prices and tend to be even lower than the average level of contract prices. Looking ahead, the extent of barter trade in energy products will hinge on progress toward reducing inflation and stabilising the ruble. For 1992 the volume of barter trade in crude oil and refined products can be put in the range of 40–50 million tons (including interrepublican barters within the FSU). Aggregate oil trade at both barter prices and contract prices in 1992 might amount to a total of some 120 million tons.

3.3.5 Interrepublican Trade Prices

In 1992 energy trade among the FSU republics (including the Baltic states) fell rapidly due largely to administrative limits imposed on Russian exports. Sales are regulated on the basis of quarterly quotas which, for the first quarter of 1992, suggest a 40 to 50 per cent fall in Russian exports of crude oil from the 1991 levels (*Kommersant*, 27 January–3 February 1992).

Interrepublican trade prices are essentially negotiated prices among the governments concerned. They are obtained by converting world prices to ruble prices at a negotiated exchange rate. In addition a sizeable amount of the interrepublican energy shipments take place through barter deals. The implicit price of these deals is unknown, but there is a growing tendency to value barter trade at world prices.

In the beginning of 1992 the bulk of Russian crude oil was sold to most of the other republics at the then prevailing state-set wholesale price of 350 rubles per ton plus the 28 per cent VAT and additional transport charges. FSU members paid just 260 rubles per thousand cubic meters for natural gas plus VAT and transport charges. However the rapidly falling value of the ruble, further domestic price increases, and the Russian government's intention to minimise energy-trade subsidisation, led to massive upward adjustments in interrepublican trade prices. Table 3.5 records the level of these prices in June 1992. During the first half of that year the average prices for oil and natural gas shipments to other FSU republics increased about eightfold. Compared with the average domestic selling price in June 1992, the average interrepublican export prices were about 40 per cent higher in crude oil and 50 per cent higher in natural gas. The Baltic states paid one fifth to one half more for Russian fuel exports than did other FSU countries. Interrepublican trade prices are expected to move relatively quickly to the world price level at the commercial exchange rate of the day. In 1992 significant quantities of Russia's primary fuels, purchased advantageously in soft-currency terms, were reexported by several other republics in the form of electricity and refined products at hard-currency world prices. Growing concern about losses stemming from what is considered 'non-equitable trade' will force Russian authorities to close the existing price gap. Certain interrepublican energy shipments are already paid for in hard currency at world prices. This is true, for instance, in the case of Russia's 1992 imports of 11.3 BCM of natural gas from Turkmenia.

3.3.6 Magnitude of Distortions in Current Energy Prices

The magnitude of energy-price distortions is hard to determine because of the lack of a realistic operational exchange rate for the ruble. The so-called commercial exchange rate (115 rubles per dollar as an average for June–July 1992 and reaching about 1000 rubles in the Autumn of 1993) is unrealistic because it severely undervalues the ruble with respect to the tradable sector as a whole. For a possibly better approximation of the 'realistic' exchange rate we have chosen the inflation-adjusted implicit ruble–dollar cross-rate of Hungary, which works out to an average 30 rubles per dollar for the first half of 1992 (see the Introduction to this book). This has been used to calculate the degree of disjunction between domestic and world energy prices in mid-1992. Two sets of domestic prices are considered, namely state-controlled wholesale prices (without the 28 per cent value-added tax) and commodity-exchange prices. Table 3.8 shows the ratios of world prices to domestic wholesale prices in June 1992 for selected fuels. For comparison, ratios based on the commercial exchange rate prevailing in mid-1992 are also given in the table.

When using the commercial exchange rate, the divorce between domestic wholesale prices and world prices works out to be enormous, despite two substantial hikes in energy prices during the first half of 1992; on average the world/Russian energy-price ratio is 7.5. At the existing exchange rate it is simply not realistic to move domestic energy

Table 3.8 Degree of distortion in selected Russian wholesale energy prices, June 1992 (ratios of world prices to domestic prices at alternative exchange rates)

	World price[1] ($/ton)	*World/domestic price ratio*			
		Official wholesale prices at:		*Commodity exchange prices at:*	
		30 rubles per US $[2]	*115 rubles per US $[3]*	*30 rubles per US $[2]*	*115 rubles per US $[3]*
Crude oil	120	1.6–2.0 1.9[4]	6.1–7.7 7.3[4]	1.4	5.3
Heavy (residual) fuel oil	96	1.0	3.8	0.6	2.3
Diesel fuel	167	0.9	3.4	0.7	2.7
Jet fuel	187	0.6	2.3		
Unleaded gasoline, AI-93	230	0.8	3.1	0.8	3.1
Natural gas	88[5]	1.7–2.4 2.2[6]	6.5–9.2 8.4[6]	0.6	2.3
Coking coal	46	1.0	3.8		
Steam coal	37	2.0	7.7	1.1	4.3
Electricity (for industry)	0.064[7]	1.6	6.1		
Total energy[8]		2.0	7.5	1.0	3.7

Notes: For the calculation of world/domestic price ratios, domestic prices exclude the value-added tax.
1. For crude oil: average world price (FOB) weighted by export volume; for refined oil products: average spot prices in Rotterdam; for jet fuel: NWE/ARA cargoes (CIF); for natural gas: average West European border price effective 1 March 1992; for coal: US export price in 1991 (FAS); for electricity: average price for industry in the European OECD countries in 1991.
2. Implicit ruble–dollar cross-rate of Hungary in 1990, adjusted for inflation differentials.
3. Average commercial ('floating market') rate in June–July 1992.
4. Ratio of world price to average selling price of June 1992.
5. Dollars per thousand m^3.
6. Ratio of world price to average selling price of June 1992.
7. Dollars per kWh.
8. Weighted average of the crude-oil, natural-gas and coal price ratios (weights: quantity of consumption in 1991). Domestic prices are average selling prices in June 1992 (first week of June 1992 for natural gas).

prices to those prevailing in market economies in the course of a short period of time, as envisaged under Scenario 1. Even commodity-exchange prices lag considerably behind world prices if the commercial exchange rate is applied.

At the assumed 'realistic' rate of 30 rubles per dollar, world energy prices are on average only two times the aggregate Russian wholesale prices. In the case of coal the difference is probably understated because the quality of Russian coal is lower than that of US export coal, which is used as a benchmark. At this exchange rate official wholesale prices for refined oil products work out to be close to international prices – in fact they even exceed them by a small margin, except for heavy fuel oil. At the 'realistic' exchange rate most of the prices registered on the commodity exchanges in Russia are very close to world levels.

These comparisons reveal a surprisingly small gap between Russian and world energy prices. It should be noted, however, that the assumed rate of 30 rubles per dollar is applicable only to the first half of 1992. Since then the PPP-adjusted rate of the ruble (per dollar) must have risen substantially due to an accelerating divergence of Russian and external inflation trends. Hence it is likely that the domestic–external price gap has widened appreciably relative to the estimate for mid-1992. Clearly an early and complete removal of the existing under-pricing of energy does not appear to be a realistic target until some measure of stability in the PPP-adjusted rate has been achieved.

The relatively small variations between the product-specific price ratios suggest that the domestic price adjustments implemented since 1990 have removed a large part of the massive traditional distortions in the structure of domestic relative prices. Historically the wholesale price ratio between coal, crude oil, natural gas and electricity, on the one hand and petroleum products on the other, was much lower in Russia than in the market economies. Steam coal was especially undervalued. Remaining interfuel price distortions at the official wholesale price level are only a fraction of the ones that prevailed prior to 1990.

Table 3.8 reveals that the remaining inter-fuel price distortions also pertain to the commodity-exchange prices. For example, while heavy fuel oil is much cheaper than crude oil in international markets, the reverse is true on the Russian commodity exchanges. These distortions are not surprising given the relatively small volumes transacted on the exchanges, the volatile nature of spot prices in a highly inflationary environment and the use of some energy products as a hedge against inflation. In the period ahead, with growing volumes traded on these markets and the easing of inflationary pressures, relative spot prices can be expected to move closer to those observed in the world markets.

At the retail level the gap between international and Russian prices in mid-1992 remained massive, even at the 30 rubles per dollar rate (Table 3.9). The reason for this is that Russian households typically pay far less for energy than do industrial users. For example, for natural gas and electricity households pay only about one fifth of the price charged to industrial consumers. In the case of district heat this ratio is as low as 6 per cent. At the 30 rubles per dollar exchange rate the average European retail price of natural gas is 40 times the Russian price (at the commercial exchange rate the difference works out to an extreme 155-fold). However gasoline appears to be a major exception; as a result of several massive retail-price increases during the first half of 1992 retail prices now stand at a higher level than wholesale prices (including taxes) and correspond to about one third of the typical price paid by Western European consumers.

Table 3.9 Degree of distortion in selected retail energy prices in Russia, June 1992 (including taxes) (ratios of market-economy prices to state-set domestic retail prices at alternative exchange rates)

	World price[1] *($/ton)*	*World price/domestic price ratio at:*	
		30 rubles per $	*115 rubles per $*
Leaded gasoline (93 octanes)	1085	3.2	12.3
Light fuel oil	442	36.8	141.0
Natural gas	352[2]	30.0	115.0
Electricity (for urban users)	0.136[3]	19.4	74.3
Electricity (for rural users)	0.136[3]	29.1	111.5
Heat (district)	32[4]	56.5	216.4

Notes:
1. For unleaded gasoline, light fuel oil and electricity: average price in the European OECD countries in 1990; for natural gas: Austrian price (the price for OECD Europe was not available; in previous years the Austrian price was very close to the West European average).
2. Dollars per thousand m^3.
3. Dollars per kWh.
4. Dollars per Gcal (the average West-European price charged to industry is used to approximate the price paid by households).

The interfuel price distortions are also much greater at the retail level than in the case of wholesale supplies. The relative prices of heat and natural gas in retail trade are low in Russia, while gasoline is overpriced vis-à-vis other refined-oil products.

3.3.7 Energy Price Outlook for the Near Future

The Russian political leadership is aware that energy prices have been among the most distorted. The need to move them to world-market levels at a realistic exchange rate and also to correct the remaining distortions in the structure of relative fuel prices is readily admitted. The need to raise energy prices in real terms is important on several grounds. First, even efficient energy producers will not be able to cover their operating costs, let alone the costs of capital replacement and expansion, unless real prices are substantially raised. Second, keeping energy prices at below world-market levels perpetuates wasteful consumption. Experiences of 1991 and the first half of 1992 reveal that consumption of energy declined by much less than GDP and industrial output, primarily because of the small increase in real prices (but also due to the continued lack of cost sensitivity of consumers).[10] Third, the major international financial agencies condition their lending operations on moving domestic energy prices to world parity level in a specified period of time.

The dilemma confronting the Russian government during 1992 concerned the choice between immediate price liberalisation and gradual decontrol. After some hesitation the government abandoned the plan of immediate decontrol, set for 20 April 1992, in favour of a more gradual phase-in of world-price levels. It is believed that, in view of the large degree of underpricing of energy at the commercial exchange rate, an immediate and full price decontrol would have had a devastating impact not only on the already depressed Russian economy but also on most of the other FSU republics.[11]

The new government policy has shifted toward a phased decontrol to be implemented in a series of sizeable real increases in prices. The government plans to partially free oil and coal prices and allow them to reach world levels gradually by the end of 1993. This, in our view, is an apparently overambitious target if the swiftly declining commercial exchange rate of the ruble is to be applied. The plan envisages tighter government control of natural-gas and electricity prices.

On 11 September 1992, under considerable pressure from domestic oil producers and the major international lending agencies, the Russian government announced that the official crude-oil prices would rise 'in the near future' (meaning the following few weeks) to between 4000 and 5000 rubles per ton, a 2.25-times increase relative to the price range (1800–2200 rubles) set in May 1992. Indications are that prices of the politically more sensitive oil products will be increased less than that planned for crude oil.

In the course of 1993 there was a distinct danger that Russia would suffer from hyperinflation. General wholesale-price increases may well reach 2000 per cent or more. Overall inflation is driven to a considerable extent by hikes in energy prices. In these circumstances, even seemingly massive increases in the nominal price of energy may leave the real price level relatively little changed, and in consequence neither energy conservation nor upstream activity would be stimulated.

We conclude that a speedy increase of domestic energy prices to the international level will be hard to accomplish under conditions of very high inflation and a free fall of the exchange rate. Even massive nominal-energy-price increases will not result in much higher real prices under such circumstances. A more overriding issue is whether it is at all desirable to force a convergence of domestic and international prices to occur at an increasingly unrealistic commercial ruble exchange rate that is completely divorced from the currency's purchasing power parity. Even with an assumed rapid success in financial and currency stabilisation in the near future, as posited in Scenario 1, the envisaged energy-price adjustments in real terms will require an extended period of time. In our view it is unlikely that these adjustments could be completed much sooner than the middle of the 1990s, even under the best of circumstances.

3.4 MARKET REFORMS AND FUTURE PATTERNS OF ENERGY CONSUMPTION

3.4.1 Methodology and Main Underlying Assumptions for Consumption Projections

The energy-consumption projections presented in the following pages are based on three alternative reform outcomes, notably Scenario 1, radical market reforms; Scenario 2, gradual market reforms, and Scenario 3, reform impasse. The contents of these scenarios are outlined in some detail in Chapter 1.

Consumption levels are projected in the following pages for the three major fuels (oil, natural gas and coal) for the period 1992–2005. Total consumption is the sum of the three fuels. Hydro-electric and nuclear power are not included in the total.

For the purpose of projection simulations, a straightforward dynamic consumption model has been specified for each fuel. The model is able to explore the effects of changes in the rate of growth of GDP, price changes (including lagged effects) and structural shifts in total output. The price- and non-price-induced changes in the composition of total output are introduced through judgmental adjustments to the historical income (GDP) elasticities. Interfuel substitution enters the model indirectly through the assumed extent of price changes and price elasticities for the individual fuels.

The general form of the model is:

$$C_i = A Y_t^b \prod_{i=1}^{n} P_{t-i+1}^{c_i}(u_t)$$

where C is energy consumption, Y is GDP, P is the real industrial wholesale price of energy, b is energy/GDP elasticity, c_i represents the structure of the lagged price-elasticity coefficients, A is a constant, t denotes year and u is the error term.

The parameters used for the simulations reflect, in broad terms, the assumptions elaborated in the three scenarios.

3.4.1.1 Growth Paths of GDP

The assumed growth profiles of GDP appear in Figure 1.1 in Chapter 1. Under each scenario GDP continues to contract in the near future, but the extent and duration of the decline varies across scenarios. Scenario 1 assumes rapid and consistent moves toward simultaneous financial stabilisation and structural reforms. Initially this causes a sharp drop in total output. The economy begins to turn around in 1994 and a vigorous recovery gets under way in the subsequent years. Because of less austere fiscal and monetary policies, in Scenario 2 retrenchment of economic activity is less than in the first scenario, turnaround is delayed and economic recovery is less rapid. The deepest slump occurs under Scenario 3 as a result of the serious disruptions that ensue from the failure to implement the market-oriented reforms. Given these disparate growth trajectories, in the year 2000 total output under the gradual scenario works out to be 14 per cent less than under the radical scenario, while the output level under the scenario of reform impasse works out to be 45 per cent less. In 2005 the respective GDP shortfalls are 18 per cent and 50 per cent.

3.4.1.2 Income Elasticity of Energy Consumption

Historical GDP elasticities were derived from regressions run for the period 1976–1990. These are vastly different for the three fuels: 2.60 for natural gas, 0.33 for oil and −0.30 for coal. For simulation purposes the historical elasticities are used in the case of oil and coal. The income coefficient for natural gas was adjusted downward on the assumption that the extremely high historical elasticity is not sustainable over the simulation period, but more importantly because gas, the dominant incremental source of energy, is assumed to absorb much of the effects of non-price-driven structural changes in total output and of the technological improvements in energy use. The downward adjustment in the income elasticity of gas varies across the scenarios to accommodate the different speeds of capital-stock turnover and the resulting energy-efficiency improvements. Thus, owing to the assumed higher rate of turnover of capital stock in Scenario 1, the downward adjustment is more pronounced in this case, at least for the second half of the 1990s. For similar reasons the extent of downward adjustment varies also among the two other scenarios.

Furthermore our investigation reveals that, except for oil, the income-elasticity relationships behave drastically differently in periods of stagnant and falling GDP than under normal economic growth. For example, the sharp drop in GDP between 1989 and 1991 did not produce nearly as much decline in fuel consumption as would be commensurate with the income-elasticity relationships observable during normal growth periods. Therefore, for the coming years of GDP declines, the observed 'crisis-period elasticities' were used (1.0 for coal and 0.1 for gas).

3.4.1.3 Extent of Energy-Price Adjustments

Under all scenarios energy prices are assumed to increase relative to the end-of-1991 levels, but the time profile and magnitude of the increases vary across scenarios and fuels, in line with the broad assumptions contained in Chapter 1. Scenario 1 embodies rapid liberalisation of prices; more specifically energy prices are supposed to reach world parity in three years, that is by the end of 1994; under Scenario 2 convergence is more gradual and is expected to be completed by the year 2000; and under Scenario 3 internal prices reach world levels only in 2005.

Thus, given the initial discrepancy between the January 1992 official wholesale prices in Russia and the average world prices at the 30 rubles per dollar exchange rate, the assumed annual average *real* price increases that are needed to reach projected world-market prices[12] in the given benchmark year, and to track international prices in subsequent years, are indicated below. The negative numbers in 2001–5 in Scenarios 1 and 2 are due to the World-Bank forecasts of declining world-oil prices for that period.

	Scenario 1		
	1 Jan 1992–4 *(per cent)*	*1995–2000* *(per cent)*	*2001–5* *(per cent)*
Oil	128	4.2	−0.9
Natural gas	137	4.2	−0.9
Coal	79	1.8	0.0
Overall	123	3.7	−0.7

	Scenario 2		**Scenario 3**
	1 Jan 1992–2000 *(per cent)*	*2001–5* *(per cent)*	*1 Jan 1992–2005* *(per cent)*
Oil	31	−0.9	19.0
Natural gas	33	−0.9	20.0
Coal	22	0.0	14.0
Overall	26	−0.7	18.0

3.4.1.4 Price Sensitivity of Energy Demand

In the market-oriented scenarios energy prices are assumed to play a key role in encouraging energy savings. Past price elasticities of energy consumption in the FSU are zero across the board and a poor guide of future demand-sensitivity to price change. With the substantial reservoir of untapped energy efficiency, the large real-price increases under Scenarios 1 and 2 may result in a sizeable demand-reducing effect. The latter will hinge upon the success of structural reforms, comprising privatisation, the imposition of financial discipline and cost-minimization pressure on energy users.

It is fair to assume that even with a consistent implementation of radical reforms, the economy of the FSU will continue to carry some anti-market legacies of the command economy, for example a concentrated industrial structure with extensive monopoly powers, an underdeveloped financial system and a weak entrepreneurial class. Therefore we believe that, within the projection period, the radical reforms will produce a semi-marketised economy at best. Probably the best proxy for such a semi-market economy is Hungary, where the short-term price elasticities are one half and the long-term elasticities are about two thirds of the typical elasticities observed in developed market economies.[13] To reflect the above assumption, Scenario 1 puts the initial FSU price sensitivity at half of that of Hungary and allows it to rise to the Hungarian levels in five years. In Scenario 2, which reflects a more gradual tightening of enterprise budget constraints, this process is assumed to be completed only by the year 2000. In Scenario 3 the assumed initial price sensitivity is set at only one fifth of that of Hungary and the period needed to fully match Hungary's price responsiveness extends to 2005.

3.4.1.5 *Structural Changes in Total Output*

Clearly, shifts in the mix of total output may exert a potentially considerable impact on future trends in energy consumption and the overall energy intensity of the FSU. But it is very difficult to foresee the direction, scope and speed of structural change resulting from the new market conditions, including market-clearing prices in energy and other factor inputs. Therefore the analysis is limited to a rough judgement of the net impact on energy demand resulting from the divergent sectoral pressures.

One view on the expected scope of sectoral restructuring is that because industry was largely built for non-economic purposes, much of the industrial output will not be needed by the new market economy. It is pointed out that the capital stock built during decades of non-market planning is grossly out of sync with the structure of capital that the market economy would call for.[14] Those holding this view consequently predict massive structural transformation, if market reforms get under way. More specifically, they anticipate a big shakeout of traditional heavy industries, many of which are energy intensive.

Some caution is needed with regard to expectations of a massive structural shakeout for several reasons. First, the highly-energy-intensive industries are the backbone of the FSU economy, with a large impact on employment. Simply for social reasons, a large-scale phase-out of these activities does not appear likely during much of the period under review, even if market forces render these activities inefficient. Second, foreign-exchange constraints are likely to remain a critical feature during a significant part of the transition period and will limit the scope for a large-scale substitution of imports for inefficient domestic activities.

Third, and most importantly, recent investigations that simulate the sectoral structure of the economy of the FSU at world-market prices suggest that while a great deal of structural misallocation of productive resources does exist, the FSU appears to be competitive in a range of energy-intensive industrial sectors, for example ferrous and non-ferrous metallurgy, heavy engineering and oil and gas production.[15] Given existing input–output relationships, although a number of industrial sectors would generate low or even negative value added at world prices (meaning that the costs of material and energy inputs absorbed by these sectors exceed the value of the goods that they produce), the most energy-intensive sectors would remain very profitable. The quoted evidence suggest that, even with existing inefficiencies in energy usage, the FSU as a whole, and the resource-rich republics – Russia, Ukraine, Kazakhstan and Turkmenia – in particular, appear to possess strong comparative advantage in a wide range of energy-intensive goods. The energy-intensive activities do not appear to be losers if world prices are taken to indicate the long-term direction of efficient industrial restructuring. The favourable competitiveness ranking (at world prices) of these industries may further improve, if one adds the energy-efficiency improvements to be brought about by successful privatisation and the creation of a competitive environment.

These findings are of major significance and argue against the view that predicts a strong contraction of energy-intensive branches. But since they are aggregative, they may hide the potential for important intrabranch restructuring in response to market reform. For example, metallurgy as a whole shows up as competitive when exposed to world prices even with current input proportions. At the same time it is clear that metallurgical firms specialising in armaments will face a substantial reduction in demand in connection with the anticipated retrenchment in the military sector. On the other hand metal-intensive goods such as automobiles and consumer durables with income-elastic, pent-up demand are projected to experience a marked upward trend. For some metal products, for example steel, the weakness in domestic demand could be offset, at least in part, by a possible upsurge in exports, similar to what has occurred on a large scale in non-ferrous metals (aluminum and nickel particularly).[16]

The expected direction and intensity of the demand effect resulting from structural change has been introduced in the following demand projections by means of judgmental adjustments of the historical income elasticity.

3.4.2 Projected Trends in Energy Consumption under Alternative Scenarios

Table 3.10 and Figure 3.7 show the broad consumption trends for oil, natural gas and coal in the FSU under the three alternative scenarios. Projected consumption figures are also provided for the major individual republics and republican groups by adopting the assumptions specified for the FSU as a whole, an admittedly crude procedure (Tables 3.10–3.14). At this point the lack of relevant information has prevented us from detailing separate sets of assumptions that reflect republican specificities such as domestic resource endowments (for example, in an attempt to suppress domestic demand, net importers may move more quickly towards world prices) or the levels of economic development (energy intensity falling faster in the most developed republics, where downsizing of industry and shifts toward the service sector will dominate structural change). It is our view, however, that many of the assumptions specified under the three scenarios for the FSU are broadly applicable to each republic embarking on market-oriented economic reforms.

The following discussion relates to the FSU as a whole.

3.4.2.1 Oil

As a result of the combined impact of macroeconomic depression and real price increases, oil consumption is shown to fall throughout much of the 1990s under all scenarios. Because of the severe slump in GDP and the intense price shock, the drop in consumption is projected to be particularly sharp in Scenario 1. The 1995 level of consumption is about 25 per cent lower than the prereform reference level (1989). Consumption bottoms out in 1998–9 when the rapidly unfolding economic recovery offsets the delayed demand-reducing effects of the price shock. In the following period oil consumption picks up at a relatively moderate pace, with changes in aggregate economic activity as the primary driving force. By 2000 and 2005 consumption levels are down by 34 per cent and 30 per cent, respectively, compared with the reference level.

Figure 3.7   The FSU: projected energy use in Scenarios 1–3 (MTOE)

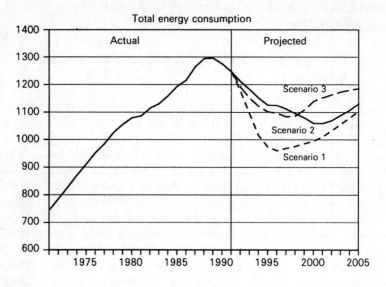

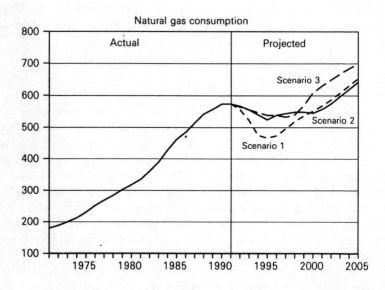

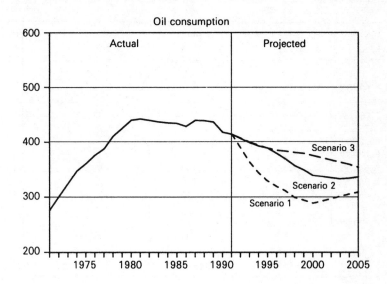

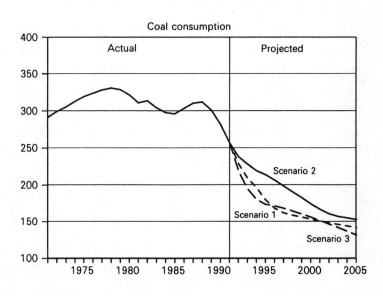

Table 3.10   Fuel consumption in the FSU, 1989–2005 (MTOE)

Year	Total	Oil	Gas	Coal
1989	1298	442	555	301
1990	1271	414	572	285
1991	1242	413	572	257
Scenario 1:				
1995	975	330	465	180
2000	990	290	550	150
2005	1100	310	650	140
Scenario 2:				
1995	1125	390	520	215
2000	1055	340	540	175
2005	1125	330	640	155
Scenario 3:				
1995	1105	390	540	175
2000	1145	380	610	155
2005	1180	350	700	130

Table 3.11   Fuel consumption in Russia, 1989–2005 (MTOE)

Year	Total	Oil	Gas	Coal
1989	802	277	355	170
1990	796	268	366	162
1991	786	268	370	148
Scenario 1:				
1995	617	213	300	104
2000	631	187	355	89
2005	703	200	421	82
Scenario 2:				
1995	712	252	337	123
2000	671	219	351	101
2005	718	217	413	88
Scenario 3:				
1995	699	252	347	100
2000	725	243	392	90
2005	756	229	451	76

Table 3.12   Fuel consumption in Ukraine, 1989–2005 (MTOE)

Year	Total	Oil	Gas	Coal
1989	224	59	89	76
1990	219	57	91	71
1991	202	54	89	59
Scenario 1:				
1995	156	43	72	41
2000	158	38	85	35
2005	173	40	101	32
Scenario 2:				
1995	181	51	81	49
2000	168	44	84	40
2005	178	44	99	35
Scenario 3:				
1995	174	51	83	40
2000	179	49	94	36
2005	184	46	108	30

Table 3.13   Fuel consumption in Kazakhstan, 1989–2005 (MTOE)

Year	Total	Oil	Gas	Coal
1989	71	19	10	42
1990	69	19	10	40
1991	67	19	11	37
Scenario 1:				
1995	50	15	9	26
2000	46	13	11	22
2005	47	14	12	21
Scenario 2:				
1995	59	17	10	32
2000	51	15	10	26
2005	49	15	12	22
Scenario 3:				
1995	53	17	10	26
2000	51	17	11	23
2005	48	16	13	19

Table 3.14   Fuel consumption in Central Asia,* 1989–2005 (MTOE)

Year	Total	Oil	Gas	Coal
1989	71	20	45	6
1990	66	14	46	6
1991	63	13	45	5
Scenario 1:				
1995	50	10	37	3
2000	55	9	43	3
2005	64	10	51	3
Scenario 2:				
1995	57	12	41	4
2000	57	10	43	4
2005	64	10	51	3
Scenario 3:				
1995	58	12	43	3
2000	63	12	48	3
2005	69	11	55	3

* Kyrgryzstan, Tadjikistan, Turkmenia and Uzbekistan

Table 3.15   Fuel consumption in Transcaucasia,* 1989–2005 (MTOE)

Year	Total	Oil	Gas	Coal
1989	42	18	23	1
1990	41	17	23	1
1991	39	17	21	1
Scenario 1:				
1995	31	13	17	1
2000	33	11	21	1
2005	37	12	24	1
Scenario 2:				
1995	36	16	19	1
2000	35	14	20	1
2005	38	13	24	1
Scenario 3:				
1995	36	15	20	1
2000	38	15	22	1
2005	41	14	26	1

* Armenia, Azerbayjan and Georgia

As a result of the less severe economic depression, a more gradual catching up with world prices and weaker price sensitivity, the initial consumption drop is less pronounced in Scenario 2, but the period of decline is more protracted. Consumption bottoms out only by the end of the projection period when GDP growth effects balance out the relatively moderate price effect. Under this scenario consumption is below the reference level by 12 per cent in 1995, 23 per cent in 2000 and 25 per cent in 2005.

Scenario 3 displays elevated levels in oil consumption throughout the period under investigation. This is caused by the slow price adjustment, and reflects the poor record of price-induced improvements in the efficiency of oil utilisation. In contrast with the other scenarios, in Scenario 3 the oil-intensity of GDP keeps rising throughout the 1990s.

3.4.2.2 Natural Gas

As expected, the sharpest temporary drop in consumption occurs in Scenario 1. The macroeconomic slump and the heavy price shock work in tandem to cause a 14 per cent reduction in consumption between 1989 and 1995. Soon, however, the price impact is overridden by the vigorous economic growth assumed in this scenario. The high GDP elasticity of gas usage, even with downward adjustments to accommodate sectoral shifts in total output, sets the stage for a fairly rapid buildup in consumption. By 2000 gas use approximates the 1989 level and exceeds it by a growing margin in the subsequent years. In 2005 consumption is about 17 per cent higher than the level registered in 1989.

In Scenario 2, the less severe early economic depression and the more moderate price impact cause only a small contraction in consumption. In 1995 natural-gas use is only 6 per cent below the reference level. However, owing to the less dynamic post-depression pickup in GDP, weaker price sensitivity and slower structural change, the buildup in gas consumption is less dramatic than in the previous case. In 2000 and 2005 consumption is very close to the levels obtained under Scenario 1, but at a considerably smaller GDP.

The least significant trend reversals are shown under Scenario 3. Here, in the absence of marked price-induced efficiency improvements and pronounced structural changes, the only substantial consumption-moderating force is the decline in economic activity. While consumption in 1995 is 3 per cent lower than that in the reference year, the 2000 and 2005 levels work out to 10 per cent and 26 per cent larger, respectively. The fact that this scenario combines the lowest level of GDP with the highest level of consumption points to the deteriorating efficiency of gas utilisation.

To illustrate the magnitude of the demand-dampening effect of the assumed price increases, Figure 3.8 isolates the price impact from other demand-shaping forces for natural gas under Scenarios 1 and 2. As expected, owing to the much greater initial price shock and the presumed stronger price responsiveness in Scenario 1, the magnitude of the price impact works out to be markedly larger in this case. Other things being equal, without the price effect the level of natural-gas consumption would be 29 per cent higher in 1995 and about one third higher in 2000 and 2005. In Scenario 2 the corresponding numbers are lower: 22 per cent in 1995 and approximately one fourth in 2000 and 2005. Clearly, with the set of assumptions underlying the two scenarios, energy-price increases drive the temporary downward shift in consumption, and they explain the relatively low growth in consumption during the projection period as a whole.

3.4.2.3 Coal

The required price adjustments are smaller for coal than for the other fuels. For this reason the consumption trends show a more uniform pattern across the scenarios through the projection period. In all three scenarios there is a considerable fall in coal usage. The steepest consumption drops are shown in Scenarios 1 and 3. In 1995 and 2005 they are about 40 per cent and 55 per cent below the 1989 level in both cases. The crisis period of the first half of the 1990s prompts the smallest contraction in consumption under Scenario 2 (28 per cent in 1995).

3.4.2.4 Total Energy Use

The 'bottom-up' approach, adding individual fuel-consumption levels, was used to derive the aggregate consumption trends. As a cross-check, separate projection exercises were performed for total energy. The projected values obtained from the two approaches follow each other closely, lending credence to the bottom-up approach.

Significant reversals in long-term total-energy-consumption trends can be expected under all scenarios, although the sharpness and timing of the reversal varies. The quickest and deepest fall occurs in Scenario 1. This scenario therefore stands out as the most effective mechanism for tapping the large reservoir of energy efficiency accumulated in the FSU

Figure 3.8 FSU natural gas consumption: magnitude of price effect under Scenarios 1–2 (MTOE)

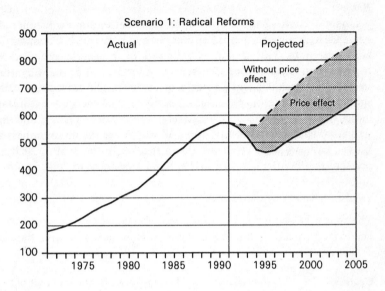

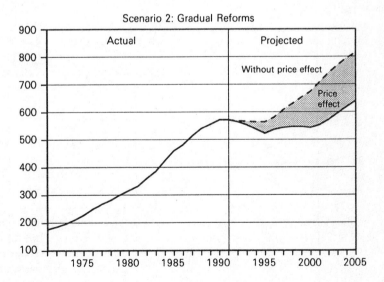

over decades. The fall in total consumption from 1989 is 25 per cent by 1995, 24 per cent in 2000 and 15 per cent in 2005. Consumption bottoms out in 1996–7, followed by a 1.6 per cent annual increase until 2005.

Under Scenario 2 the drop in aggregate consumption is smaller and stretches over a longer period of time than in Scenario 1. Consumption hits bottom in 2001–2 and is followed by moderate growth. The consumption decline from 1989 reaches a total of 13 per cent by 1995, 19 per cent in 2000, and 13 per cent in 2005. The least-pronounced shifts in the long-term consumption paths of total energy are displayed under reform impasse. A relatively weak price impact and few structural shifts in the composition of output are the main underlying causes. Consumption levels are down relative to the 1989 level by 15 per cent in 1995, 10 per cent in 2000 and 9 per cent in 2005.

3.4.2.5 Changes in the Fuel Mix

The shares of major fuels in total fossil-fuel consumption were able to be derived directly from the consumption projections, and they are

Figure 3.9 The FSU: fuel shares in total energy consumption (per cent of total fossil fuel use)

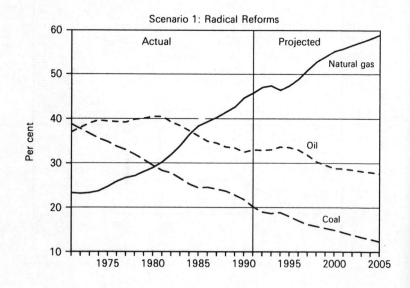

Figure 3.9 continued

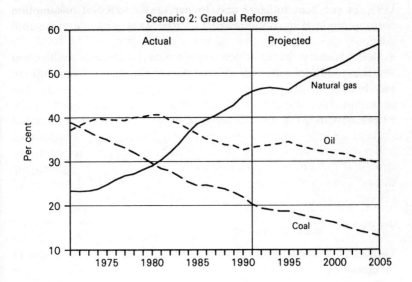

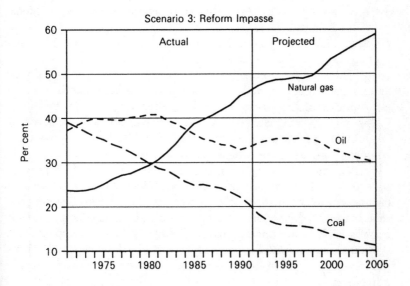

shown in Figure 3.9. No major differences can be discerned across the scenarios; in all cases the pattern observed in the past two decades (the 1980s in the case of oil) appears to be sustained. Thus natural gas is predicted to increase further its already high share of the total fuel market whilst the gas-for-oil and gas-for-coal substitution continues in a parallel fashion, although at a somewhat slower pace than experienced in the 1980s.

3.4.2.6 Aggregate Energy-Efficiency Trends

These trends were derived from the projection results and the assumptions about the future paths of GDP. Figure 3.10 reveals the contrasting patterns in the alternative Scenarios. Unit energy requirements continue to rise at a rapid rate under Scenario 3 until the mid-1990s, and even with the subsequent reversal they stay at levels exceeding those of the late 1980s. Relatively small and protracted price adjustments, attenuated cost sensitivity and moderate structural changes are the key factors underlying this poor performance in energy efficiency.

A very different picture emerges in the other two scenarios. In both cases a decoupling of energy use and economic growth seems possible. Energy-intensity trends display a sharp departure from those of the past. In Scenario 1, large energy savings are quickly generated. Between 1990 and 2005, energy intensity shows an annual 2.6 per cent decrease, the same as experienced in Japan between 1973 and 1990. Given the large scope for energy savings, the plausibility of such an outcome cannot be seriously challenged. However, even with the 2.6 per cent rate of improvement in energy efficiency, in 2005 the energy intensity of the FSU economy would be only at the level achieved by the OECD countries in the late 1970s, some 20 per cent above these countries' current energy intensity.

In Scenario 2, unit energy requirements fall at an annual 1.9 per cent between 1990 and 2005, which is somewhat higher than the 1.7 per cent decline registered for the OECD between 1973 and 1990. This suggests that a marked reversal in the long-standing energy-efficiency paths is possible even with phased, partial market reforms, provided that systematic steps are taken toward market-based pricing and micro-incentives are put in place for energy consumers to act as cost minimisers.

Figure 3.10   The FSU: energy-efficiency paths under Scenarios 1–3

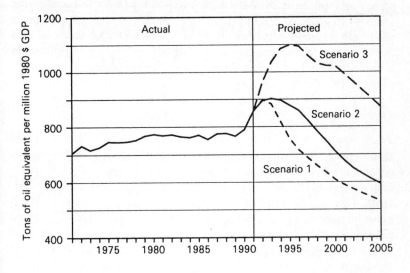

4   FSU Energy Exports, International Markets and Eastern Europe

4.1   INTRODUCTION

This chapter looks at the international-market implications of alternative resolutions of the energy-sector crisis in the FSU. The following subjects are dealt with. Section 4.1 sets the scene by reviewing the significance of the FSU as an exporter of energy in 1989, the last 'normal' year under the old regime. It also provides a brief historical perspective of the FSU's energy-export performance. In Section 4.2 we pull together the results of the production and consumption analyses contained in Chapters 2 and 3 and project the FSU's export performance under our alternative scenarios. Section 4.3 juxtaposes these export projections against an extension of historical export trends and discusses the price impact on the international market of the anticipated alternative export outcomes. In Section 4.4 we focus on Eastern Europe, a region that is very heavily dependent on energy imports from the FSU, and explore the problems that this region would encounter in the event of failing FSU supplies.

4.2   SIGNIFICANCE OF THE FSU AS ENERGY EXPORTER PRIOR TO THE REFORMS

In the late 1980s the FSU was by far the world's largest exporter of energy. Table 4.1 depicts the country's importance in the international energy markets in 1989. Net FSU fossil-fuel exports in that year corresponded to 3.8 per cent of world total primary energy supply (TPES), and 11.2 per cent of global exported supply. The share of FSU exports amounted to 4.7 per cent of world TPES, if the country's own consumption is excluded.

The dominance of the FSU was greatest in the international natural-gas market. FSU gas accounted for more than 30 per cent of all international trade, but only 4.8 per cent of consumption, given that

Table 4.1   Significance of net FSU exports in world fuel markets in 1989 (MTOE)

	Coal	Oil	Gas	Total
World TPES	2231	3098	1707	7036
World exports	255	1900	260	2415
FSU exports	19	170	81	270
FSU exports, % share in:				
World TPES	0.9	5.5	4.8	3.8
World exports	7.5	9.0	31.2	11.2

Sources: BP (1990); IEA (1990); OPEC (1991).

this is a commodity with very limited trade. FSU exports of oil, though accounting for no more than 9 per cent of world trade, nevertheless corresponded to 5.5 per cent of world consumption. The oil exports alone approached the volume lost through the embargo of Iraq and Kuwait in 1990–1 (about 200 million tons on an annual basis).

Table 4.2 compares the volume of gross fuel exports from the FSU in 1989 with that generated by other major energy exporters. The volume of FSU sales, expressed in oil equivalents, was 39 per cent above that of Saudi Arabia, the second most important exporting nation at the time. The FSU and Canada were the only truly diversified exporters, supplying large amounts of all three fuels. But then Canada's total exports were only one third as large.

Table 4.2   Exports (gross) of fuels from leading supplying countries in 1989 (MTOE)

	Coal	Oil	Gas	Total
FSU	24	200	81	305
Saudi Arabia		220		220
Iraq		120	3	123
Canada	22	50	34	106
Iran		103		103
UAE		90	3	93
Norway		66	26	92
Venezuela		80		80
Australia	69	8	1	78
Kuwait		77		77
UK	1	68		69

Sources: BP (1990); IEA (1990); OPEC (1991).

Exports of energy from the FSU have always had a strong geographical concentration. In 1989 almost 85 per cent of the total was sold in Europe, with the East and West taking roughly equal shares. Table 4.3 reveals that in 1989 almost 12 per cent of Western Europe's TPES of the three fuels was satisfied by supplies from FSU, and that the corresponding import dependence was 20 per cent. In the case of gas the figures were substantially higher.

Table 4.3   The significance of imports from the FSU in the West European fossil-fuel markets in 1989 (MTOE)

	Coal	*Oil*	*Gas*	*Total*
WE TPES	258	592	208	1058
WE total imports[1]	86	461	65	612
WE imports from FSU	5	78	40	123
Imports from FSU, % share in:				
WE TPES	1.9	13.3	19.2	11.6
WE total imports[1]	5.8	16.9	61.5	20.1

Note:
1.   Excluding intra-area trade.
Sources: BP (1990); PlanEcon (1990); IEA (1990).

Eastern Europe consumes only one third as much energy as Western Europe. Hence its dependence on imports from the FSU is far greater, both in total and for each fuel individually. This warrants a special detailed investigation (Section 4.4).

To provide a further perspective on FSU energy exports, Table 4.4 documents the development of the country's foreign sales of each fuel since 1980. The figures reveal a small and relatively steady volume of coal exports through the 12–year period, except for a three-year dip in the early 1980s. They show very impressive growth in the export of gas, which roughly doubled in volume over the period under study. They also depict a slow and unstable growth in oil, the dominant export product, between 1980 and 1989, followed by a dramatic decline in the ensuing two years. When measured in terms of export performance, the energy crisis of the FSU over the recent years is an exclusively oil phenomenon. Net exports of coal declined only moderately in 1990 and 1991, those of gas recorded historical highs in the 1989–91 period.

Table 4.4   FSU net exports of fossil fuels (MTOE)

	Coal	*Oil*	*Gas*	*Total*
1980	14	156	43	213
1981	13	156	46	215
1982	10	163	47	220
1983	9	173	47	229
1984	10	170	53	233
1985	13	153	54	220
1986	16	170	63	249
1987	17	180	67	264
1988	18	184	69	271
1989	19	170	81	270
1990	18	147	86	251
1991	15	100	81	196

Sources: PlanEcon (1990); PlanEcon (1992).

4.3   PROJECTIONS OF ENERGY EXPORTS FROM THE FSU

The analyses of production prospects until 2005 contained in Chapter 2 yielded feasible ranges of future output for coal, oil and gas in Scenarios 1–3. Judgment and qualified guesses were used to reduce these ranges into single figures for each scenario at different points in time. In determining the plausible production levels for gas, we also took account of existing limitations in the capacity to transport this fuel to foreign borders, and the ability of foreign markets to absorb FSU gas. Our consumption projections were derived from the model exercises, conducted in Chapter 3, of what may happen to energy usage in the FSU under the alternative scenarios. The present section pulls together these production and consumption projections for each fuel separately. Potential export capability is simply the difference between production and consumption. The export series obtained in this way, constitute the main input into the following analyses of what may happen in the international energy markets as a consequence of shifting FSU export supply. Table 4.5 summarises the projected statistics, along with historical figures for 1989–91. Figure 4.1 provides a graphical representation for oil and gas, which together account for an overwhelming share of total production, consumption and exports. A few caveats should be borne in mind when the table and figure are scrutinised.

Table 4.5 FSU energy: projections of production, consumption and exports under alternative scenarios (MTOE)

	Total fossil fuels			Oil			Gas			Coal		
	Prod.	Cons.	Exp.	Prod.	Cons.	Exp.	Prod.	Cons.	Exp.	Prod.	Cons.	Exp.
1989	1567	1298	269	610	442	168	644	555	89	313	301	12
1990	1527	1271	256	570	414	156	660	572	88	297	285	12
1991	1435	1242	193	515	413	102	658	572	86	262	257	5
Scenario 1: shock therapy												
1995	1170	975	195	390	330	60	580	465	115	200	180	20
2000	1375	990	385	460	290	170	710	550	160	205	150	55
2005	1550	1100	450	550	310	240	800	650	150	200	140	60
Scenario 2: gradual reforms												
1995	1235	1125	110	390	390	0	620	520	100	225	215	10
2000	1330	1055	275	450	340	110	660	540	120	220	175	45
2005	1485	1125	360	520	330	190	760	640	120	205	155	50
Scenario 3: reform impasse												
1995	1220	1105	95	380	390	-10	615	540	75	205	175	30
2000	1290	1145	145	430	380	50	670	610	60	190	155	35
2005	1385	1180	205	500	350	150	705	700	5	180	130	50
Scenario 4: reform impasse and war												
1993	–	–	20	–	–	0	–	–	20	–	–	5
1995	–	–	50	–	–	0	–	–	40	–	–	10
200	–	–	105	–	–	20	–	–	60	–	–	25
2005	–	–	175	–	–	120	–	–	5	–	–	50

Figure 4.1   FSU oil and gas: projections of production, consumption and exports under alternative scenarios (MTOE)

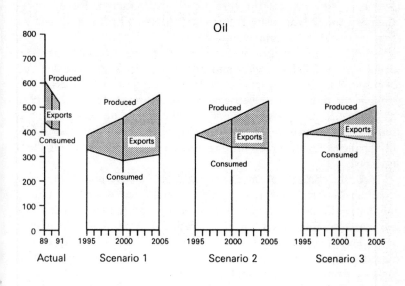

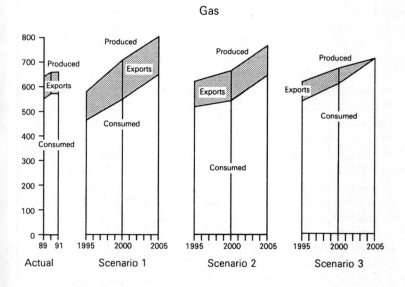

First, our picture of the FSU energy sector is incomplete in that it does not include hydro-electric and nuclear power, nor exported electricity. Nevertheless the three fossil fuels account for an overwhelming proportion of total energy produced and consumed, and an even greater share of total energy exports.

Second, all our export figures are simply the difference between production and consumption and no account is taken of losses and inventory change. This, and the difference between the sources used, explains the discrepancies between the export figures for 1989 to 1991 in Table 4.5, and those contained in the preceding section. For a longer-term perspective like that considered in the present study, such discrepancies would be of little consequence and we have left them unresolved.

Third, the analyses of the preceding chapters have not devoted any attention to Scenario 4: reform impasse and internal war. A military conflict could have a variety of dimensions, and the incertitudes of a war scenario reduce the value of any penetrating analysis of its impact on the energy sector. For this scenario, therefore, we show only a set of plausible export figures as a reminder of the shocks that could ensue if such a scenario were to unfold.

Several broad findings, most of which were touched upon in the production and consumption chapters, emerge from the figures.

We are pessimistic about the developments of oil production. The socialist authorities of the FSU have long practiced a marked *raubwirtschaft* in relation to the country's oil resources. With sharply falling investments in recent years, the *raubwirtschaft* has worsened. Even under the most favourable circumstances the damage will take a long time to repair. Our analysis also suggests that new production will be developed under less favourable geological and economic conditions than has been the case in past decades.

Falling oil output will sharply suppress exports early in the projection period. We project zero exports by the mid-1990s in Scenarios 2 and 3. Over the longer term we are much more optimistic about the export performance, especially in Scenarios 1 and 2. Though oil production will remain below the peaks of the late 1980s in all scenarios throughout the period under consideration, we see exports recovering to the earlier peak levels and rising above them, from the turn of the century in Scenario 1 and by 2005 in Scenario 2, primarily as a consequence of substantially reduced consumption levels.

We see much less of a physical–technological constraint on gas output, and expect production volumes by the turn of the century to be higher than in Scenarios 1 to 3. Consumption of gas will rise impressively as the FSU economy recovers after the mid-1990s. Nevertheless we foresee a steady and substantial expansion of exports in Scenarios 1 and 2 over the levels of 1989. In these scenarios the transport capacity, and the capability of foreign markets to absorb FSU gas, and not the ability to produce it may in fact constitute the binding constraint on output.

Foreign support to liquidate the emergent 'gas bubble' (defined as unused production potential) arising from successful economic and political reforms would strengthen the FSU's foreign-currency earnings, and thus reduce the need for non-commercial assistance from the West. Such support could involve the financing and construction of additional export pipelines to remove any emerging transport bottlenecks, and – even more importantly – a complete opening-up of the West-European gas market to increasing FSU supplies.

Production of coal will decline in all scenarios as a market-oriented economy is established. Just like Germany, the UK and Poland, the FSU has long maintained a significant segment of coal production that will not be able to survive once the umbrella of public protection is withdrawn. Consumption of coal is predicted to decline even more, and exports in all scenarios by the turn of the century and beyond work out at higher figures than currently. However these exports constitute a minor proportion of total FSU energy exports, especially in value terms, given that coal is the cheapest of the three fuels per unit of energy. Furthermore the anticipated coal exports will continue to represent a small fraction of global trade in this fuel.

The quantitative forecasts contained in Table 4.5, along with current and forecast international prices of energy (World Bank, 1991a; see also the discussion in Section 4.3.2 below), permit us to estimate anticipated FSU export revenues from fossil fuels under the alternative scenarios, assuming that all such exports will be paid for in convertible currency at the going international price. The projected export proceeds are summarised in Table 4.6.

To gauge whether our revenue projections are high or low, we provide the hypothetical export-revenue numbers for 1989 for comparison, on the assumption that all exports in that year too had been paid for in dollars at the international prices of the day. In fact more than 40 per cent of these exports were sold to socialist countries for rubles at special low prices. In 1990 global convertible currency revenues from exported FSU goods and services amounted to $34 billion, with oil and gas accounting for 52 per cent of the total (IMF, 1992b).

Table 4.6   The FSU: projected export revenue from fossil fuel sales under
alternative scenarios (billion 1990 $)

	Oil	*Gas*	*Coal*	*Total*
1989	21.2	8.2	0.8	30.4
Scenario 1:				
1995	7.5	10.8	1.2	19.5
2000	26.9	19.0	3.6	49.5
2005	36.0	17.0	4.0	57.0
Scenario 2:				
1995	0	9.4	0.6	10.0
2000	17.4	14.3	3.0	44.7
2005	28.5	13.6	3.3	45.4
Scenario 3:				
1995	−1.3	7.1	1.8	7.6
2000	7.9	7.1	2.3	17.3
2005	22.5	0.6	3.3	26.4

Note: The following international prices (1990 $/TOE) were used to obtain
the above revenues (World Bank, 1991a):

	Oil	*Gas*	*Coal*
1989	126	94	65
1995	125	94	59
2000	158	119	66
2005	150	113	66

Table 4.6 provides interesting insights into plausible developments,
both over time and across fuels and scenarios.

Our projections indicate a large revenue dip in the mid-1990s,
followed by impressive improvements at the end of the century and
beyond. The potential for increased export earnings is substantial. By
2005 anticipated energy-export earnings will be approaching the
exaggerated hypothetical 1989 revenue level reported in Table 4.6,
even in the pessimistic Scenario 3.

In line with the quantitative conclusions, our export-revenue
projections indicate that oil will suffer the most severe, though
temporary, decline. In 1995 even the optimistic Scenario 1 projects
oil revenues only one third of the hypothetical level in 1989, while in
Scenarios 2 and 3 oil sales fall to zero. A noteworthy observation

pertains to gas in 2005. In Scenario 1 in that year, gas revenues are twice as large as the hypothetical level in 1989, but the high domestic consumption levels foreseen for Scenario 3 reduce gas exports to insignificance. Coal revenues expand over time in all scenarios, but remain quite small in absolute terms.

A vast difference in aggregate export earnings emerges across the three scenarios. Revenues in Scenario 3 will be less than half of the earnings envisaged in Scenario 1 throughout the time horizon of our study. The inferior outcome of Scenario 3 becomes more accentuated over time. In the mid-1990s an annual export-revenue loss of $10 billion is incurred in this scenario compared with Scenario 1. By the end of the century and beyond this loss expands to $30 billion.

This difference across scenarios points to the dramatic importance of reforms to improve export performance. But given the great significance of energy production and trade in the macroeconomy of the FSU, the causal relationship operates in the opposite direction too. A healthy energy sector with a strong export performance is a crucial precondition for the maintenance of successful economic and political reforms.

The main purpose of this chapter is to discuss the implications for the rest of the world of changing exports from the FSU as a whole. However, the analysis of earlier chapters makes it possible to throw some interesting light on exports by individual FSU republics.

Virtually all exportable surpluses of energy in the FSU are generated by Russia, Kazakhstan, and Central Asia (comprising the republics of Kyrgyzstan, Tadzikistan, Turkmenia and Uzbekistan). Several of the following tables, which have the same format as Table 4.5 above, provide actual production, consumption and exportable surplus for each of the three areas during 1989–91, as well as projections until 2005 under the first three of our scenarios.

Table 4.7 and Figure 4.2 reveal, unsurprisingly, that Russia dominates the total exportable surpluses generated by the FSU, and that it is projected to continue to do so under all scenarios throughout the period under study. In the case of fossil fuels in aggregate, as well as of oil and gas separately, Russian exportable surpluses are much larger than the corresponding FSU totals. The difference reflects Russian net supplies to the importing FSU republics. In the case of coal a somewhat different picture emerges. Russia has been a net importer of this fuel, and such imports are projected to continue in the medium term. By the turn of the century, at the latest, the Russian republic is expected to generate net coal exports, accounting for around one half

Table 4.7 Energy in Russia: projections of production, consumption and exports under alternative scenarios (MTOE)

	Total fossil fuels			Oil			Gas			Coal		
	Prod.	Cons.	Exp.	Prod.	Cons.	Exp.	Prod.	Cons.	Exp.	Prod.	Cons.	Exp.
1989	1214	802	412	555	277	278	495	355	140	164	170	−6
1990	1187	796	391	516	268	248	515	366	149	156	162	−6
1991	1116	786	330	461	268	193	517	370	147	138	148	−10
Scenario 1: shock therapy												
1995	894	617	277	335	213	122	463	300	163	96	104	−8
2000	1050	631	419	380	187	193	560	355	205	110	89	21
2005	1207	703	504	460	200	260	632	421	211	115	82	33
Scenario 2: gradual reforms												
1995	948	712	236	340	252	88	498	337	161	110	123	−13
2000	1006	671	335	370	219	151	521	351	170	115	101	14
2005	1150	718	432	440	217	223	595	413	182	115	88	27
Scenario 3: reform impasse												
1995	929	699	230	332	252	80	492	347	145	105	100	5
2000	1005	725	280	370	243	127	530	392	138	105	90	15
2005	1075	756	319	420	229	191	555	451	104	100	76	24

Figure 4.2   Russian oil and gas: projections of production, consumption and exports under alternative scenarios (MTOE)

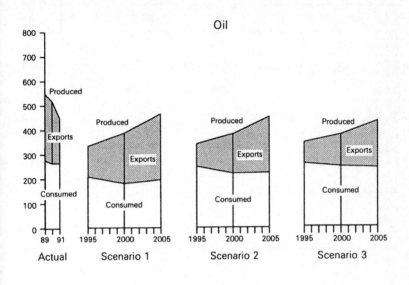

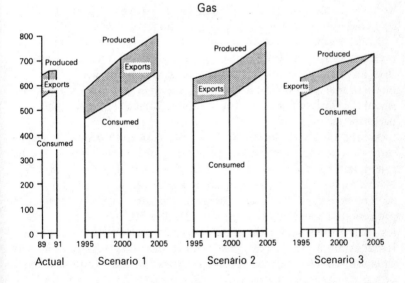

Table 4.8   Russia: projected export revenue from fossil fuel sales under alternative scenarios (billion 1990 $)

	Oil	Gas	Coal	Total
Scenario 1: shock therapy				
1995	15.3	15.3	−0.5	30.1
2000	30.5	24.4	1.4	56.3
2005	39.0	23.8	2.2	65.0
Scenario 2: gradual reforms				
1995	11.0	15.1	−0.8	25.3
2000	23.9	20.2	0.9	45.0
2005	33.5	20.6	1.8	55.9
Scenario 3: reform impasse				
1995	10.0	13.6	0.3	23.9
2000	20.1	16.4	1.0	37.5
2005	28.7	11.8	1.6	42.1

of the FSU total. However, the importance of this shift in the coal balance should not be exaggerated. Both in Russia and in the FSU, coal trade accounts for a minute proportion of total fuel trade.

Table 4.8 projects, analogously with Table 4.6, the energy-export revenues of Russia. The numbers are based on the crucial assumption that all exports, including those within the FSU, will be sold at international prices. For Russia, too, the data in Tables 4.7 and 4.8 reveal the stark importance of successful reforms for the energy sector's performance.

Among the disaggregated FSU regions considered below, Kazakhstan is the second most important in terms of net fuel exports, and its role is seen to increase over our forecast horizon (Table 4.9). In 1989–91 this republic's total fuel surplus corresponded to around 5 per cent of that generated by Russia. Beyond the turn of the century, our projections suggest that the figure will be closer to 10 per cent. Coal has accounted for a very large proportion of exportable fuel supplies in Kazakhstan in the recent past. Our projections suggest that this situation will change. The surpluses of coal are seen to remain more or less constant in all scenarios, while petroleum will undergo a large expansion as Tenghiz is developed, making oil the dominant fuel export at the end of our time horizon. Kazakhstan has been a net importer of gas in the recent past, but our projections point to significant exportable surpluses by the turn of the century and beyond. In 1991, Kazakhstan's net material product was estimated at 7.5 per cent of that of Russia (IMF, 1992a). In that year, therefore, the Kazakhstani economy's dependence on energy exports was less than that of the Russian economy. This ranking will change if our scenarios prove correct, and the two economies grow in parallel.

Table 4.10 displays production, consumption and exportable surpluses in Central Asia. Near-balance prevails and is projected to remain in oil and coal, while a sizable and constant surplus is foreseen in the case of gas. There are large differences in the energy balances of individual republics in Central Asia. Uzbekistan accounts for 60 per cent of the region's energy consumption, but it produces very little itself. Turkmenia, in contrast, produces more than 60 per cent of the region's energy output but consumes only 25 per cent of the regional total. This makes Turkmenia a sizable net energy exporter, a role that is projected to continue throughout the time horizon of our study. Turkmenia stands out as the most energy-export-dependent among the FSU republics. In 1991 its energy exports/net material product ratio was twelve times higher than in Russia (IMF, 1992a).

Next to Russia, Ukraine is by far the largest economy in the FSU, and we have constructed Table 4.11, again in the same format as the preceding ones, to show this republic's energy balances, even though it does not contribute to the net export of fuels. On the contrary, it appears that Ukraine has been a very large importer of energy (in excess of 100 MTOE in the recent past). In broad terms, roughly one quarter of the exportable surpluses generated by Russia in 1989–91 have been consumed by Ukraine. The traditional exportable surpluses of Ukrainian coal are projected to decline over time, and the magnitude of the republic's energy-import needs is forecast to remain through our time horizon.

The exportable surpluses generated by Russia, Kazakhstan and Central Asia recorded in the preceding tables, have been reorganized in Tables 4.12–4.14, to make it easier to observe the provenance of net exports of each fuel. Russia's dominance is supplemented by significant net supplies from Kazakhstan in the case of oil, and by an important net contribution from Central Asia in the case of gas. In coal Kazakhstan plays the major role, with important current contributions by Ukraine (not shown in the table) and future ones by Russia.

Table 4.9 Energy in Kazakhstan: projections of production, consumption and exports under alternative scenarios (MTOE)

	Total fossil fuels			Oil			Gas			Coal		
	Prod.	Cons.	Exp.	Prod.	Cons.	Exp.	Prod.	Cons.	Exp.	Prod.	Cons.	Exp.
1989	94	71	23	26	19	7	5	10	−5	63	42	21
1990	90	69	21	26	19	7	6	10	−4	58	40	18
1991	91	67	24	27	19	8	6	11	−5	58	37	21
Scenario 1: shock therapy												
1995	84	50	34	30	15	15	6	9	−3	48	26	22
2000	114	46	68	52	13	39	16	11	5	46	22	24
2005	131	47	84	60	14	46	26	12	14	45	21	24
Scenario 2: gradual reforms												
1995	83	59	24	27	17	10	6	10	−4	50	32	18
2000	114	51	63	48	15	33	18	10	8	48	26	22
2005	128	49	79	58	15	43	22	12	10	48	22	26
Scenario 3: reform impasse												
1995	79	53	26	26	17	9	6	10	−4	47	26	21
2000	97	51	46	37	17	10	17	11	6	43	23	20
2005	115	48	67	51	16	35	23	13	10	41	19	22

Table 4.10 Energy in Central Asia: projections of production, consumption and exports under alternative scenarios (MTOE)

	Total fossil fuels			Oil			Gas			Coal		
	Prod.	Cons.	Exp.	Prod.	Cons.	Exp.	Prod.	Cons.	Exp.	Prod.	Cons.	Exp.
1989	118	71	47	9	20	−11	105	45	60	4	6	−2
1990	116	66	50	9	14	−5	103	46	57	4	6	−2
1991	117	63	54	10	13	−3	103	45	58	4	5	−1
Scenario 1: shock therapy												
1995	105	50	55	10	10	0	92	37	55	3	3	0
2000	129	55	74	14	9	5	112	43	69	3	3	0
2005	133	64	69	18	10	8	115	51	64	0	3	−3
Scenario 2: gradual reforms												
1995	108	57	51	9	12	−3	96	41	55	3	4	−1
2000	123	57	66	15	10	5	105	43	62	3	4	−1
2005	130	64	66	17	10	7	111	51	60	2	3	−1
Scenario 3: reform impasse												
1995	106	58	48	8	12	−4	95	43	52	3	3	0
2000	118	63	55	10	12	−2	104	48	56	4	3	1
2005	125	69	56	13	11	2	108	55	53	4	3	1

Table 4.11 Energy in Ukraine: projections of production, consumption and exports under alternative scenarios (MTOE)

	Total fossil fuels			Oil			Gas			Coal		
	Prod.	Cons.	Exp.	Prod.	Cons.	Exp.	Prod.	Cons.	Exp.	Prod.	Cons.	Exp.
1989	118	224	−106	5	59	−54	25	89	−64	88	76	12
1990	109	219	−110	6	57	−51	23	91	−68	80	71	9
1991	92	202	−110	5	54	−49	20	89	−69	67	59	8
Scenario 1: shock therapy												
1995	71	156	−85	4	43	−39	15	72	−57	52	41	11
2000	62	158	−96	6	38	−32	12	85	−73	44	35	9
2005	56	173	−117	9	40	−31	15	101	−86	32	32	0
Scenario 2: gradual reforms												
1995	79	181	−102	4	51	−47	17	81	−64	58	49	9
2000	69	168	−99	5	44	−39	11	84	−73	53	40	13
2005	56	178	−122	7	44	−37	11	99	−88	38	35	3
Scenario 3: reform impasse												
1995	70	174	−104	4	51	−47	16	83	−67	50	40	10
2000	56	179	−123	6	49	−43	11	94	−83	39	36	3
2005	52	184	−132	7	46	−39	10	108	−98	35	30	5

Table 4.12   Oil in the FSU: exportable surpluses by major republic or republican group under alternative scenarios (MTOE)

Year	Russia	Kazakhstan	Central Asia	Total
1989	278	7	−11	274
1990	248	7	−5	250
1991	193	8	−3	198
Scenario 1: shock therapy				
1995	122	15	0	137
2000	193	39	5	237
2005	260	46	8	314
Scenario 2: gradual reforms				
1995	122	15	0	137
2000	193	39	5	237
2005	260	46	8	314
Scenario 3: reform impasse				
1995	80	9	−4	85
2000	127	10	−2	135
2005	191	35	2	228

Table 4.13   Gas in the FSU: exportable surpluses by major republic or republican group under alternative scenarios (MTOE)

Year	Russia	Kazakhstan	Central Asia	Total
1989	140	−5	60	195
1990	149	−4	57	202
1991	147	−5	58	200
Scenario 1: shock therapy				
1995	163	−3	55	215
2000	205	5	69	279
2005	211	14	64	289
Scenario 2: gradual reforms				
1995	161	−4	55	212
2000	170	8	62	240
2005	182	10	60	252
Scenario 3: reform impasse				
1995	145	−4	52	193
2000	138	6	56	200
2005	104	10	53	167

Table 4.14   Coal in the FSU: exportable surpluses by major republic or republican group under alternative scenarios (MTOE)

Year	Russia	Kazakhstan	Central Asia	Total
1989	−6	21	−2	13
1990	−6	18	−2	10
1991	−10	21	−1	10
Scenario 1: shock therapy				
1995	−8	22	0	14
2000	21	24	0	45
2005	33	24	−3	54
Scenario 2: gradual reforms				
1995	−13	18	−1	4
2000	14	22	−1	35
2005	27	26	−1	52
Scenario 3: reform impasse				
1995	5	21	0	26
2000	15	20	1	36
2005	24	22	1	47

We now return to an aggregate analysis of the FSU. Section 4.3 below aims to assess the possible impact on the international market of the alternative FSU energy-export outcomes derived from our scenarios. To accomplish that task we require a set of 'normal' export values with which to compare our outcomes. Only with such a yardstick will it be possible to determine whether the projected export figures for the whole of the FSU, contained in Table 4.5, result in a surplus or a deficit in international energy supply compared with what has been 'anticipated'. Such surpluses and deficits, in turn, are needed to gauge whether the scenario outcomes will tend to suppress international prices or push them to higher levels than would have otherwise occurred.

For want of a better yardstick we have established the 'normal' export supply of each fuel from the FSU by simply extending the 1980–9 trend of actual exports until 2005, the time horizon for our investigations. The results show what a reasonably informed observer of international markets in 1989 might have expected in terms of future FSU supply. They are presented graphically in Figure 4.3. Actual exports for 1990 and 1991 have been plotted in the figure but are regarded as abnormal, and hence have been omitted when determining

Figure 4.3 Fuel exports from the FSU, 1993–2005, projected on 1980–9 trend

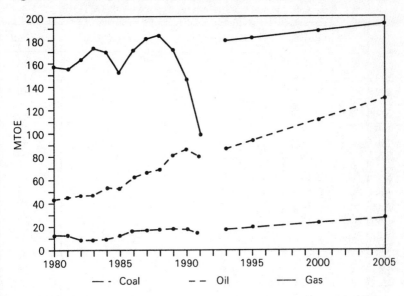

the anticipated export trend figures for 1993 to 2005. The significance of this omission is negligible for the trends in gas and coal but quite important in the case of oil.

These trend projections are juxtaposed in Table 4.15 with our scenario export outcomes to determine whether the outcomes represent surpluses or deficits compared with the 'normal', expected trend. The table reveals a disappointing oil-export performance in all our scenarios and over most of the time period under scrutiny. Scenario 1 forecasts for gas are substantially above the 'normal' trend, while Scenario 3 yields deficits, which increase over time. For coal our scenarios predict higher than 'normal' exports in most cases.

4.4 FSU EXPORT SUPPLY AND WORLD ENERGY MARKETS

Having assessed the significance of the FSU as an energy supplier to the international markets and presented forecasts of its future export prospects, we are now ready to investigate how these export prospects might influence the price of fossil fuels in international markets.

Table 4.15 FSU fuel export forecasts: scenario results compared with projected 1980–9 trends (MTOE)

impasse	1980–9 trend projection	Scenario 1: shock therapy		Scenario 2: gradual reforms		Scenario 3: reform	
		Forecast	Difference from trend projection	Forecast	Difference from trend projection	Forecast	Difference from trend projection
Oil							
1995	181	60	−121	0	−181	−10	−191
2000	187	170	−17	110	−77	50	−137
2005	193	240	47	190	−3	150	−43
Gas							
1995	94	115	21	100	8	75	−19
2000	112	160	48	120	8	60	−52
2005	131	150	19	120	−9	5	−126
Coal							
1995	20	20	0	10	−10	30	10
2000	23	55	32	45	22	35	12
2005	27	60	33	50	23	50	23

We begin with a general analysis of price formation in international energy markets, continue with a brief presentation of the method we intend to use for the task at hand, and then apply this method to each of the fuels in turn. The section ends with a brief summary of our findings.

4.4.1   International Energy Market Reactions to Changes in Supply

The base mechanism for price change in an international energy market is quite simple. A reduction in the supply of, for example, oil will initially lead to a price increase. This will in turn reduce the quantity demanded and increase the quantity supplied from other sources, if slack capacity exists, until a new equilibrium between demand and supply is established.

In a longer-term two additional factors will make themselves felt as a consequence of the higher price. First, producer incentives will emerge to expand capacity and supply. Second, consumer incentives will emerge to reduce overall energy use and to replace oil with other materials, for example coal and gas. This should result in reduced demand for oil. For these reasons the initial price impact of the supply cut will be curbed over time. Substitution in favour of other fuels will in turn raise the demand for these materials and therefore indirectly lead to some increase in their prices.

The reverse would apply in the event of an oil-supply increase, with an initial price fall followed by a slight rise as producers and consumers adjust to the initial price change. The base mechanism could also be employed to analyse a series of consecutive supply declines, each having both a short-term and a long-term price impact.

Econometric studies suggest short-term price elasticities of demand for individual fuels at -0.1 to -0.3, with long-term values at -0.5 to -1.0 or more. The elasticities would be lower for total energy, reflecting the loss of opportunity to substitute among the fuels. Such studies also suggest very high short-term price elasticities of supply when unused capacity is available, declining to near-zero as full capacity utilisation is approached. Long-term supply elasticities could be close to zero at very low prices, but approach infinity at very high prices.

The above relationship suggests that the market reaction to changes in anticipated supply, such as those that can be expected in future FSU exports, could be determined with the help of a model employing empirically tested short-term and long-term price elasticities of demand and supply.

We do not intend to follow such an approach. Many models of this nature have been constructed; for a variety of reasons their predictive success has not been great. First, elasticities are hard to measure. They exhibit considerable instability over time. Their values change with the price level, and not necessarily in a smooth manner. Hence there is little uniformity in the elasticity numbers obtained from different studies. Second, the relationship between supply, demand and price may not function as described above if there is producer collusion, and such collusion is clearly present in the international oil market and the European gas market. The reactions of a cartel to a cut in outsiders' supplies are difficult to predict and model. For example Saudi Arabia and other OPEC members quickly compensated for the shortfall caused by the embargoes on Iraqi and Kuwaiti oil in 1990, but this reaction was politically prompted and had little to do with standard economic rationale. A third problem has to do with expectations, which are also very difficult to model. A price increase will raise demand, not reduce it, if it creates expectations of further price increases, for then consumers and speculators will want to add to inventories. Conversely consumers will not adjust to a higher price, and the long-term price elasticity of demand will remain low if there are persistent expectations that the higher price will not last.

Our analysis of the impact of FSU export change will be more qualitative. While not ignoring price elasticities, a more informal approach will permit us to identify and consider intricacies such as the ones outlined in the preceding paragraph.

4.4.2 The Price Impact of Changing FSU Exports

The international markets for coal, oil and gas, considered in the following pages, will be influenced in coming years by a number of external events other than the evolution of FSU export supply. For example, world economic expansion will be a key determinant of the overall rate of demand growth. Environmental concerns, expressing themselves through differential taxes and regulations, are likely to reduce the use of coal and favour the consumption of gas. Technical change, such as the introduction of gas-fired combined-cycle power generation, can likewise be expected to improve the competitiveness of gas and increase the relative market share of this fuel. Events of this nature will obviously impact on the development of demand and supply, and on price in each fuel market.

The following analysis has no ambition to provide comprehensive overviews of the international energy markets and their development, and does not explore 'external' factors such as the ones mentioned above. It is exclusively concerned with the impact of varying FSU supply on each of the markets. The narrow focus permits a clearer scrutiny of the issue under investigation.

Other anticipated events in each energy market are nevertheless included in the analysis by our use of World-Bank material to establish total internationally traded quantities and the international prices of the three fuels. Forecasted volumes of global trade have been taken from a thorough and comprehensive study of world energy markets (World Bank, 1990), while the base-price forecasts (excepting gas) have been extracted from World Bank, 1992c, which presents revisions of the price series contained in the earlier document. Since these revisions are small, no serious inconsistencies arise in combining the quantitative forecasts in the former document with the price forecasts in the latter.

Coal and oil are treated identically in our analysis. Both fuels are traded in truly global markets. For the reasons detailed below, the analysis of gas requires a regional (European) approach.

The initial stage of our analysis is somewhat mechanistic and is intended to give a feel of the orders of magnitude. In the case of coal and oil, the surpluses or deficits in FSU exports in 1995–2005, obtained from a comparison of our scenario forecasts of exports with the projected (1980–9) export trends (Table 4.15), are expressed as a percentage of world gross exports (World Bank, 1990a) in the same year. Assuming, next, a uniform price elasticity of demand equal to 0.2, with all else remaining unchanged, the percentage changes in global exported supply permit us to recalculate the price-forecast series for each scenario, using the World-Bank forecasts as the starting point. Only Scenarios 1–3 are considered.

This exercise is illustrated in Figure 4.4. Q_1 is the world export figure and P_1 the price, both given by the World Bank. Q_1Q_2 is the difference (shortfall) between the FSU export volume derived from a projection of the actual 1980–9 trend and that forecast in our alternative scenarios. With everything else remaining unchanged, price will slide up to P_2 along the demand curve D, which has been drawn to represent a price elasticity of 0.2 in the price range under scrutiny. Expressed in per cent, the price move from P_1 to P_2 is five times as large as the quantity move from Q_1 to Q_2.

Figure 4.4   Initial price adjustment to a fall in FSU supply

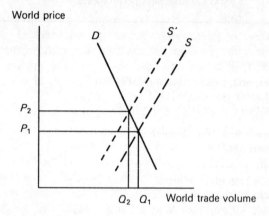

The consecutive steps of this analysis are summarised in Tables 4.16 and 4.17 for coal and oil. The tables also present the price results. The initial analysis for gas basically follows the same approach, with some alterations that are detailed below. The gas results are summarised in Table 4.18.

The price deviations from the World Bank forecast, that emerge from these exercises can be considered as the upper limit of what might occur in the relatively short term if FSU exports change as indicated. The price elasticity of demand would tend to be higher if a collapsing FSU supply is anticipated in advance, for then consumers would have had time to prepare for the event before it occurred. In addition, unless all capacity was fully used, one would expect at least some positive supply reaction from other supply sources. For example, if the supply curve is shaped like *S* in the figure before the FSU collapse, it would be like *S'* after the event. The figure demonstrates that added supply from other sources would establish a new equilibrium between supply and demand, with a price increase less than one half of $P_1 P_2$.

In the following steps of our investigations of each of the fuels, we therefore modify the price findings on the basis of qualitative analyses that take into consideration the specific circumstances characterising the markets for coal, oil and gas.

4.4.2.1 Coal

The mechanistic assessment of the price impact of FSU export variations on the anticipated trend for internationally traded coal in

Table 4.16   Measuring the international price impact of variations in the
FSU's coal export performance

	1995	2000	2005
Base assumptions			
FSU exports, trend projection (MTOE)	20	23	27
World gross exports (MTOE)	317	356	388
International price (1990 $/ton FOB)	39	44	44
Difference from base assumptions in FSU exports (MTOE)			
Scenario 1: shock therapy	0	32	33
Scenario 2: gradual reforms	−10	22	23
Scenario 3: reform impasse	10	12	23
Difference in FSU exports (in per cent of world gross exports)			
Scenario 1: shock therapy	0	9.0	8.5
Scenario 2: gradual reforms	−3.2	6.2	5.9
Scenario 3: reform impasse	3.2	3.4	5.9
International price, assuming ceteris paribus, price elasticity of demand=(−)0.2, 1990 $/ton			
Scenario 1: shock therapy	39	24	25
Scenario 2: gradual reforms	45	30	31
Scenario 3: reform impasse	33	37	31

Sources: World gross exports and base international prices from World Bank,
1990, 1992; FSU exports, trend projections from Table 4.15; scenario data from
Table 4.5.

our scenarios is summarised in Table 4.16. Some of the results clearly
exaggerate what is likely to occur.

The international market for coal is competitive, and is likely to
remain so for the foreseeable future. Exported supply in such markets
will be determined, by and large, by the marginal cost of existing
capacity in the short term, and by the total cost of expanding that
capacity in the longer term.

Most of the coal produced worldwide is domestically consumed, and
coal exports constitute a small proportion of global output. The
possibility of shifting between domestic and export markets is

significant. Even a very large shortfall in international supply is easily
made up for by such shifts. Hence, once a threshold price level is
exceeded, the price elasticity of exported coal supply is quite high. For
the same reason a capacity limit for exported coal production is hard to
identify. As international prices rise, more output will be allocated to
exports. At levels above $40 per ton FOB (1990 dollars) the export
supply schedule for steam coal becomes virtually horizontal (Doyle,
1988; IEA, 1990). However a capacity constraint does exist for
exported coal in the form of limited harbour and transport facilities.

On these grounds we conclude that this assessment exaggerates the
price impact of supply variations from the FSU. The excess supply in
Scenario 1 would hardly result in the low prices reported in Table 4.16
for 2000 and 2005 because a price fall of the indicated magnitude
would lead to curtailed export supply from elsewhere, and probably
also from the FSU itself. For similar reasons an FSU shortfall, such as
indicated in Scenario 2 for 1995, could raise prices to $45 (FOB) only in
the relatively short term.

4.4.2.2   Oil

Since the early 1980s the international price of oil has been effectively
determined by OPEC, or more precisely by the cartel's Middle-East
core. Variations in capacity utilisation over this period of time have
been used as the tool to pursue varied price objectives. Shifts in world
demand and changes in supply outside the cartel have been countered
by OPEC's output decisions, in defence of a very high price in the first
half of the decade and of a much lower one since 1986.

Substantial unused capacity in 1989–90 enabled the cartel to make
up not only for the decline in FSU exports of some 70 million tons
between 1989 and 1991, but, with a few months' delay, also for the
huge deficit of about 200 million tons on an annual basis that arose in
August 1990 in consequence of the embargo against Iraq and Kuwait.
Because of increased capacity utilisation in Saudi Arabia and other
countries, global supply remained relatively stable and prices in the
latter half of 1991 were not very different from those that prevailed in
early 1990.

These experiences point to three questions that must be addressed
when revising the price impact of future changes in FSU supply,
reported in Table 4.17. First, would the indicated prices in the three
scenarios be agreeable to OPEC, or would they tend to provoke
offsetting action to keep supply and prices stable? Second, is it likely

Table 4.17   Measuring the international price impact of variations in the FSU's oil export performance

	1995	2000	2005
Base assumptions			
FSU exports, trend projection (MTOE)	181	187	193
World gross exports (MTOE)	2028	2167	2247
International price (1990 $/ton FOB)	17.1	21.6	20.6
Difference from base assumptions in FSU			
exports (MTOE)			
Scenario 1: shock therapy	−121	−17	47
Scenario 2: gradual reforms	−181	−77	−3
Scenario 3: reform impasse	−191	−137	−43
Difference in FSU exports (in per cent of			
world gross exports)			
Scenario 1: shock therapy	−6.0	−0.8	2.1
Scenario 2: gradual reforms	−8.9	−3.6	−0.1
Scenario 3: reform impasse	−9.4	−6.3	−1.9
International price, assuming ceteris			
paribus, price elasticity of			
demand = (−)0.2, 1990 $/bl			
Scenario 1: shock therapy	22.2	22.5	18.4
Scenario 2: gradual reforms	24.7	25.5	20.6
Scenario 3: reform impasse	25.1	28.4	22.6

Sources: World gross exports and base international prices from World Bank, 1990, 1992; FSU exports, trend projections from Table 4.15; scenario data from Table 4.5.

that OPEC will continue to operate with sufficient excess capacity to enable it to stabilise prices by increasing production in the event of an FSU supply shortfall? And third, could the anticipated shifts in FSU exports occur so suddenly and be so large that time would be needed for OPEC to implement compensatory movements to restore the desired price level?

There are many views about the price level that the OPEC core would prefer[1]. Economic rationale suggests (Radetzki, 1991) a price of about $20 per barrel (constant 1990 dollars), because above this level the demand curve for OPEC oil becomes very elastic as non-cartel oil and other fuels become competitive. Hence a price above $20 is not desirable since it would involve sharp reductions in market share. By the same token there is little incentive for letting prices fall below $20 because demand for OPEC oil then becomes quite inelastic. If correct, this argument would suggest that the OPEC core might want to make up for the FSU shortfall in the early periods of Scenarios 2 and 3 in order to maintain prices at the desired level.

The historical experience of excess capacity in OPEC during the 1980s may not be of relevance when examining the future. The excess capacity was the result of a sharp shrinkage of OPEC's market in the first half of the decade, not of conscious expansion efforts.

Looking at the 1990s and beyond, it is nevertheless clear that each member of the OPEC core does have an incentive to maintain production capacity beyond its immediate needs. On the one hand such capacity is not very costly in the Middle East (Adelman, 1992). On the other a large capacity provides the members with an advantage in the cartel's quota negotiations. For OPEC collectively, too, there is a point in having excess capacity, since such capacity helps the cartel manage the market by enabling it to prevent price explosions, and by constituting a tool for potential retaliation against insiders or outsiders who are seen to overproduce. Despite the very substantial excess capacity that was revealed during the Middle-East crisis in 1990, forceful efforts were already underway at the time the crisis broke out to expand production capability even more.

On these grounds we conclude that OPEC will normally have not only the desire, but also the means to make up for FSU shortfalls that bring prices to levels above $20.

The anticipated shifts in FSU supply under Scenarios 1 to 3 are seen to be gradual, both in their downward and upward moves. Hence, if the OPEC core has the will and the capacity, no problem should arise in compensating for the changes in FSU supply. According to our reasoning the will to do so in full measure would be limited in 1995, given that the base assumption prices are significantly below $20, the price that OPEC is thought to desire to maintain.

We conclude our oil-price analysis by noting that the variations in FSU exports detailed in our scenarios are unlikely to create havoc in the international oil market. The prices given for our scenarios in Table 4.17 constitute the maximum deviations from the base-price assumptions contained in the World-Bank study. This is what might occur if OPEC and other oil producers do not react at all to the fluctuations in FSU exports, for instance because there is no spare capacity to draw upon.

We deem it more probable that the deviations would be substantially smaller, since other producers, and the OPEC core in particular, can be expected to adjust their output to make up for the varied FSU export performance. Based on historical experience, the OPEC core alone could easily replace all conceivable FSU shortfalls and steer prices to the levels it finds desirable.

Prospects for a continued increase in FSU exports, as in Scenario 1 towards the end of our time horizon, would provide a strong incentive to the oil cartel to coopt the FSU into its international market management. From the FSU's point of view the ideal would be to act as a free rider, increasing its export supply while others (OPEC) adjusted their exports downwards to maintain price levels. Such a policy would become untenable with an increasing dominance of FSU oil in the international market. At some stage, probably beyond the time horizon under consideration, OPEC might threaten to let prices fall unless the FSU agreed to constrain its supply. The advantage to the FSU of active involvement in market management, along with OPEC, would have to be judged in the light of the seriousness of the threat, and of the production constraints that the FSU would have to implement.

4.4.2.3 Gas

For at least two reasons it is necessary to adopt a different format for our treatment of the natural-gas market. First, no global market for gas has yet emerged; neither is one likely to be established within the time horizon of this study. Instead, natural-gas trade takes place in three regional markets. In the early 1990s these markets were separated by very high transport costs and had only indirect interconnections, mainly through the world price of oil.

In 1990 (BP 1991) North American trade, amounting to 43 BCM, consisted almost exclusively of Canadian exports by pipe to the US. The Pacific trade (52 BCM) consisted entirely of LNG imports by Japan, Korea and Taiwan, predominantly from South-East Asia and Australia. European gas imports (including intraregional trade) were by far the largest, with a total of more than 200 BCM. The FSU was the most important supplier, accounting for 96 BCM, close to half of overall European imports. All East-European imports originated in the FSU. In Western Europe, supplies from the FSU accounted for 35 per cent of all purchases from abroad. Remaining imported supply to Western Europe came from Algeria, Libya, the Netherlands and Norway.

The claim that no global market exists is supported by Figure 4.5, which depicts monthly developments of import prices in the three markets from July 1990 to October 1992. Both the discrepancies in levels and the absence of synchronization in price moves point to the independence of each market vis-à-vis the others.

Figure 4.5   Gas import prices

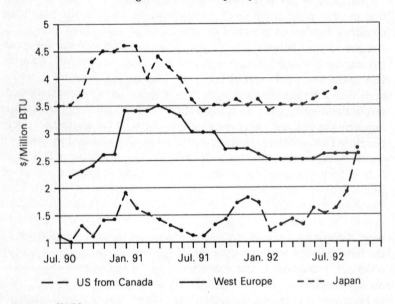

Source: WGI.

All FSU exports have so far ended up in Europe. With one possible exception this export concentration is likely to prevail until 2005. By early next century it is possible that some Russian gas (Sakhalin) will be traded by pipe or as LNG in the Pacific market, but the quantities are unlikely to be large enough to have a significant influence on prices in that market. For these reasons our investigations of how a shifting FSU export performance will impact on prices focuses entirely on the European market.

A second reason why a different format is needed in our discussion of gas is that no World Bank price forecasts exist that could be used as a base assumption from which to calculate alternative future price paths.

We propose the following approach to circumvent this base-price unavailability. The traditional CMEA pricing arrangements can be disregarded in considering the future. These arrangements have disintegrated and are being replaced by "international" pricing formulas that are closely related to those employed in Western Europe. Hence we take the West-European gas prices as our starting point.

Contracts for gas imports to Western Europe through the 1980s have tied the gas price per unit of energy content (c.i.f. at the importing country's border) to the price of oil and oil products, but with a lag. For the 11-year period 1980–90, the ratio between the West-European gas import price and the average price of crude oil imported into the IEA countries, works out at $0.75 (BP, 1991). The discount has been needed to keep gas competitive with oil products at final consumption, given the higher cost of transporting and distributing gas in the importing countries. This practice has yielded considerable monopoly benefits. Through the pricing arrangements gas producers have enjoyed the monopoly prices that are reaped by OPEC (Radetzki, 1992).

It is widely assumed that the link between European gas and oil prices will be maintained in the foreseeable future (IEA, 1991e). Combining this assumption with the World Bank's oil-price forecasts permits us to derive a price-forecast series for gas that can be used as a base assumption for our analysis. We simply posit, for the purpose of the base assumptions, that the price of gas will remain at 75 per cent of oil prices throughout the time horizon. Table 4.18 has been constructed on this basis.

The content of this table raises several points that require discussion. The first concerns price formation in the West-European gas market. The prices derived from our exercises in Table 4.18 assume that the West-European gas-price levels will move up or down in response to gas-supply changes until a market equilibrium is reached. This is not the way the gas market has operated in the past two decades. As noted above, the price of gas in Western Europe has been tied to the price of substitutes, and equilibrium in the gas market has been achieved primarily by producers being obliged to restrain supply (Radetzki, 1992). With this price-formation system in force an emergent gas-supply shortage would require rationing to be imposed.

In contrast with the views expressed by the IEA and others (IEA, 1991e), we believe that the price tie between oil and gas is being undermined by a number of factors, and that a break might well occur before the end of the century (Radetzki, 1991). Such a break could

Table 4.18   Measuring the impact on European price levels of variations in the FSU's natural gas export performance

	1995	2000	2005
Base assumptions			
FSU exports, trend projection (MTOE)	94	112	131
Gross exports to Europe (MTOE)	200	239	266
European price (1990 $/Mn BTU)	2.4	3.0	2.8
Difference from base assumptions in FSU exports (MTOE)			
Scenario 1: shock therapy	21	48	19
Scenario 2: gradual reforms	8	8	−9
Scenario 3: reform impasse	−19	−52	−126
Difference in FSU exports (in per cent of gross imports to Europe)			
Scenario 1: shock therapy	−10.5	−20.1	7.1
Scenario 2: gradual reforms	4.0	3.3	−3.4
Scenario 3: reform impasse	−9.5	−21.8	−47.3
European import price, assuming, ceteris paribus, price elasticity of demand = (−)0.2, 1990 $/Mn BTU			
Scenario 1: shock therapy	1.2	0.0	1.8
Scenario 2: gradual reforms	1.9	2.5	3.3
Scenario 3: reform impasse	3.5	6.3	9.4

Sources: Gross exports to Europe from World Bank, 1990; base prices taken at 75 per cent of oil price forecast by World Bank, 1992c; FSU exports, trend projection from Table 4.15; Scenario data from Table 4.5.

plausibly be triggered by a sudden and large shift, up or down, in FSU supply, causing a market disequilibrium that could not be managed without an independent adjustment in gas prices. It may nevertheless be instructive to consider a case where the price link is maintained in the wake of an FSU supply cut, and where rationing is used to come to grips with the ensuing gas shortage.

To put rationing into perspective, one can note that total consumption of gas in Europe (excluding FSU) was around 300 MTOE in 1990, and is forecast to rise to some 400 MTOE in 2000 and perhaps 450

MTOE in 2005 (IEA, 1991e). Consider a deficit of 50 MTOE in 2000, roughly corresponding to the level indicated for our Scenario 3 in Table 4.18, and equal to about 13 per cent of consumption.

In the case of rationing, such a shortfall would in all probability not be evenly spread throughout Europe. The Netherlands, a large and self-sufficient consumer, might not be affected at all. The shortfall experienced by the UK and Romania, which are only marginally import-dependent, would be less than the Continental average, if these two countries succeeded in obtaining any imports at all. The burden of adjustment for remaining countries would consequently exceed the 13 per cent level. Even among these countries there would be variations in import availability, depending on the origin of the imports and contract conditions.

For oil, rules have been set by the IEA to share the burden of shortfalls among members. No corresponding framework has been designed for gas in Western Europe, or on the Continent as a whole, so a supply disruption would probably be dealt with by each nation independently. Since the rationing process among nations would be politically determined, it is by no means clear that a link-up of, say, Poland or Hungary or Bulgaria with the West-European gas grid would provide security against an FSU shortfall. In the event of shortage, decision-makers in Germany, Austria and Italy would tend to give priority to their own national interests, with regard to the gas that entered their territory. A corollary is that a reduced gas flow from the FSU could be retained to satisfy the transit countries' needs. Czechoslovakia would have a particularly favoured position in this regard.

Rationing within the nations would vary depending on the role and importance of gas, and on the preferences of politicians. Where imported gas accounts for a significant share of TPES, as is the case in Germany and Italy, a cut in traded supply of the magnitude considered would indubitably have important negative repercussions, both on industrial output and household comfort.

A second issue arising from the content of Table 4.18 is that both the volume and price deviations from the base assumptions are much larger in relative terms than those for oil and coal. This follows from the fact that the deviations are compared with European gross imports, not world trade as in the case of the other fuels, and that FSU gas supply is so important in Europe.

The figures reveal that the immediate price impact would be very large if prices rather than rationing were to be used to restore balance in the European gas market after a surprise change in FSU supplies. For example, the figures indicate that the market would have problems in swallowing the "gas bubble" that emerges in Scenario 1 in the latter half of the 1990s. Similarly, with the disappointing export levels of Scenario 3 in 2000 and 2005, prices could attain, in the extreme case, twice or even three times the level posited in the base assumptions.

Far more moderate price changes can be expected if the changes in FSU exports are anticipated in advance, or if time is allowed for gas consumers and non-FSU suppliers to adjust to the initial shortfall and its price impact. Take the price figures emerging in Scenario 3 as an illustration. The disappointing FSU export figures at the end of the century will cause a market imbalance that will break the price link between gas and oil. With rising prices, gas will become uncompetitive in many uses. Those who can substitute quickly, for example those with dual fuel power capacity, will do so, and there will be a relatively speedy one-time shrinkage in consumption, reducing the initial price rise to below that indicated in Table 4.18.

Longer-term forces will come into play if a continued shortfall in FSU supply is revealed. Gas-using equipment will not be replaced as it becomes old, wherever alternative fuels offer a better option than the more expensive gas. The prospect of a continuing higher price will stimulate expansion from existing supply sources, for example from Norway and Algeria, or from new ones in the Middle East and West Africa. This will result in lower Scenario 3 prices than indicated in Table 4.18, at the turn of the century and beyond, when these adaptations come into effect. But prices will remain more elevated than in the base assumptions because the cost of supply from alternative sources is higher than the cost of FSU gas exports over a wide range of volumes (IEA, 1991e; Little, 1991; see also Section 4.4). With a high gas price in Scenario 3, gas consumption will become more concentrated in market segments that can afford to pay more, for example in running peak-power generation and in operating household appliances (Julius and Mashayekhi, 1990).

The longer-term adjustments among producers and consumers outlined here will ensure that the gas price does not rise too far above the oil price, even in the absence of an established link between the two. If it did, the longer-term result would be a shrinkage of the gas market into insignificance as gas became uncompetitive with alternative fuels.

A secondary effect of the reduced gas demand would be an expansion of the demand for alternative fuels, including oil and coal. But given the size and versatility of the world market for each of these products, their prices would not be much influenced by a partial shift away from gas in Europe.

It may be interesting to consider a variation beside our scenario framework, in which FSU exports exhibit a considerable and persistent instability. Sharp annual fluctuations could be caused, for instance, by an unsettled regulatory framework governing gas production and exports, or by continuing interrepublican disputes about gas transit.

Gas consumption requires very heavy capital outlays on transmission and distribution and on the facilities that use gas. Hence predictability and reliability of supply are highly valued by importers. The prevalence of long-term contracts is an expression of consumer preference in this respect. The unreliability of FSU gas supply in the case under consideration would reduce the value of that gas to importers. This in turn would probably lead to the development of a two-tier market. The first tier, comprising reliable supply, would be traded under long-term contracts at premium prices. The second-tier supply would record lower average prices and slower demand growth, as importers revealed their preference for stability. Since the purpose of long-term contracts is diluted when suppliers cannot control volumes, the second tier would also be distinguished by including a high proportion of spot transactions.

We conclude that alternative gas-export volumes from the FSU could have a very strong impact on the European gas market. If gas supplies become abundant, such as in the case of the 'gas bubble' posited in Scenario 1, prices may be pushed to very low levels and high-cost gas, for example from Norway, could be driven out of the market. If gas supplies shrink the initial effect may be a doubling or even tripling of price above the base assumption level. Gas prices could remain quite high for half a decade or longer, necessitating painful adjustments among gas consumers and stimulating alternative gas supply expansion. Gas prices would decrease but could still remain substantially above the base-assumption levels as long as the FSU supplies continue below expectations, as these adjustment efforts take effect.

4.4.2.4 A Summary of Findings on International Market Implications

The FSU export outcomes for coal, oil and gas in our scenarios have been juxtaposed against trend projections of export volumes and World-Bank forecasts of prices to obtain an idea of the impact that alternative FSU export performances might have on the international energy markets. These exercises have been followed up by qualitative discussions to illuminate the implications for each fuel market.

We conclude that, in the case of coal and oil, the alternative FSU export paths derived in our scenarios are unlikely to make more than a temporary dent in global traded availability and international price. The main ground for this conclusion is that past and prospective FSU exports of coal and oil constitute limited proportions of world trade in these products, so even large changes in FSU sales will have only a small impact on the global total. But there are additional arguments, specific to each of the two markets, in support of our view.

In the case of coal we note that global trade constitutes only a small fraction of global output, so the price elasticity of traded supply is bound to be very high. Hence a deficiency caused by failed exports from any one supplier would soon be made up by supply from elsewhere.

In the case of oil an argument of crucial importance for our conclusion is that the OPEC core has maintained considerable unused capacity in its market management. We deem it probable that the cartel will continue to pursue such a policy throughout the time horizon of the present study. Variations in FSU exports will then be made up for by OPEC in support of the price that the cartel chooses to defend. Hence OPEC's price objective, not FSU export variations, will be the principal determinant of oil prices. If FSU exports experience a substantial and sustained expansion, one may foresee attempts by OPEC to coopt the FSU producers into the cartel.

The situation is quite different in the case of gas. The European market leads an independent life, with insignificant exchange with the North American and Pacific markets. Supplies from the FSU have a very dominant position in European imports, which in turn constitute a major proportion of total consumption. Hence disruptions in FSU supply could have a dramatic impact on the European gas market and on gas prices, in turn leading to painful adjustments among gas consumers as they try to substitute in favour of other fuels.

The above analysis has treated each fuel in turn. We should add that the international-market outcomes would be quite similar if, as is probable, the FSU energy export fortunes develop in parallel for the three fuels. For example there is a high probability that the sudden and dramatic cut in all FSU energy exports following from an internal FSU war, would soon be made up for by increased coal and oil exports from elsewhere, restoring order in these two markets and restricting the period of higher prices caused by the initial shortfall. The problems in the European gas market would of course be amplified and prolonged if the short-term efforts to substitute are hampered by higher coal and oil price levels.

4.5 IMPLICATIONS FOR EASTERN EUROPE

4.5.1 Introduction

The East-European countries need to be treated separately, when the implications of varying FSU energy-export performances are explored. This follows from Eastern Europe's exceptionally high reliance on supplies from the FSU, but even more from the inflexible infrastructural ties that effectively hinder switching to other suppliers in many cases. In many East-European countries the risk of collapsing energy exports from the FSU, and the serious economic and social consequences that would follow, have prompted lively activity, which is mainly at the discussion and planning stage, aimed at reducing the reliance on FSU energy.

The purpose of this section is to gauge the nature and dimensions of Eastern Europe's dependence on energy supplies from the FSU, to discuss existing vulnerabilities and to explore realistic and economically worthwhile actions that could reduce the strain if a collapse in FSU exports were in fact to occur.

1989 is used throughout as the benchmark year for the analysis. This is partly because of the serious delay in which data become available. A more important reason for choosing 1989 as the benchmark year is that for Eastern Europe it was the last 'normal' year of the preceding era. The subsequent dramatic changes included (a) the collapse of COMECON trade, (b) the halting of cheap energy imports from the FSU, (c) the commencement of far-reaching economic reforms and (d) a dramatic decline in economic activity. The period of change is far from ended. Hence it seems to us that it would be inappropriate to use any of the transient and unstable years after 1989 as a base to assess the future.

Our alternative scenarios for economic and political development in the FSU provide a variety of energy-export paths, some indicating quite buoyant export volumes. In the following we largely disregard the cases where FSU energy exports, both worldwide and to Eastern

Europe, remain sufficient. Instead attention is focused on the drastic export declines predicted in some of our scenarios and on the problems caused by the ensuing unsatisfied East-European import needs.

4.5.2 The Impact of FSU Export Shortfalls

Over the past few decades the East-European countries have become very heavily dependent on FSU energy supply. The measures of dependence for 1989 are detailed in Table 4.19, for the group of six countries in aggregate and for each individual country in turn. Figure 4.6 provides a pictorial overview. (Note that 'gross availability' in Figure 4.6 comprises the exported volumes that are excluded from the TPES concept used in Table 4.19.) Several comments are prompted by these compilation:

First, overall reliance on energy imports is about the same in East and West Europe (40–50 per cent of total consumption).

Second, with a GDP of $653 billion in 1989 (see Table 4.19), the energy intensity of the country grouping works out at 559 TOE per million dollars. In Western Europe the figure is only 252, suggesting a very large potential for energy savings in Eastern Europe.

Third, while the world's dependence on FSU energy amounted to 4 per cent of total primary energy supply (TPES) and Western Europe's to 12 per cent (Tables 4.1 and 4.3), in Eastern Europe as a whole the figure was 31 per cent, rising to highs of 68 per cent in Bulgaria and 48 per cent in Hungary. Even in Romania, the least dependent country, imports from the FSU constituted 18 per cent of TPES, substantially more than in Western Europe.

Fourth, coal accounts for one half of TPES in Eastern Europe compared with 25 per cent in the western part of the continent. It is coal that provides the East-European countries with some measure of energy independence. In all cases domestic production accounted for a major share of consumption. In aggregate, imports account for less than one tenth of coal consumption, and slightly more than one half of the import needs were satisfied by the FSU. Poland, alone in the group, records coal exports on a significant scale (IEA 1991a).

Fifth, three quarters of the total East-European demand for oil was satisfied by the FSU. Romania and Yugoslavia were the only countries with a limited reliance on FSU oil. All six countries recorded oil-product exports; those of Bulgaria, Czechoslovakia, Hungary and Poland being reexports of FSU supplies, mainly in processed form.

Romania was by far the largest oil-product exporter, but the oil it sold was predominantly of non-FSU origin.

Sixth, all imports of gas originated in the FSU. These imports accounted for one half of Eastern Europe's gas consumption. Bulgaria and Czechoslovakia have no significant domestic gas production, so their reliance on FSU gas is virtually total.

Seventh, the figures in Table 4.19 underestimate the FSU's importance in supplying electricity. A large part of Eastern Europe's electricity is generated in power stations using fossil fuels imported from the FSU. The way we have structured the figures is intended to clarify the immediate implications of cuts in FSU electricity deliveries. The table reveals that 27 per cent of the electricity consumed in Hungary was supplied by the FSU. In Bulgaria, Romania and Czechoslovakia the share was between 6 per cent and 9 per cent.

The motivations for establishing the strong energy bonds between the FSU and Eastern Europe were predominantly political. Their establishment was accomplished through a combination of political coercion and trade terms for energy imports that favoured Eastern Europe.

The economic advantage of energy imports from the FSU has recently been quantified by Kenen (1990). In a thorough analysis, the author asserts that fuel, which dominated the East-Europeans imports from the FSU in the late 1980s, was priced about 60 per cent below world-market prices, while machinery and transport equipment, the most important category of East-European exports to the FSU, were priced about 15 per cent above world-price levels. Under such circumstances the economic lure of energy imports from the FSU must have been quite strong.

From 1990 onwards steps were taken to dismantle the special COMECON trading arrangements and to use world-market prices in trade transactions. By 1991 a major share of Eastern Europe's fuel imports from the FSU was priced at world-market levels and paid for in convertible currency. However a significant remaining proportion of these imports continued to be traded at special prices, or under barter deals, involving, for instance, FSU energy supply in compensation for past East-European deliveries of goods or services. This was particularly common in the case of gas, where imports were paid for through a reduction of the debt incurred by the FSU through East-European involvement in building the FSU gas industry. Table 4.20 provides a simple and rough measure of the losses incurred by the East-European economies in consequence of the change in the pricing arrangements.

Table 4.19 Significance of imports from the FSU in the East-European energy markets in 1989

	Coal (MTOE)	Oil (MTOE)	Gas (MTOE)	Other (MTOE)	Total (MTOE)	Electr. (TWH)
All six countries						
TPES	186.4	86.6	70.9	20.9	364.8	493.2
Gross imports	16.5	92.6	34.8	6.0	149.9	48.4
Imports from FSU	9.7	65.6	34.8	3.8	113.9	31.6
Imports from FSU, % share in						
TPES	5.2	75.8	49.1	18.2	31.2	6.4
Gross imports	58.8	70.8	100.0	63.3	76.0	65.3
Poland						
TPES	93.2	16.1	9.5	0.3	119.1	145.1
Gross imports	0.7	18.2	6.4	1.0	26.3	12.1
Imports from FSU	0.6	15.2	6.4	1.0¹	23.2¹	3.9
Imports from FSU % share in						
TPES	0.6	94.4	67.4	333.3	19.6	2.7
Gross imports	85.7	83.5	100.0	100.0	88.6	32.2
Czechoslovakia						
TPES	41.2	15.7	9.2	6.6	72.7	91.9
Gross imports	2.9	17.2	9.4	0.8	30.3	10.4
Imports from FSU	1.7	16.6	9.4¹	0.51	28.2	5.8
Imports from FSU, % share in						
TPES	4.1	105.7	102.2	7.6	38.8	6.3
Gross imports	58.6	96.5	100.0	62.5	93.1	55.8
Hungary						
TPES	7.2	8.6	9.4	4.6	29.8	40.6
Gross imports	1.9	7.8	4.9	1.0	15.6	11.1

Imports from FSU	0.6	7.81	4.9	1.0	14.3	11.0
Imports from FSU, % share in						
TPES	8.3	91.0	52.1	21.7	48.0	27.1
Gross imports	31.6	100.0	100.0	100.0	91.7	99.0
Yugoslavia						
TPES	17.8	16.5	5.8	3.2	43.3	83.1
Gross imports	2.7	12.9	3.4	2.0	21.0	2.2
Imports from FSU	1.5	9.6	3.4[1]	0.2	14.7[1]	0.6
Imports from FSU, % share in						
TPES	8.4	58.2	58.6	6.3	33.9	0.7
Gross imports	55.6	74.4	100.0	10.0	70.0	17.3
Romania						
TPES	17.2	17.4	31.9	1.8	68.3	83.7
Gross imports	4.6	21.6	5.8	0.7	32.7	7.8
Imports from FSU	1.6	3.9	5.8[1]	0.7[1]	12.0[1]	5.8
Imports from FSU, % share in						
TPES	9.3	22.4	18.1	38.9	17.6	6.9
Gross imports	34.8	18.1	100.0	100.0	36.7	74.4
Bulgaria						
TPES	9.8	12.3	5.1	4.4	31.6	48.8
Gross imports	3.7	14.9	4.9	0.5	24.0	4.8
Imports from FSU	3.7[1]	12.5	4.9[1]	0.4[1]	21.5	4.5
Imports from FSU, % share in						
TPES	37.8	101.6	96.1	9.1	68.0	9.2
Gross imports	100.0	68.2	100.0	80.0	89.6	93.8

Notes: TPES = total primary energy supply.
1. PlanEcon figures adjusted to tally with gross figures provided by IEA.
Sources: TPES and gross imports from IEA, 1991b; imports from FSU from PlanEcon, 1990, 1992.

Figure 4.6   Fossil fuels in Eastern Europe in 1989: shares of gross availability by type and source

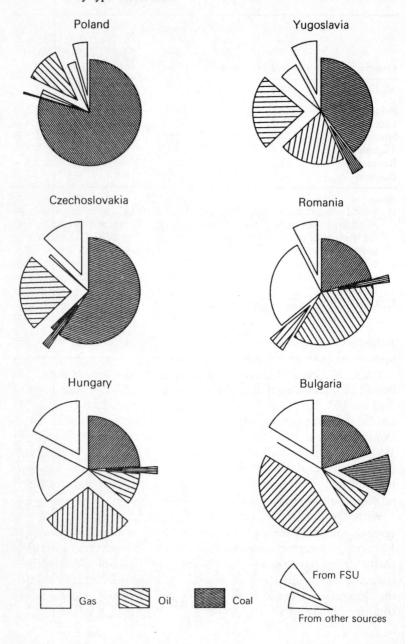

Table 4.20 Eastern Europe: an assessment of the economic impact of higher prices for fuels imported from the FSU (1989 values)

Country	Imports from FSU (MTOE)	Valued at world price ($bn)[1]	Valued at 40% of world price ($ bn)[2]	Diff. ($bn)	GDP ($bn)[3]	Diff. as share of GDP (%)
All six	113.9	12.3	4.9	7.4	653	1.1
Poland	23.2	2.5	1.0	1.5	183	0.8
Czechoslovakia	28.2	3.1	1.3	1.8	131	1.4
Hungary	14.3	1.5	0.6	0.9	68	1.3
Yugoslavia	14.7	1.6	0.6	1.0	135	0.7
Romania	12.0	1.3	0.5	0.8	83	1.0
Bulgaria	21.5	2.3	0.9	1.4	53	2.6

Notes:
1. World price of oil in 1989 = $17.2 per barrel. Assume coal price = 40 per cent of oil price, gas price = 75 per cent of oil price, all per unit of energy. Then the East-European mix of fuel imports from the FSU should have an average world price of $14.8 per barrel of oil equivalent.
2. It is assumed that the East-European countries paid 40 per cent of the world-market price for fuels under the traditional arrangements (Kenen, 1990).
3. GDP data from Directorate of Intelligence (CIA), 1991.

Bulgaria, with the highest dependence on imports from the FSU, appears to have been hardest hit by the change.

Since 1989 the FSU economy has experienced a serious crisis. The demand for manufactured imports from Eastern Europe has collapsed. And the FSU's inability to maintain oil and coal production after 1989 has led to a substantial shrinkage of its energy-export capability. Gross exports of fossil fuels in 1988 and 1989 amounted to 300 MTOE. By 1991 these exports had shrunk to around 200 MTOE. Virtually all destinations experienced declines, but the most severe cuts were implemented in oil contracts that stipulated payment through barter or other 'soft' arrangements.

With the dissipating advantage of bilateral trade, and with the uncertainties of FSU supply capability, East-European dependence on FSU energy has emerged as starkly excessive. Forceful and sometimes costly efforts have been initiated in all the countries under study to reduce this dependence, by cutting down on consumption, by increasing domestic energy output or by establishing alternative supply sources, thereby alleviating the threat of sharp cuts in FSU supply.

Such East-European efforts can be easily understood against the background of long-standing political sensitivities vis-à-vis the FSU, and of the economic and physical supply disruptions that actually occurred after 1989.

Nevertheless the design of economically rational actions to reduce dependence requires a careful and objective look at several questions. First, with the evolving political realities, is there any ground to believe that purely political considerations in the FSU could cause a disruption in energy supply to Eastern Europe specifically? Second, what is the probability of further sharp declines in the FSU's energy-export capability, and when are such declines likely to occur? Third, how much damage would be caused to the East-European economies by further shortfalls in FSU energy supply? Fourth, assuming all energy imports into Eastern Europe to be world-market priced, if alternative sources were to be used what would be the additional costs incurred as a result of greater transportation distances and the need to establish new infrastructure? Fifth, how long would it take to put such new infrastructure in place?

In the following paragraphs we provide a few general comments, which seem to us to have equal validity for Eastern Europe collectively.

There is little ground to believe that the FSU or its constituent parts will be using energy exports to Eastern Europe to accomplish political objectives. The FSU's preoccupation with internal political issues and the introduction of a market economy leave little scope for international political pursuit in the foreseeable future. The overriding objective of energy exports, it seems to us, will be to maximise the revenue that such exports can bring. So long as East-Europeans countries are prepared to pay the international price, we see little likelihood of politically inspired intervention. The likelihood of the FSU imposing embargoes or making exports conditional on the satisfaction of some political ends does not appear to be significantly greater than the likelihood of similar action being taken by other exporters of energy to Eastern Europe.

The above should be distinguished from the supply disturbances that may be caused by political tensions and disagreements within the FSU. The ultimate consequence, if such tensions are allowed to mount, would be an outbreak of internal war, with a collapse of export capability, as outlined in Scenario 4. Supply disturbances have already occurred, for example because of interrepublican disagreements about transit fees. Such tensions should presumably be resolved over time, as the FSU republics sort out the problems caused by their independence and learn to coexist.

Energy production and the energy-export capability of the FSU fell sharply between 1989 and 1992. This has been discussed in detail in earlier parts of our study. The impact of this on East-European countries has clearly been detrimental. We foresee further substantial declines in oil-export capability, down to zero in Scenarios 2 and 3 by the middle of the decade. At the same time we expect exports of coal and gas to be maintained throughout the 1990s (Scenario 4, internal war, excepted). Of greater significance for our investigations is the fact that the mid-1990s are seen to be the turning point in all scenarios. The likelihood of further export shortfalls subsides after 1995. Oil-export capability is forecast to start recovering after that date, even in pessimistic Scenario 3, and the occurrence of a crippling internal war, an improbable event at any time, becomes increasingly unlikely with each passing year. Protection against FSU supply shocks is most needed in the very near future, but the more ambitious East-European plans to diversify supply will require several years to become operational.

As indicated in our scenario outcomes, it is the supply of oil, not gas and coal, that is in the greatest danger of further decline. FSU oil exports fell from 170 million tons in 1989 to 100 million in 1991. Even in optimistic Scenario 1 oil exports are predicted to fall further: to only 60 million tons by 1995, less than the volume exported to Eastern Europe exclusively in 1989 alone. Further sharp reductions in sales to that region are therefore probable. But geographical proximity and existing pipeline connections mean low transportation costs, and thus makes Eastern Europe highly attractive to FSU producers. Hence supplies to this area may be the last to be cut, so long as the East-European countries are prepared to pay the international price.

Two factors would tend to lessen the impact on Eastern Europe of reduced oil deliveries from the FSU. The first is that, under the old regime, the region imported in excess of its own needs in order, to generate product exports to the West. Crude imports can be reduced without impairing domestic consumption by discontinuing these product exports. Any damage will be limited to underemployment of overexpanded refining capacities and lost export revenues. The second is that oil probably offers the widest scope for fungibility among the major fuels. Existing harbour and pipeline facilities permit several East-European countries an easy and rapid replacement of significant amounts of FSU oil by supplies from elsewhere.

Eastern Europe's high dependence on gas from the FSU, and the inflexible gas-import infrastructure, have aroused particular concern in that region. Increasing the number of sources from which gas could be obtained is seen as an insurance policy well worth paying for. Since roughly the same alternative sources are being considered by most of the countries, this is the proper place to assess the size of the premium. In 1989 Eastern Europe consumed 94 BCM of gas, of which 45 BCM was imported (BP, 1990). By 2000 import needs may have grown substantially because of expanding consumption and falling output.

Earlier analyses in this study led us to the conclusion that the FSU's export capability would grow from recently recorded levels until the end of the century in the first two scenarios. Serious problems with export capability would arise only in the unlikely Scenario 4, 'reform impasse and internal war', and in Scenario 3 from about the end of the century. In Scenarios 1 and 2, export increases of 30–40 BCM between 1990 and 2000 are anticipated, even if FSU production remains unchanged during that period, and much more if production increases. The probability that supplies from the FSU will be available to satisfy Eastern Europe's needs therefore appears reasonably high. There may nevertheless be a desire to adopt costly measures to diversify supply. After all, insurance is taken out precisely to protect against the unlikely. But how large would the insurance premium be?

One way of approaching this issue is by looking at the cost of alternative supply, assuming that some relationship exists between the cost of the sources chosen and the price paid. For the FSU we focus on Scenario 2 in this comparison. In that scenario FSU gas production in 2000 will remain at 790 BCM (660 MTOE), about the same as in 1990, with exports increased by almost 40 BCM to a total of 145 BCM.

Disregarding all caveats, the analyses of FSU gas conducted in Chapter 2 suggested an average cost of supply, at city gate or East European border in 2000, of $0.95 (1990)/per mmBTU, if production remains unchanged throughout the 1990s at 790 BCM, but that it would increase to $1.2 if production is raised to 850 BCM (Table 2.8, Chapter 2). The average cost of the additional 60 BCM supply works out at $4.4 per mmBTU. In the absence of better information we assume, bravely, that the total cost of marginal supply at the lower, 790 BCM level, is $1.30 per mmBTU, that is, one third above the average cost of that supply. We further assume that the total cost of marginal supply rises linearly from that level to reach $4.40 at an output of 820 BCM, the mid-point of the 790–850 BCM range. If these figures are correct, we obtain the following cost data for FSU export supply in 2000, over and above the 105 BCM exported in 1990 (Table 4.21):

Table 4.21   FSU gas export supply cost in the year 2000

Production range (BCM)	Export range (BCM)	Cumulative addition to exports over 1989 level (BCM)	Total average cost within range ($/mmBTU)	Total cost of range ($ million)	Cumulative cost of additional exports ($ million)
750–790	105–145	40	1.30[1]	1870	1870
790–800	145–155	50	1.80	650	2520
800–810	155–165	60	2.85	1030	3550
810–820	165–175	70	3.90	1400	4950

Note:
1. For want of better information, we assume that the average cost within this range equals the cost at the margin. This exaggerates the total cost figure for this range.

The costs of alternative sources of gas to Eastern Europe have recently been assessed by Arthur D. Little (1991). Neatly summarised, the findings of this study suggest the following quantities and costs (1990 dollars, including 10 per cent real return on capital) of additional supply by 2000 (Table 4.22).

Clearly, if our cost estimates and those of Arthur D. Little are correct, few of these alternatives could compete in cost terms with additional supplies from the FSU. A number of somewhat artificial assumptions have to be made in order to compare a feasible least-cost solution for satisfying Eastern Europe's gas-import needs by 2000, with an alternative providing for a diversification of supply sources. An attempt to do that may nevertheless be illustrative. Assume therefore that Eastern Europe's gas import demand rises by 30 BCM between 1989 and 2000, or from 45 to 75 BCM.

In the first case all of the additional supply is provided by the FSU, but we introduce the supplementary assumption that overall FSU exports have to increase by twice as much because of obligations to satisfy West-European customers' growing needs. Our estimates of FSU gas costs indicated that raising exports by a total of 60 BCM would involve total average costs of $1.3 per mmBTU for the first 40 BCM increase, $1.8 for the following 10 BCM tranche, and finally,

Table 4.22 Costs of alternative sources of gas to Eastern Europe

	BCM	Cumulative (BCM)	Total average cost ($/mmBTU)	Total cost of supply ($ million)	Cumulative cost of supply ($ million)
Iranian gas via pipe through Turkey, at Bulgarian border	20	20	2.00	1440	1440
Algerian gas via additional pipe through Italy, at Yugoslav border	5	25	2.10	380	1820
Algerian and Libyan LNG (including ships and regasification), at Yugoslavian harbour	10	35	2.40	860	2680
LNG from Qatar at Yugoslavian harbor	5	40	3.00	540	3220
Norwegian gas via new pipe through Denmark, at Polish border	10	50	3.10	1110	4330
Norwegian gas through new pipes via Emden, at Czechoslovak border	10	60	3.40	1220	5550
Norwegian LNG (incl. ships and regasification), at Polish harbour	5	65	4.50	810	6360

Source: Little (1991).

$2.85 for the final 10 BCM tranche. With the total costs equally attributed to West and East Europe, the East European cost of an additional annual supply of 30 BCM works out at $1800 million.

In the second case it is assumed that the FSU' share of Eastern Europe's imports is forced to shrink from 100 per cent to 60 per cent. Hence the entire import expansion, 30 BCM in all, will be provided by sources other than the FSU. More precisely, we take it that one half, or 10 BCM of the new supply of Iranian gas will be at the disposal of Eastern Europe, the rest being shipped onwards to Western Europe, but that the 20 BCM of Algerian, Libyan and Qatar gas listed above will be available for Eastern Europe since it will be handled through facilities exclusively dedicated to this region. This arrangement will raise Eastern Europe's sources of supply from one to four, with the annual cost of 30 BCM of additional gas amounting to $2500 million. Thus the insurance premium in this calculation amounts to $700 million per year.

The cost levels indicated above would provide the minimum needed to make the establishment of the respective supply capacities worthwhile. What prices would be is another matter. If all existing supply capacity is fully utilised by 2000 there will be a tendency for all prices to move up to the cost of marginal supply, and little economic advantage will be reaped from relying on low-cost gas from the FSU. In contrast, those gas buyers who are committed to take delivery of high-priced gas from costly supply sources may incur very heavy losses if there is surplus capacity by the turn of the century and if low-cost gas producers compete by lowering their prices.

Adopting a more speculative view, one may conjecture that such East-European initiatives to increase their sources of supply should make the European gas market more competitive. The addition of Iran and Qatar to the list of gas suppliers would complicate producers' efforts to take monopolistic market control. The split-up of FSU deliveries into separate supplies from Russia and Turkmenia, or even from several independent companies in these republics, would increase the competitive pressures even more. All else being equal, such producer proliferation should lead to lower gas prices in the whole of Europe and a reduction in the importance of large, long-term supply contracts, much as has occurred in the US gas market in recent decades. It is difficult to assess the value of the ensuing importer advantages, to be juxtaposed against the additional costs determined above. It is also hard to justify why the East-European importers in particular should take the initiative and assume the sizable initial costs when the conjectured benefits will accrue to all European gas consumers.

Yet another point of general applicability to Eastern Europe has to do with the elevated energy intensities in the region, as demonstrated in Table 4.23, and with the consequent energy-savings potential. Though one must be cautious when interpreting the figures because of problems in measuring GDP, and because of the doubtful reliability of energy consumption data, the numbers suggest an average energy intensity in Eastern Europe that is twice the level of Western Europe's and on a par with that recorded in the FSU (Chapter 3). One of the major theses of this study is that FSU energy consumption will experience a substantial decline in the early phases of a thorough reform programme, in response to falling GDP, to the increasing relative price levels of energy, and to economic restructuring in which the size of the energy-intensive sectors of industry is reduced. Similar declines in energy demand should occur in the East-European economies even earlier, given that the reform programmes in most of these countries have preceded those of the FSU. It is highly probable that further efforts to increase energy savings in Eastern Europe, for instance by dismantling the sizable and often uneconomic heavy-industry sectors, particularly in the chemical, fertiliser and metals branches, will yield a higher social benefit per unit of expenditure than the marginal ventures to increase domestic energy production or expand alternative imports. Lower levels of energy consumption would automatically reduce the dependence on FSU supplies and improve Eastern Europe's ability to handle future supply curtailments from that source.

Table 4.23   Energy intensities in East and West Europe in 1989

	GDP ($bn)	TPES (MTOE)	Intensity (TOE/m$)
OECD Europe	5635	1418	252
East Europe Six	653	364.8	559
Poland	183	119.1	651
Czechoslovakia	131	72.7	555
Hungary	68	29.8	438
Yugoslavia	135	43.3	320
Romania	83	68.3	823
Bulgaria	53	31.6	596

Sources: Table 4.20; IEA, 1992; OECD (1992) *Economic Outlook*, December.

There is no doubt that energy consumption in Eastern Europe fell dramatically after 1989, even though definite data are not yet available. Preliminary figures suggest a decline in apparent consumption between 1989 and 1991 of 31 per cent for oil products, 17 per cent for natural gas and 11 per cent for electric power (PlanEcon, 1992). But it is not clear to what extent this is due to the reforms themselves, to the ensuing contraction in economic activity, assessed by the OECD to have led to GDP declines between 1989 and 1992 of 35 per cent in Bulgaria, 17 per cent in Czechslovakia, 11 per cent in Hungary, 20 per cent in Poland and 22 per cent in Romania (OECD, 1992a), or simply because energy supplies have been physically unavailable. In all probability a complex recursive process is going on, where the reform process, the GDP contraction and the cuts in FSU energy deliveries are simultaneously the cause and effect to the ongoing change.

4.5.3 Conclusions

We conclude by noting that some of the ambitious East-European investment plans to reduce the dependence on imports of energy from the FSU may have a weak economic rationale. The likelihood of further large declines in the FSU's export capability beyond 1995 is small. Many of the projects to reduce dependence are costly and a take long time to implement, while the supply shortcuts are most likely to occur in the near future. The greatest probability for further reduction in supply arises in the case of oil, where existing infrastructure in several countries permits a fair scope for substitution in favour of alternative import sources. Finally, declining East-European energy consumption will reduce the need to import from the FSU, thereby shielding these economies from the potential damage that failed FSU supply could cause.

In the end it may turn out that acceptance in Eastern Europe of continued and heavy dependence on FSU energy will be a rational economic choice even in the absence of political bonds and pricing favours, given the geographical proximity of the energy sources, the abundance and reasonable reliability of long-term supply, and the costly infrastructure that is already in place.

Notes and References

2 Production Constraints and Prospects

1. In 1990 average well yield in the FSU was 8.88 tons per day, and in Russia 11.5 tons per day. Wells commissioned in Russia before 1991 will pump only about 3.3 tons by 2000. In that year. the average new well in Russia will pump less than six tons per day, because of the exhaustion of high-yielding reservoirs (Information from NIIEng., 1992). The average well yield outside Russia was 4.8 tons in 1990, with a further decline anticipated everywhere except Kazakhstan (Oil ministry statistics from Birman, 1992).

2. Samotlor, Romashkino, Sutorminsk and Tallinskiy, with almost 33 000 wells (Arbatov *et al.* 1991, p. 26; *The Oil and Gas Journal*, 7 October 1991, p. 28; Taganskiy *et al.*, 1991, pp. 4–7; Khalimov, 1991, p. 14.

3. All the maps and charts in this chapter were drafted by Messrs Phil Reed, Cary de Wit and Greg Hughes at the University of Kansas Cartographic Service.

4. By the end of 1991, West Siberia produced 38 per cent of the Soviet cumulative total (Maksimov, 1989, vol. I, pp. 12–14; USGS, 1975). Cumulative production in European and Caucasian provinces of the FSU computed as total minus those in West Siberia and Sakhalin (Riva, 1991, p. 62; Dinkov, 1987, p. 255; *Surgutskaia tribuna*, 26 May 1992, p. 2; Panfilov, 1990, p. 25; API, *Basic Petroleum Data Book,* various recent issues).

5. The following provides a summary of Russian/Soviet definitions of oil reserves.

> 'Active reserves': oil reserves with permeability of greater than 50 millidarcies; with viscosity of less than 30 centipoise (or millipascals × second); and crudes without heavy gas cuts.
>
> 'Hard-to-recover reserves': all reserves other than active. Defined as reserves with permeability lower than 50 millidarcies; or with viscosity of less than 30 centipoise (or millipascals); or with heavy gas cuts.
>
> A + B reserves: theoretically this corresponds to proven, recoverable reserves of oil and gas in the API classification. A + B reserves have production wells. For oil, however, Russian/Soviet reserve estimates in this category are significantly overstated. Usually, they have been calculated with an initial 0.45 recovery coefficient, on the average. This is much higher than justified by Western experience. In the US reserves are considered proven only when the production methods have been shown to be effective in a given deposit over the long term. Extraction coefficients thus rise gradually, and so do proved reserves, the size of which is also influenced by a host of economic and legal considerations.
>
> A + B + C_1 reserves. Usually referred to as explored reserves. The C_1 category corresponds to probable reserves in the API classification.

220

C_2 reserves: this roughly corresponds to possible reserves in the API classification. It represents preliminary estimates based on a test well that shows the presence of oil or gas. In restricted cases, C_2 reserves may also be interpolated from geophysical and analogue data between and along productive strata.

6. The reservoirs of gas fields in which oil forms a significant proportion of reserves are also difficult. In 1992, for example, the oil ring of Urengoy produced only 1.5 million tons. Even slight variations in reservoir saturation lead to very large drops in well yields. The large Novoportovskoe deposit at the base of the Yamal Peninsula, discovered in 1967, remains undeveloped (Kucherov and Ponomarev, 1992, pp. 8–9; Remizov, 1991, p. 3). Drilling for new reserves has proved very disappointing: the 165 structures tested in this northern 40 per cent of the province and deep drilling below 3000 meters revealed the presence of only meagre quantities of oil (Yermakov and Skorobogatov, 1988, pp. 17–22; Skorobogatov and Fomichev, 1988, pp. 1–5).

7. A special commission of the then Soviet Academy of Sciences concluded in 1990 that from 0.2 to 6.4 million tons of oil could be produced in East Siberia by 2000, under various assumption of investment and priorites, and from 9 to 13 million tons by 2010 (Rudenko and Makarov, 1990, p. 49).

8. That ratio for 'active' reserves alone was over 14 both in Russia as a whole and in West Siberia through the 1980s (Tables 2.2 and 2.3). When reserve/production ratios fall below about 11, a steady output cannot be sustained. Historically, reserves in the US have been extracted at a maximum rate, but when that ratio dropped below 11, production began to decline. 'Hard-to-recover' reserves cannot be produced at such rates. Nonetheless these reserves can substantially supplement high-flow reserves.

   In Russia's case, however, even the reserve/production ratio of 14 does not guarantee stable production. The approximate 11-year floor of the reserve/production ratio applies to fully proven reserves. For Russia the 14-year 'active-reserve' cushion refers to proven *plus* probable reserves. The latter are not fully explored, nor prepared for production. In recent years downward revisions in the volume of reserves have been common. The large Var'yega and Sutorminskoe fields in West Siberia are two particular examples.

9. 'Hard-to-recover' reserves have so far contributed only about 6 per cent of cumulative output both in Russia and in West Siberia alone. Only about one fifth of the initial produceable reserves in this category have been extracted in Russia and a mere 10–12 per cent in West Siberia; the corresponding share for high-flow reserves are 63 per cent and 51 per cent (Khalimov, 1990, pp. 99–104).

10. The Russian oil institute data actually provide a breakdown for only a 342 million tons output in 2000. To reach 370 million tons in 2000, most of the extra would have to come from new wells and from idle wells restored. If extraction from wells producing before 1991 were to be intensified, the share of output from these wells would be even less than shown in Figure 4.

11. We subdivided the total West-Siberian reservoir data set into four parts for separate regression analysis. By this means we avoided excessive mingling of different reservoir populations, enhancing the predictive power of the resultant equations. Three of these follow closely S.P. Maksimov's subdivisions of the West Siberian Province into geological subregions. The fourth is a somewhat more diverse grab bag, in part an unavoidable compromise.

12. We are indebted to the Kansas Geological Survey for the use of the regression and MDS models. Special thanks are due to Professors John Davis and John Doveton for running the programmes and interpreting the results. The pertinence of the conclusions in the specific Russian and FSU context are our responsibility.

13. Less than 1 per cent of West Siberia's cumulative production of 5.8 billion tons originated from geological beds associated with pools of severe underproduction, that is, 41–42 million tons. Our multiple regressions suggest a degree of underproduction of about 45 per cent of that predicted. That works out to about 50 million tons from these pools. Underproducing reservoirs, which could not be included in the regression equations, could certainly contain at least half as much. However only a portion of this will be recoverable. Destructive production practices have caused inorganic salts and expanded clay particles to block reservoir pores in many damaged reservoirs. Reserves in such pools have been converted to non-recoverable reserves for the most part (*Surgutskaia tribuna*, 26 May 1992, p. 2; Khalimov, 1991, p. 103).

14. By 1991, 15 000 wells were drilled cumulatively in the greater Salym area of the Bazhenov Formation. Salym itself was subjected to an underground nuclear explosion. Yet Greater Salym can show a mere 265 000 tons of *cumulative* production for all that effort (Khalimov *et al.* 1990, p. 102).

15. The Middle and Lower Jurassic underlies most of West Siberia. High petroleum potentials were assigned to these Jurassic beds at depths of 3–4000 meters in the Nadym-Pur subregion, an area 6–900 km north of the Middle Ob'. Here a transitional zone of continental and marine facies, and the presence of deltaic, prodeltaic and other shoreline features was assumed to have been very conducive to the formation of productive oil accumulations (Yekhanin, 1990, pp. 2–4; Suleimanova *et al.*, 1990, pp. 13–15). However the Jurassic sandstones have turned out to be very poorly sorted, generally tight and sealed with clay particles, which makes the extraction of the existing fluid very difficult. In addition, the large quantities of clay in the interstices of the sandstones means that the volume of *recoverable* oil would be small indeed.

    Experts now believe that only 14 per cent of all potential wells in the Middle and Lower Jurassic could be expected to yield more than 10 cubic meters of fluid. A mere 3–5 per cent of the areal extent of the complex will be relevant for production in the 1990s and even later (Nemchenko and Kulaeva, 1988, pp. 9–13; Surkov *et al.*, 1990, pp. 21–6; Samoletov *et al.*, 1989, pp. 9–12).

16. 250 BCM out of a total of 280 BCM in 1991 at Urengoy (Geresh, 1992, p. 6). At Yamburg the share is probably somewhat higher still. In April 1992 a senior geologist told us that the deep Valanginian beds in West

Siberia have much less than half the well yields of the Cenomanian (contrary to earlier expectations), and that yearly extraction from these strata in West Siberia will not exceed 40 BCM (I. P. Zhabrev, interview).

17. Ideally production from hundreds of wells would need to vary according to the rate of incursion through the various strata, in order to minimise the loss of gas. Given the size of the fields in production, the necessary information for that is inadequate. Where it exists, capital investment to put wells on such production regimes will be very significant (Geresh, 1992, p.6; Yermilovyi, 1991).

18. There is a growing literature concerning the problems of Yamal. Much of the no. 5, 1991 issue of *Gazovaia promyshlennost'*, for example, is devoted to it, but the most authoritative recent source is E. D. Yershov, *Geokriologiia SSSR. Zapadnaia Sibir*. In summer Yamal is 80 per cent flooded. The permafrost of the Peninsula is ice-saturated; in places the ground contains 70 per cent water. The high salt content of the ground lowers the freezing temperature. The transported gas will have to be cooled to as much as -5 to -7 degrees C (Shembraev, 1991, pp. 6–7). Air and permafrost temperatures in north-west Siberia have gone through cyclical changes, with the cold phase now ended. In the next three to five years the beginning of the next warming cycle is expected, lasting until 2020–25. This will further increase the uncertainty of environmental consequences associated with construction in the far Arctic (Povilenko, 1990, pp. 155–74).

19. The discount formula employed is

$$MC = \frac{\sum\limits_{1992}^{2000} \dfrac{K_t + O_t}{(1+i)^t}}{\sum\limits_{1992}^{2000} (1+i)^t}$$

where: MC is marginal cost, K is yearly capital investment, O is operating cost, assumed here to be a constant 35 per cent of total cost, and i is the discount rate.

The proper discount rate, in fact, is the crux of the problem. Though the investment forecasts are in constant prices, they were made in the extreme inflationary environment of 1991–2. In that situation the margin of error for the constant price estimate is very large, and a higher discount rate than 10 per cent may be appropriate, raising marginal costs significantly.

20. The initial Chevron–USSR protocol called for an investment of \$26–31 billion over 40 years, according to three variants, for 681–765 million tons of crude oil. Cumulative exploitation costs would total from \$52–84 billion, according to three different variants of operating regimes. The original Soviet technical–economic study also foresaw cumulative exploitation costs twice as high as capital investments. To estimate the cost of

output at the beginning of the next decade, we used the discounted value of investment and operating cost by the end of 2000 (amounting to $8.8 billion) and the similarly discounted value of cumulative production reaching 22 million tons at the end of 2000.

Notwithstanding the difficult geology of Tenghiz, the projected cost inflation between 1992 and 2005 should not affect that deposit more than the FSU average. The reason: no other field will be capable of such high, sustained production and consequent scale economies. A large number of mature deposits elsewhere must increase their input requirements per ton even more than Tenghiz. In addition, most of the equipment at Tenghiz is already foreign made, moderating the upward cost pressure as imported inputs substitute for domestic ones.

21. Other studies indicate that some new projects in operation by 2000 may have costs even higher than Tenghiz. A decade long major study of the Nizhnevartovsk oil region of West Siberia examined all reserves promoted from the possible to the probable categories (from C_2 to C_1 categories). 43 per cent of those reserves, with well flows of 20 tons per day, could produce four million tons from 830 wells over a ten-year period. The remaining reserves, with initial well flows of less than 20 tons per day, could produce almost twice that volume, but only with 10 400 wells. In other words, a more than six-fold difference exists between the two groups (Khalimov *et al.*, 1990, p. 173). With 5 per cent of the wells replaced, the capital cost per ton would amount to about 150 rubles in 1990 prices. (Well costs in Tyumen' for 1988 from Arbatov *et al.*, 1991, p. 65). Six times the number of wells for the remaining reserves, however, almost certainly would make the costs higher than at Tenghiz.

22. Special thanks are due to Albina Tretyakova, who provided us with the detailed ruble estimates. We consolidated and simplified them, reconciled discrepancies, and converted them to dollars.

23. The stock of fixed capital in Russian industry was revalued in 1992. In view of the volume of new capital necessary even to stabilise oil production at a lower level, and the need to stimulate investment by producers, the original depreciation rate for 1995 in Table 2.7 was raised substantially. For 2000 the rate of depreciation is assumed to fall back to the 9 per cent that prevailed in the late 1980s.

24. Steep cost increases in extraction is a familiar feature of production in all mature provinces. In the FSU, however, and especially in West Siberia, the crumbling capital stock doubtless exacerbates the problem, since obsolete equipment and decaying structures cannot use energy and materials efficiently. Such obsolescence and the rapidly worsening quality of the resource base will also demand wholesale replacement and a host of new, complex equipment. These will command premium prices, a larger import component and priority of delivery.

25. The exponential increase of cost from 380 to 450 million tons (from Variant *A* to *B*) is slightly above 1 per cent per million tons.

26. Ruble costs from ministry data in 1990 are supported by the more detailed input coefficients of the 1987 input-output table. Ruble data for 1990 are carried forward in real terms, based on cost multiples and the volume of physical inputs. See also the text discussion concerning Table 2.7.

27. Until 2000 we project development in the cost structure as if it applied only to gas itself, in order to simplify the analysis. In fact, some condensates are also produced, but the determination of their costs requires quite complex computations. All net increments in the volume of gas extracted till 2000 represent free gas, that is, gas not associated with oil production. The likely decline in crude oil production will result in a decrease in the volume of associated gas as well.
28. Gazprom's latest statistical volume distinguishes 28 pipeline trusts. It provides data concerning the lengths of pipelines of seven different diameters. The system works with 29 poorly matching compressor types.
29. An entire helicopter brigade is on red alert along this corridor, with several machines in the air at all times to watch for any spark or other signs of danger.
30. Sources for data: Birman, 1992; Arbatov *et. al.*, 1991, Tables 2.18 and pp. 50–1; Wilson, 1991, Table 2.9; Ikonnikov and Fayzullin, 1991, p. 3; Rudenko and Makarov, 1990, p. 26.
31. Sources: Birman, 1992; VNIIKTEP, 1989, pp. 62–3; Wilson, 1991, Tables 47–50.
32. Sources: Birman, 1992; Arbatov, 1991; Filimonov, *Neftianoe khoziaistvo*, 1990b; Neverov and Igolkin, 1991–2; Churilov, 1991.

3 Prospects for FSU Energy Consumption

1. FSU experts put the share of technically obsolete thermal power generating capacity at 100 gigawatts, about 40 per cent of total capacity (Dobrokhotov, 1990, p. 3). According to the latest national inventory, in April 1986, 61 per cent of steam turbines were outdated, being below the acceptable 'national standard', let alone the best world technology. About half of the steam turbines were older than 20 years and around one-fourth had been in operation between 11 and 20 years (Gosudarstvennii Komitet, 1988, pp. 227–8).
2. Among the major industrial nations, only Japan's pattern of final energy use shows some resemblance to the FSU pattern, with the share of industry in final consumption being nearly as high (45.9 per cent) and ferrous metallurgy being even more dominant. Another similarity between the two countries is the low share of the residential sector.
3. It is not entirely clear what explains the sharp rise in unit energy consumption of the agricultural sector. There is some evidence for the growing use of field equipment to transport goods because of unavailability or unreliability of a common trucking service. The poor quality and inadequate maintenance of the aging stock of equipment and vehicles may be an additional factor (Cooper and Schipper, 1992, pp. 12–13). The marked switch from Caterpillars to wheel tractors is also believed to increase specific fuel consumption because of the higher slippage of tractors (Sinyak 1990, p. 56).
4. The average rate of decline in industrial total factor productivity was 0.6 per cent in 1971–80 and 0.9 per cent in 1981–1990 (Directorate of Intelligence, 1991, p. 66).

5. The predictive equation specified for the market-economy reference group is the following (t-ratios in parentheses):

$$\ln \text{ENCONS} = -1.176 + 0.995 \ln \text{GDP} + 0.134 \ln \text{OUTPMIX}$$
$$(2.03) \quad (21.07) \qquad (0.34)$$
$$+ 0.226 \ln \text{SOLFUEL} - 0.016 \text{NETIMP},$$
$$(3.58) \qquad\qquad (1.79)$$

Standard error $= 0.293$ R^2 (adj.) $= 0.948$

where ENCONS is total primary energy consumption, GDP is gross domestic product; OUTPMIX is a proxy for share of energy-intensive sectors (paper and paper products, chemicals, petroleum and coal products, glass, iron and steel, non-ferrous metals) in manufacturing value added, SOLFUEL is the proportion of solid fuel in total energy consumption and NETIMP is the proportion of net energy imports in total consumption.

The 27 market economies included in the reference group are Argentina, Australia, Austria, Belgium–Luxembourg, Brazil, Canada, Denmark, West Germany, Finland, France, Greece, Italy, Japan, Mexico, Netherlands, New Zealand, Norway, Portugal, South Korea, Republic of South Africa, Spain, Sweden, Switzerland, Turkey, UK, USA.

6. New research conducted at the Ministry of Fuels and Energy of the Russian Federation puts the energy-savings potential of the Russian economy at 500 million tons of standard fuel (about 350 MTOE). This corresponds to about 60 per cent of overuse, a ratio very close to that we estimated for the FSU as a whole. The energy-savings potential was calculated as the size of possible reduction in energy use (at unchanged level of total output or standard of living) attainable through the massive adoption of already existing energy-efficient technologies and production processes. This technological definition of the savings potential is similar to that of the Makarov–Chupiatov study referred to above. The sectoral composition of the savings potential is as follows (in MTOE): energy and fuel complex, 105–130; industry, 105–125; residential and municipal, 70; agriculture, 35–42; and transport, 32–35 (*Ekonomika i zhizn'*, no. 37 [September, 1992]).

7. Wholesale prices refer to the so-called 'industry wholesale price', which includes the wholesale enterprise price (wellhead price in the case of oil) and transportation charges, but excludes turnover taxes.

8. The 40 per cent proportion of freely marketable output includes the 10 per cent share that local-government authorities of producing territories can buy from enterprises under their jurisdiction at the state-set price. Forty per cent of the production disposed of by local authorities can be sold on the domestic (Russian) market at free prices, while the remaining portion can be exported independently outside the FSU.

9. At the beginning of 1992 the Russian government levied substantial export duties, payable in rubles, on all tradable energy products. Under

strong pressure from exporters and Western investors in joint ventures, the export tariffs were reduced on 1 March. On 1 July 1992 they were raised again. In October 1992 a set of tariffs, payable in ECUs (European Currency Units) was imposed. Expressed in dollars per ton, these tariffs had the following levels: Crude oil $50 (equivalent to about 35 per cent of the international price); gasoline and jet fuel, $73; Kerosine, gasoil and diesel, $69; heavy fuel oil, $28; bunker oil, $33. For natural gas the tariff was $52 per thousand m^3. There is evidence of exemptions from these taxes, provided largely on an ad hoc basis.

10. The continued softness of the budget constraint facing energy users preserves their insensitivity to price changes. There is evidence that authorities in the FSU provide highly concessional credits as a means to offset the increased cost of energy. As an example, in September 1992 in Russia's Vladimir region (oblast), 500 million rubles of government credit was issued to enterprises to help cover the increased energy expenditures (*Ekonomika i zhizn'*, no. 38 [September, 1992]). These 'energy credits' carry only 10 per cent interest, which is highly negative in real terms and is only a fraction of the interest charged by Russian commercial banks. Such soft credits are equivalent to a hidden price subsidy and thus act to reduce the effective price of energy for those having access to them.

11. Even the abandoned package of immediate price liberalisation envisaged retaining the regulation of gas and electricity prices on a temporary basis.

12. The projected world prices for oil and coal were taken from World Bank, 1991. Since this source did not provide a price forecast for gas, we calculated the projected world price on the assumption that gas prices will closely follow those of the projected oil prices.

13. The Hungarian elasticities were available from Dobozi (1988) and from new regression runs performed for this project. The elasticities (all statistically significant) in their distributed lag forms are as follows:

	Aggregate energy	Oil	Natural gas	Coal
Current year	−0.100	−0.083	−0.050	−0.030
Lagged 1 year	−0.090	−0.074	−0.060	−0.120
Lagged 2 years	−0.070	−0.064	−0.050	−0.140
Lagged 3 years	−0.060	−0.055		
Lagged 4 years		−0.045		

14. Such views were expressed, among others, by two Harvard University researchers, Jeffrey Sachs (*Fortune*, 13 January 1992) and Joseph Berliner (*The New York Times*, 10 January 1992).

15. Senik-Leygonie and Hughes, 1992. The authors based their calculations on the 1987 FSU input-output table. The 'social-profit ratios' (defined as the ratio between the value of output at world price and the cost of factors and intermediate inputs, valued at shadow prices) for the most energy-intensive sectors have the following values in the former USSR and three major republics with favourable resource endowments:

	USSR	Russia	Ukraine	Kazakhstan
All traded sectors (average)	1.14	1.23	1.13	1.04
Energy-intensive sectors:				
Oil and gas production	1.55	1.55	1.79	1.51
Coal mining	1.08	1.16	1.02	1.22
Ferrous metals	1.78	1.87	1.62	2.14
Non-ferrous metals	1.57	1.60	1.72	1.52
Chemicals	1.17	1.17	1.25	1.04
Paper and paper products	1.45	1.49	1.42	1.26
Non-metal minerals	1.39	1.43	1.53	1.32

A study by Thornton and Mikheeva (1991), using the 1982 estimated input–output transactions table for the FSU Far East, provides further evidence for the underlying competitiveness of energy-intensive industrial branches. They found that at the existing input proportions, ferrous and non-ferrous metallurgy and heavy engineering would enjoy higher gross profits at world prices than they did at the actual domestic prices.

16. Recent studies suggest that the FSU might be among the cheapest steel producers in the world and that it may take advantage of this condition to boost future exports (Economic Commission for Europe 1990, p. 61).

4 Energy Exports, International Markets and Eastern Europe

1. For a summary of prevailing views, see Griffin, 1985.

Bibliography

Adelman, M. (1992) 'Oil Resource Wealth of the Middle East', *Energy Studies Review*, vol. 4, no. 1.

Albychev *et al.*, (1989) 'Ratsional'no razvivat' transportnuiu set' Yamala', *Gazovaia promyshlennost'*, no. 1, pp. 22–5.

AN, IKARP SSSR, (Akademiia nauk SSSR) (1991) Institute Kompleksnovo Analiza Regional'nykh Problem, Far Eastern Branch. Unpublished study of the infrastructure of the Far East.

API, *Basic Petroleum Data Book*. Several issues.

Arbatov, Alexander *et al.*, (1991) *Soviet Energy. An Insider Account* (London: The Centre for Global Energy Studies), May, mimeo.

Baranovsky (1992) 'Energetika vstupaet v gazovoiu pauzu', *Stroitel'stvo truboprovodov*, no. 2, pp. 11–12.

Baraz, V.I. (1990) 'Otsenka energoemkosti neftegazovogo proizvodstva', *Neftianoe khoziaistvo*, no. 6, pp. 13–17.

Baraz, V.I. (1991) 'Vid privoda dlia GPA: energeticheskii aspekt,' *Gazovaia promyshlennosti*, no. 3, pp. 12–13.

Birman, Igor (1992), computer data-base file on Soviet and FSU fuel industries, Silverspring, Maryland, USA.

BP (1990) *BP Statistical Review of World Energy 1990* (London).

BP (1991) *BP Statistical Review of World Energy 1991* (London).

Brilliant, L.C., P.M. Kuramshin and N.N. Gubareva (1989) 'Sovershenst-vovanie geologo-technicheskoi modeli razrabotki produktivnykh plastov Samotlorskogo mestorozhdeniia', *Neftianoe khoziaistvo*, no. 3, pp. 35–8.

Chernomyrdin, Viktor C. (1991) 'Gazovaia promyshlennost'. Trevogi i nadezhdy 1991 goda', *Gazovaia promyshlennosti*, no. 3, pp. 1–4.

Chousa Geppou Rosia Touou Bouekikai (1992), June, pp. 22–1.

Churilov, L. (1991) 'Neft' i liudi', *Pravitel'stvennyi Vestnik*, no. 35 (August).

Cooper, R.C. and L. Schipper (1992) 'The Efficiency of Energy Use in the USSR – An International Perspective', *Energy*, no. 1.

Crouse, Philip C. (1989), 'Reserve potential due to horizontal drilling is substantial', *World Oil* (October), pp. 47–9.

Dienes, Leslie (1992) 'Energy, Minerals, and Economic Policy', Chapter 5 in I.S. Koropeckyj (ed), *The Ukrainian Economy* (Cambridge, Mass: Harvard Ukrainian Research Institute).

Dikenshtein, G.Kh., S.P. Maksimov, and V.V. Semonovich (1983) *Neftega-zonosnye provintsii SSSR* (Moscow: Nedra).

Dinkov, V.A. (ed.) (1987) *Neft' SSSR (1917–1997 gg.)* (Moscow: Nedra).

Directorate of Intelligence (CIA), *Handbook of Economic Statistics* (Washington, DC), annual, various issues.

Dobozi, I. (1988) 'The Responsiveness of the Hungarian Economy to Changes in Energy Prices', in J.C. Brada and I. Dobozi (eds), *The Hungarian Economy in the 1980s: Reforming the System and Adjusting to External Shocks* (Greenwich, Conn.: JAI Press).

229

Dobrokhotov, V. N. (1990) 'Energosberezheniye: problemy i resheniya', *Teplo-energetika*, no. 1.
Doyle, G. (1988) 'The International Coal Trade and Price Outlook', *Energy Exploration and Exploitation*, no. 6.
Duchene, Gerald and Claudia Senyk-Leygonie (1991) 'Price Liberalization and Redeployment in the USSR: The Soviet Economy in World Prices', *European Economy*, Autumn.
Dzhangirov, V. A. *et al.* (1991) 'Toplivno-energeticheskaia baza', *Teploenerge-tika*, no. 1, pp. 12–16.
EBE, Eastern Bloc Energy (a monthly review of oil and energy in the USSR and Eastern Europe), several issues.
Economic Commission for Europe (1990) *The Steel Market in 1989* (New York: United Nations).
Ekon. gazeta (Ekonomicheskaya gazeta), weekly, several issues.
Ekonomika i zhizn', weekly, several issues.
Ericson, Richard (1991) 'The Mirage of Soviet Economic Reform', *Economic Change* (East and Central Europe Special Report), April.
Eskin, Vadim I. (1991) 'The First Step on the Way to the Energy Resource Market in the USSR: Prices, Taxes, Rental Payments, Credits'. Unpublished paper.
Fadeyev, V. T. (1987) 'Effektivenost' gazotransportnoy sistemy: rezervy tekhnicheskogo obnovlenie', *Gazovaia promyshlennost'*, no. 10, pp. 2–5.
FBIS-SOV (1992) 23 January, p. 64.
Filimonov, L. I., (1990a) 'Uslovye problemy otrasli', *Neftianoe khoziaistvo*, no. 4, pp. 3–9.
Filimonov, L. I. (1990b) 'Povyshenie nefteotdachi plastov – nastoiatel'naia neobkhodimost', a ne dan' mode', *Neftianoe khoziaistvo*, no. 9, pp. 3–8.
Financial Times International Gas Report (1992), February, p. 8.
FSRC News (1992) (Foreign System Research Center of Science Application International Corporation), June 1.
Gazovaia promyshlennost' (1991), no. 5.
Geresh, P. A. (1992) 'Perspektivy razvitiia Urengoiskogo mestorozhdeniia', *Gazovaia promyshlennost'*, no. 1, pp. 6–7.
Gorst, I. (1991) 'Back to Baku Development', *Petroleum Economist* (December), pp. 14–17.
Gosudarstvennii Komitet SSSR po Statistike (1988) *Materialno-tekhnicheskoye obespecheniye narodnogo khoziastva SSSR* (Moscow: Finansy i statistika).
Grace, John D. and George Hart (1983) *Natural Gas Resources of the Northern West Siberian Basin* (Baton Rouge: Lousiana State University), preprint, October.
Griffin, J. M. (1985) 'OPEC Behavior: A Test of Alternative Hypotheses', *American Economic Review* (December).
Grigor'yeva, V. A., M. M. Ivanova and A. F. Kolesnikov (1992) 'Geologiches-koe stroenie Karachaganakskogo mestorozhdenie v sviazi s zadachami ego osvoenie', *Geologiia nefti i gaza*, no. 1, pp. 10–14.
Hughes, Gordon and Paul Hare (1991) 'Industrial Restructuring in Eastern Europe: Policy and Prospects', paper presented at the European Economic Association Meeting, 2 September.
IEA (1989) *World Energy Statistics and Balances* (Paris: OECD).

IEA (1990) *IEA Coal Information 1990* (Paris: OECD).
IEA (1991a) *Energy Policies Poland, 1990 survey* (Paris: OECD).
IEA (1991b) *Energy Statistics and Balances of Non-OECD Countries 1988–1989* (Paris: OECD).
IEA (1991c) *Monthly Oil Market Report*, December (Paris: OECD).
IEA (1991d) *Energy Balances of OECD Countries 1980–1989* (Paris: OECD).
IEA (1991e) *Natural Gas Prospects and Policies* (Paris: OECD).
IEA (1992) *Energy Statistics and Balances of Non-OECD countries 1989–90* (Paris: OECD).
IEA Coal Research (1990) *Coal Prospects in Eastern Europe* (London, December).
Ikonnikov, Yu. A. and N. M. Fayzulin (1991) 'Analiz ispol'zovaniia fonda neftianykh skvazhin v ob' edineniia Minneftegasproma SSSR za 1986–1990 gg.', *Neftianoe khoziaistvo*, no. 10, pp. 2–4.
IMF *et al.* (1991) (International Monetary Fund, World Bank, Organisation for Economic Cooperation and Development) *A Study of the Soviet Economy*, vol. 3 (Paris: OECD).
IMF (1992a), *Common Issues and Interrepublic Relations in the Former USSR* (Washington DC).
IMF (1992b), *The Economy of the Former USSR in 1991* (Washington DC).
Istomim, V. I. *et al.* (1991), 'Analiz sostoianiia i kontrol' razrabotki gazovykh, gazokondenzatnykh mestrozhdenij', *Gazovaia promyshlennost'*. Vypusk 4. Seriia: *Geologiia, burenie, razrabotka i ekspluatatsiia gazovykh i gazokondenzatnykh mestorozhdenij*, no. 1, pp. 1–8.
Ivantsov, O. M. (1990) 'Trebovaniia k trubam dlia magistral'nykh truboprovodov', *Stroitel'stvo truboprovodov*, no. 11., 39–41.
Ivantsov, O. M. (1991) 'Nadezhnost' i nenadezhnost' truboprovodov', *Stroitel'stvo truboprovodov*, no. 4, p. 21; no. 11, pp. 4–9.
Izvestiya, several issues.
Julius DeAnne and A. Mashayekhi (1990) *The Economics of Natural Gas* (Oxford Institute for Energy Studies).
Kenen, P. (1990) 'Transitional Arrangements for Trade and Payments Among the CMEA Countries', IMF working Paper WP/90/79, Sept.
Khalimov, E. M. *et al.* (1990) *Resursy nefti i gaza i effektivnoe ikh osvoenie* (Moscow).
Khalimov, E. M. (1991) 'Kachestvo podgotovki neftianykh mestorozhdeniy k razrabotke', *Neftianoe khoziaistvo*, no. 2, pp. 13–16.
Khrilev, L. and O. Makarov (1991) 'Trevoga energetikov', *Ekonomist*, no. 1, pp. 62–7.
Kochnev, A. V. (1991) 'Neftianoe i gazovaia promyshlennost' v 1990 godu', *Neftianoe khoziaistvo*, no. 5, pp. 2–7.
Kommersant, several issues.
Konoplianik, A. A. (1992a) 'O formakh privlecheniia inostrannogo kapitala v neftianuyu promyshlennosti Rossii', *Neftianoe khoziaistvo*, no. 3, pp. 2–4.
Konoplianik, A. A. (1992b) 'Problemy osvoeniia Sakhalinskogo shel'fa', (Parts I and II), *Neftianoe khoziaistvo*,, no. 6, pp. 2–4; no. 7, pp. 2–5.
Kucherov, G. G. and A. N. Ponomarev (1992) 'Sostoianie razrabotki neftianykh otorochek', *Gazovaia promyshlennost'*, no. 1, pp. 8–9.

Leonidov, B. Z. *et al.* (1992) 'Sovershenstvovanie organizatsionnoi struktury po osvoeniiu neftegazovykh resursov Timano-Pechorskoi provintsii', *Neftianoe khoziaistvo*, no. 6, pp. 5–7.

Little, A. D. (1991) 'The Future of Natural Gas in Eastern Europe', final report to the World Bank, December.

Makarov, A. A. and V. P. Chupiatov (1990) 'Potentsial i realniye vozmozhnosti energosberezheniya', *Teplo-energetika*, no. 1.

Maksimov, S. P. (1989) *Neftianye i gazovye mestorozhdeniia SSSR: Spravochnych v dvukh knigakh*. Vols. I and II. References from JPRS-UEA translation.

Material'no-tekhnicheskie obespechenie narodnogo khoziaistva SSSR. (1988) Statisticheskii sbornik. Goskomstat SSSR (Moscow: Financy i statistiki).

Mayak Radio Network in Russian 0330 GMT1 (1992) 15 January. Reported in FBIS-SOV (Foreign Broadcasting Information Service – Soviet Union), 23 January, p. 64.

Moldovanov, O. I. (1992) 'Razvitie toplivno-energeticheskogo kompleksa Dal'nego Vostoka Rossii', *Stroitel'stvo truboprovodov*, no. 6, pp. 26–7.

Moskovskoe novosti (Business), October 91.

Mukhametzianov, R. N. and V. P. Sonin (1992) 'Osobennosti stroeniia i optimizatsiia razrabotki zalezhei nefti Noiabr'skogo raiona', *Neftianoe khoziaistvo*, no. 8, pp. 40–2.

Narkhoz (Narodnoe khoziaistvo SSSR), statistical yearbook of the USSR, various issues (Moscow).

Neft' Piob'ia (1992) September, p. 2.

Nehring, Richard (1978) *Giant Oil Fields and World Oil Resources* (Santa Monica, CA.: R-2284-CIA. June).

Nemchenko, N. N. and T. P. Kulaeva (1988) 'Differentsiia prognoznykh resursov nefti po velichine nachal'nykh debitov v iurskikh otlozheniiakh Zapadnoi Sibiri', *Geologicheskaia nefti i gaza* (May), pp. 9–13.

Nekrasov, A. and A. A. Troitskij (eds) (1981) *Energetika SSSR v 1981–1985 godakh* (Moscow: Energoizdat).

Neverov, Valeriy and Aleksandr Igolkin, (1991–2) 'Neft' Rodiny', *Ekonomika i zhizn'*, special issue, December 1991, pp. 8–9; no. 9, 1992, pp. 4–5.

Neverov, Valeriy and Aleksandr Igolkin (1992) 'Rossiiskaia neft' v mirovoi politike', *Ekonomicheskaia gazeta*, no. 41 (October), pp. 1, 5.

'News Notes', *Soviet Geography*, (1965–1992), various issues.

Nezavisimaia gazeta (1991) 30 October, p. 4.

NIIEng. (1992) (Scientific Research Institute of the Economics of the Oil and Gas Industries), unpublished material.

Nikolaev, B. (1992) 'Bor'ba za energoresursov', *Ekonomicheskaia gazeta*, no. 14 (April), p. 13.

OECD, *Main Economic Indicators* (monthly).

OECD (1992), *Economic Outlook* (December).

OPEC (1990), *Annual Statistical Bulletin 1989* (Vienna).

OPEC (1991) *Annual Statistical Bulletin 1990* (Vienna).

Paik, Keun-Wook (1992) 'Towards a Northeast Asian Energy Charter,' *Energy Policy*, (May), pp. 433–3.

Panfilov, I. (1990) 'Iz pervoi konnoi', *Neftianik*, no. 3, pp. 14–16.

PIW, *Petroleum Intelligence Weekly*, various issues.

PlanEcon Energy Report (quarterly), several issues.

PlanEcon (1990) *Soviet and East European Energy Databank* (Washington DC).
PlanEcon (1992) *The Russian Economy During the First Half of 1992*, nos 33–4 (September).
Pliakov, G. N. *et al.* (1992) 'Issledovanie effektivnosti vodogazovogo vozdeiftviia . . .', *Neftianoe khozkiaistvo*, no. 1, pp. 38–41.
Povilenko, R. P. (1990) *Katastrofa* (Moscow: Nedra).
Radetzki, M. (1991) 'Price Prospects in Western Europe for Internationally Traded Fossil Fuels Until 2000', *Natural Resources Forum* (November).
Radetzki, M. (1992) 'Pricing of Natural Gas in the West European Market', *Energy Studies Review*, vol 4, no 2.
Remizov, V. V. (1991) 'Kogda net analoga', *Gazovaia promyshlennost'*, no. 5, p. 3.
Riva, Joseph P. (1991) 'Dominant Middle East oil reserves critically important to world supply', *The Oil and Gas Journal* (23 September), pp. 62–8.
Rudenko, Yu. N. and A. A. Makarov (1990) 'Vozmozhnye stsenarii razvitiia energetiki SSSR. Otsenki nakanune perekhoda k rynochnoi ekonomike', Akademiia nauk and GKNT SSSR, (Moscow: November), unpublished.
Sagers, Matthew (1992) 'News Notes', *Soviet Geography*, (March 1991); *Post-Soviet Geography*, (April 1992).
Samoletov, M. V. *et al.* (1989) 'Prognozirovanie perspektivnykh ob' ektov v doiurskikh i nizhne-sredneiurskikh otlozheniiakh Krasnoleninskogo svoda Zapadnoi Sibiri', *Geologiia nefti i gaza*, no. 4, pp. 9–12.
Semenov, B. N. (1977) *Ekonomika stroitel'stva magistral'nykh gazoprovodov* (Moscow: Nedra), p. 72.
Senik-Leygonie, S. and Gordon Hughes (1992) 'Industrial Profitability and Trade among the Former Soviet Republics', paper presented at the Economic Policy Panel in Lisbon, Portugal, 1–2 April.
SG. Soviet Geography (monthly).
Shembraev, G. A. (1991) 'Sposoby stoitel'stvo v arkicheskoi zone strany', *Gazovaia promyshlennost'*, no. 5, pp. 6–7.
Shenkov, A. S. ed. (1988) *Ekonlmika neftegazovogo stroitel'stva*. (Moscow: Nedra).
Shirkovskiy, A. Y. (1992) Doktor tekhnicheskich nauk. Deputy director of training and research, Central Interbranch Institute of Advanced Training and Requalification for Oil and Gas Industry Specialists, Moscow, Soviet Metallurgy Industries. Interview in May.
Sinyak, Ju. (1990) *Energy Efficiency and Prospects for the USSR and Eastern Europe* (Tokyo: Economic Research Center).
Skobtsov, L. and Ye. Chernova (1992) 'Sibirskiy gaz v setiakh intrig', *Stoitel'stvo truboprovodov*, no. 1, pp. 16–8.
Skorobogatov, V. A. and V. A. Fomichev (1988) 'Perspektivy neftegazonosnosti iurskikh i melovykh otlozheniy Yamala i Gydana', *Geologiia nefti i gaza*, no. 2, pp. 1–5.
Solomatin, V. I. and L. A. Zhigarev. (1992) 'Osnovnye problemy geologii krylidtozony', *Stoitel'stvo truboprovodov*, no. 6, pp. 10–13.
Suleimanova, L. O., F. M. Kuanyshev and M. E. Merson (1990) 'Prognoz kintsentratsii UV v porovom prostranstve kollektorov v Zapadno-Sibirskoi i Prikaspiiskoi GNG', *Geologiia nefti i gaza*, no. 8, pp. 13–15.
Surgutskaia tribuna (1992), 26 May, p. 2.

Surkov, V. S., *et al.* (1990) 'Prognoz krupnykh zone neftegazonakopleniia v nizhnesredneiurskikh otlozheniiakh Zapadno-Sibirskoi plity', *Sovetskaia geologiia*, no. 8, pp. 21–6, esp. 26.

Taganskiy, V. M., *et. al.* (1991) 'Opyt braboty Sutorminskogo UBR', Neftianaia promyshlennost'. Seriia: *Stroitel'stvo neftianykh i gazovykh skvazhin na sushe i na more*, vol. I, no.. 12, pp. 1–58.

Thornton, J. and N. Mikheeva (1991) 'Structural Change and Integration of the Soviet Far East into the World Market: The Case of Negative Value Added', Seattle, Institute for Economic Research, University of Washington, discussion paper series no. 91–14 (October).

Tiumenskie izvestiia (1992) 24 September, p. 3.

Tretyakova, Albina and Meredith Heinemeier (1970–1990) *Cost Estimates for the Soviet Gas Industry* (Washington DC: Center for International Research), CIR staff paper no. 19, 1986.

Tretyakova, A. (1986) US Bureau of the Census, Center for International Research, personal communication.

Trud (1990) (Daily) 12 December, p. 1.

TsNIEI Ugol' (1991) (Central Scientific Research Institute of the Coal Industry). Statistical material.

Turevskiy, Ye. N. *et al.* (1990) 'Siykling process poglotitel' regeneratsiia – teplovaia Karachaganakskoe GKM', EI Gazprom. Seriia: *Podgotovka, pererabotka i ispol'sovanie gaza*, no. 3, pp. 1–5.

Ugol' Ukrainy. (1990) (monthly), no 6, pp. 2–4.

UNCTAD (1991) *Handbook of International Trade and Development Statistics 1990* (New York: United Nations).

US Congress, Joint Economic Committee (1990) 'Measures of Soviet Gross National Product in 1986 Prices' (Washington DC).

US News and World Report (1992) 13 April, p. 43.

USGS Geological Survey Circular 725 (1975) *Geological Estimates of Undiscovered Recoverable Oil and Gas Resources in the United States.*

Vechernyi Kiev, several issues.

Vestnik Statistiki (1990), no. 4, p. 51.

VNIIE Gazprom (1991) (All Union Scientific Research Institute of the Gas Industry), *Gazovaia promyshlennost' SSSR '90* (Moscow).

VNII ekonomiki gazovoi promyshlennosti. Unpublished *Doklad.*

VNIIKTEP (1989) (All Union Scientific Research Institute of Complex Energy Problems) *Toplivno-energeticheskii kompleks* (Moscow).

Vol'skiy, E. L. (1990) 'Povyshenie effektivenosti yedinoy sistemy gazosnabzhneiia strany', *Stroitel'stvo truboprovodov*, no. 8, pp. 1–5.

Vol'skiy, E. L. (1992) 'Magistral'nyi transport gaza: problemy i perspektivy', *Stroitel'stvo truboprovodov*, no. 1, pp. 14–16.

Von Flatern, Rick (1991) 'Technology Keeps Pace With Horizontal Drillers', *Petroleum Engineer International* (November), pp. 16–22.

WGI (World Gas Intelligence) (monthly), several issues.

Wilson, Cameron D. (1991) *Soviet and East European Energy Databook* (Tadcaster, UK: Eastern Block Energy Ltd).

World Bank (1990) *Price Prospects for Major Primary Commodities*, report no. 814/90 (December).

World Bank (1991a) IECIT, 'Revision of Primary Commodity Price Forecasts', office memorandum, 5 November.
World Bank (1991b) *World Development Report 1991* (Washington DC).
World Bank (1991c) IECT, 'Revision of Primary Commodity Price Forecasts', office memorandum, March.
World Bank, *World Tables*, various issues (Washington, DC).
Yekhanin, A. Ye. (1990) 'Perspektivy poiska zalezhei raznogo fazovogo sostava v nizhnesredneiurskom neftegazonosnom nadkomplekse Zapadnoi Sibiri', *Geologiia nefti i gaza*, no. 4, pp. 2–4.
Yeremenko, P. T. and N. A. Vorob'ev (1989) *Razvitiie truboprovodnogo transporta v SSSR i za rubezhom* (Moscow: Nedra).
Yermakov, V. A. and V. A. Skorobogatov (1984) *Obrazovanie uglevodo-rodnykh gazov v uglenosnykh i subuglenosnykh formatsiikh* (Moscow: Nedra).
Yermakov, V. I. and V. A. Skorobogatov (1988) 'Termoglubinnye usloviia gazoneftenosnosti iurskikh otlozhenii severnykh raionov Zapadnoi Sibiri', *Geologiia nefti i gaza*, no. 11, pp. 17–22.
Yermilovyi, O. M. (with Ye. M. Nanivskiy) (1991) *Regulirovanie razrabotki gazovykh mestorozhdeniy Zapadnoy Sibiri* (Moscow: Nedra).
Yershov, E. D. (ed.) (1989) *Geokriologiia SSSR. Zapadnaia Sibir'* (Moscow: Nedra).
Yershov, Yu. (1992) 'Skoraia pomoshch dlia neftedollarov', *Ekonomika i zhizn'*, no. 28 (July), p. 17.
Yufin, V. A. (ed.) (1978) *Truboprovodnyi transport nefti i gaza* (Moscow: Nedra).
Zhabrev, I. P., Doktor tekhnicheskikh nauk. Senior scientist, Institute of Oil and Gas Problems of the Academy of Sciences and State Education Committee SSSR/Russia (Moscow).
Zolotov, A. N. and F. K. Salmanov (1992) 'Mineral'no-syr'evaia baza nefti i gaza v SSSR i pervonachal'nye zadachi nauka', *Geologiia nefti i gaza,* no. 3, pp. 2–7.
Zoteev, Gennadii (1991) *The Soviet Economoy in 1991* (Moscow: Economic Institute of Ministry of Economy and Forecasting of the USSR).

Index